The Rhetoric of the New Political Documentary

Edited by Thomas W. Benson
and Brian J. Snee

Southern Illinois University Press
Carbondale

Copyright © 2008 by the Board of Trustees,
Southern Illinois University
Printed in the United States of America

Chapter 4, "Vietnam Flashbacks," copyright © 2008 by Roger Stahl

11 10 09 08   4 3 2 1

Library of Congress Cataloging-in-Publication Data
The rhetoric of the new political documentary / edited by Thomas W.
Benson and Brian J. Snee.
      p. cm.
Includes bibliographical references and index.
ISBN-13: 978-0-8093-2836-9 (pbk. : alk. paper)
ISBN-10: 0-8093-2836-4 (pbk. : alk. paper)
   1. Documentary films—United States—History and criticism. 2. United
States—Politics and government—2001– I. Benson, Thomas W. II. Snee,
Brian J.
PN1995.9.D6R495 2008
070.1'8—dc22   2007036644

Printed on recycled paper. ♻
The paper used in this publication meets the minimum requirements of
American National Standard for Information Sciences—Permanence of
Paper for Printed Library Materials, ANSI z39.48-1992. ∞

Contents

Thomas W. Benson and
Brian J. Snee

New Political Documentary

Rhetoric, Propaganda, and the Civic Prospect

The Rhetoric of the New Political Documentary explores the most visible and volatile element in the 2004 presidential campaign—the partisan documentary film. This collection of original critical essays by leading scholars and critics analyzes a selection of political documentaries that appeared during the 2004 election season, when President George W. Bush ran as the Republican candidate, campaigning for a second term; the Democrats nominated Senator John Kerry of Massachusetts after a long and vigorously contested primary season; and the country was at war with Iraq. We examine the new political documentary with the tools of rhetorical criticism, combining close textual analysis with a consideration of the historical context and the production and reception of the films.

Throughout the 2004 presidential campaign, evolving technological capabilities and a variety of emerging political techniques were exploited in surprising and effective ways. Refined methods of data analysis and distribution permitted targeted, face-to-face persuasion and get-out-the-vote activities.[1] Broadcasting was supplemented with new forms of "narrow-casting." Focus groups, word testing, push-polling, and voter surveys permitted television and Internet advertising to reach new levels of sophistication with targeted persuasion on wedge issues. Internet sites that ranged from objective news outlets to partisan Web logs circulated news, advertising, commentary, rumor, and gossip, and the Internet was used to raise money in unprecedented amounts for major party campaigns.[2] Together, these developments and others created new vehicles for campaign organizing and fund-raising that led to unprecedented successes but also widespread concern about further distortion of the public sphere by money, power, and technology.

A fascinating and unexpected development in the 2004 campaign was the reemergence of the feature-length documentary film as an outlet for partisan and polemical messages. Documentaries have always held the power to influence public opinion, and historians and critics of documentary have always emphasized its social and political functions, but seldom have documentaries been a major force in a national political election. The films considered in this project do not fit perfectly into the genre of social documentary—it can be argued that they are not "really" documentaries at all—but they do appropriate the form of documentary to lend structure and authenticity to their appeals, even as they draw on other genres and hybrids to create a rhetoric that is a mix of documentary, propaganda, political advertising, and news forms. In this sense, generic "documentary" provides both a source of forms that filmmakers can emulate and adapt to their own uses and a set of reading practices that viewers employ to make sense of these films. The new political documentaries went beyond the broad objectives of earlier eras of documentary filmmaking, such as spreading nationalism, examining social problems, or insinuating military superiority, and instead addressed issues and audiences in ways seldom seen before the 2004 election.

Michael Moore's *Fahrenheit 9/11* announced with its release in June 2004 that the era of the new political documentary had begun. Moore's film was an unexpected financial and critical success, and it quickly became a focal point of charges and countercharges throughout the campaign. In this sense, *Fahrenheit 9/11* and the responses to it marked some of the most distinguishing features of the new political documentary—its ability to be produced and distributed quickly enough to engage other films in partisan, cinematic debate, to create the impression and perhaps the reality of significant effects on public opinion, and to influence the campaign agendas of both major parties.

Fahrenheit 9/11 was the most visible of a number of films that shaped the national conversation about—and perhaps the outcome of—the 2004 presidential campaign. The majority of these films were originally prepared for theatrical release, made front-page news, then circulated widely in videotape and DVD or on the Internet; in some cases, they were broadcast on local and national television and, even more frequently, became fodder for television news reports—all before the November 2004 election.

The year 2004 was an especially important election year for the United States. The country faced the first presidential campaign since the electoral confusion of 2000, the terrorist attacks of 2001, the bitterly partisan midterm elections in 2002, and the invasion of Iraq in 2003. The campaign offered the hope of restoring some sense of stability and trust.

The rhetorical influence of the new political documentary appears to be mixed. The films of 2004 raised issues thought by campaigners to be too hot to handle, and they helped set the agenda for the campaign. The films were produced cheaply and quickly, they emerged unexpectedly, they were distributed widely, and they appeared to be made for the sole purpose of influencing the outcome of the election. But they often resorted to sensationalism and oversimplification, descending to partisan diatribe that sometimes distracted the attention of the campaign from discussion of more important matters.

The release of *Fahrenheit 9/11* in June 2004 was followed until November by a controversial mix of documentaries that added to and shaped the already highly charged atmosphere of the campaign. George Bush's religious convictions, John Kerry's service in Vietnam, the passage of the USA PATRIOT Act, the invasion of Iraq, minority voter disenfranchisement in election 2000—all became the subjects of widely circulated films.

The Documentary Idea

The cinema began with documentary. The term "documentary" itself was first applied to motion pictures in a 1926 review by John Grierson of Robert Flaherty's *Moana*.[3] A generation earlier, the very first commercial films seemed to record everyday life as it happened and presented it to audiences, who marveled at the magic of moving pictures. In films like *Workers Leaving the Factory* (1895) and *Arrival of a Train* (1895), artistry appeared to be deliberately avoided.[4] The first films seemed to work their magic on their own. The concept of a "political" documentary was an oxymoron—briefly.

Even before the turn of the century, politicians recognized the potential benefits of moving pictures. *William McKinley at Home* (1896) reminds us how quickly film began to be employed by politicians all the way to the White House. This one-minute Auguste and Louis Lumière short offered no direct political argument but provided citizens the thrill of seeing a president on film. Film was thus absorbed into the presidential spectacle, framed in an aesthetic of factuality, which was in itself a political effect, much as the many photographs of Abraham Lincoln had been almost a half century earlier.

Soon filmmakers and politicians began to explore the persuasive possibilities of film, in both fiction and documentary. What today might be called political documentaries began to circulate, as did fiction films about political issues and politicians. Lincoln was depicted as early as 1903 in the Edison Film Company's production of *Uncle Tom's Cabin*. He reappeared dozens of times, often in strikingly different portrayals, in both documentaries and docudramas during this early era of the cinema.[5] As the U.S. film industry concentrated on famous men and historic moments with films like D. W. Griffith's *Birth of a Nation* (1915), a rapidly developing international industry was using the cinema, often in documentary mode, to address social and political issues.

Revolutionary Cinema

Starting in the 1920s, the Soviet Union began to explore the political potential of documentary film. Long before the emergence of a state-sanctioned style known as Soviet "socialist realism," the early Russian cinema produced documentaries and historical fictions supporting Marxist ideology and the Communist state.

Like Griffith in the United States, with whose work he was well acquainted, Sergei Eisenstein narrated the history of his society, reconstructing it from a distinctive ideological perspective. Among his most famous films are *Strike* (1925), *Battleship Potemkin* (1926), *October* (1928), *Alexander Nevsky* (1938), *Ivan the Terrible, Part I* (1945) and *Ivan the Terrible, Part II* (1948). The content was historical; the forms were daringly experimental. Adapted from the concept of the Marxist dialectic, Eisenstein's "theory of montage" was a radical new means of visual expression—so radical that Soviet bureaucrats soon accused him of abandoning the cinematic party line and indulging in bourgeois formalism.

The 1920s Soviet cinema and its characteristic style had international influence. Bill Nichols notes:

> This particular blending of elements took root in other countries in the late 1920s and early 1930s as governments . . . saw the value of using film to promote a sense of participatory citizenship and to support the role of government in confronting the most difficult issues of the day, such as inflation, poverty, and the Depression. Answers to these problems varied widely from democratic Britain to fascist Germany and from a New Deal United States to a Communist Russia, but in each case, the voice of the documentarian contributed significantly to framing the national agenda and proposing courses of action.[6]

In the years that followed the Soviet-led revolution in the cinema, the political documentary came to be regarded by nations around the world as an essential weapon.

Government Propaganda

Grierson defined documentary as the "creative treatment of actuality" and insisted that documentary film had an obligation to society. Erik Barnouw writes that Grierson feared "that expectations once held for democracy were proving illusory. Problems facing society had grown beyond the comprehension of most citizens; their participation had become perfunctory, apathetic, meaningless, often nonexistent." Grierson "saw a solution. The documentary film maker, dramatizing issues and their implications in a meaningful way, could lead the citizen through the wilderness. This became the Grierson mission."[7] Grierson and his followers deplored documentary that mythologized man and nature as outside the realm of society, history, and politics. Their primary example of one who participated in such mythologizing was Robert Flaherty, whom Grierson identified as the father of documentary but whose *Nanook* (1922) and *Man of Aran* (1934) were dismissed as romantic evasions by the committed documentarians of the Grierson movement. Nevertheless, Flaherty's patient humanism and gift for image and rhythm were deeply influential for the documentary movement. In the United States, Pare Lorentz followed the Griersonian model in his support of the New Deal with films like *The Plow That Broke the Plains* (1936) and *The River* (1938).[8] So too did Ralph Steiner and Willard Van Dyke, directors of *The City* (1939), a film that shares both Grierson's commitment to political filmmaking and Eisenstein's commitment to visual argument through montage.[9] The Griersonian tradition has been challenged in many ways, and documentary film has evolved since Grierson's days; nevertheless, rhetoric and politics have remained at the core of documentary and documentary scholarship.

In World War II, the documentary film and its close relative, the newsreel, were regarded as military assets. On December 18, 1941, just days after the attack on Pearl Harbor, President Franklin D. Roosevelt established the Bureau of Motion Picture Affairs within the Office of War Information. Hollywood, in turn, established its own War Activities Committee "to coordinate American filmmaking activity with the propaganda and morale-boosting programs of the government."[10] Hollywood produced fictional films that supported the war, and Hollywood sent some of its best film artists to work in the government documentary project, where they created films of enduring influence. Classics from the war era include Frank Capra's "Why We Fight" series (1943–45); John Ford's *The Battle of Midway* (1942) and *December 7* (1943), shot by Ford while he headed the Field Photographic Branch of the Office of Strategic Services; William Wyler's *Memphis Belle* (1944); and John Huston's *Report from the Aleutians* (1943) and *The Battle of San Pietro* (1944).

Other allied nations were also delivering the war to film audiences. In Great Britain, the social documentary tradition of the 1920s and 1930s was extended into a series of distinguished war films, including such classics as *Target for Tonight* (1941), *Fires Were Started* (1943), and *Desert Victory* (1943).

The British enlisted "Master of Suspense" Alfred Hitchcock, who had commented on the war effort in films like *Foreign Correspondent* (1940), *Saboteur* (1942), and *Lifeboat* (1944). In 1944, he was persuaded by the British Ministry of Information to direct two short French-language propaganda films: *Bon Voyage* and *Aventure Malgache.*

Nazi Germany aggressively sponsored propaganda films as an instrument of domination and intimidation. "Why should I demoralize the enemy by military means," Adolf Hitler once asked, "if I can do so better or more cheaply in other ways?"[11] Joseph Goebbels, Hitler's infamous Minister of Propaganda, captured the Reich's attitude when in 1934 he said, "We are convinced that in general film is one of the most modern and far-reaching methods of influencing the masses. A regime thus must not allow film to go its way."[12] Hitler and Goebbels seized control of UFA, Germany's legendary government-sponsored film production studio, and in 1933 created the Reich Film Chamber. Hitler and Goebbels used fictions like *Jew Suss* (1940) and *The Eternal Jew* (1940) to spread their anti-Semitic ideology, while most of their documentaries seemed content to praise Hitler and Germany. Nevertheless, those documentaries are among the most effective examples of war propaganda ever made.

Leni Riefenstahl's *Triumph of the Will* (1935) documents the 1934 Nazi party rally at Nuremberg and casts Hitler as the savior of Germany, who literally descends from the heavens by airplane to walk among his people. The film's most striking and, to modern viewers, unexpected feature is its comparative lack of overt hate speech, though even at the time the film's constant verbal and visual celebration of purification and unanimity, in the context of Hitler's widely reported campaign of anti-Semitism, was legible as part of a consistent pattern. Riefenstahl understood her task to be the glorification of Hitler and the German state, not the explicit condemnation of Jews. Her images were thought to possess such power that the film was banned in several countries, including the United States, whose own propagandists studied *Triumph of the Will* as a model of filmic persuasion.

Fighting alongside the feature-length documentary was the short series film, shown mostly in theaters before the full-length, usually fictional, feature. In the United States, the "March of Time" newsreel series addressed global political issues in the 1930s and 1940s. A defining feature of the "March of Time" series was its insistence on presenting more than one side of every issue but then suggesting, at least implicitly, which side seemed most logical. In this sense, the series was both like and unlike the new political documentary, which always makes its agenda known but only rarely acknowledges the validity of opposing points of view. The "March of Time" ended in 1951, having reached at its peak a weekly audience of 20 million Americans and an international audience estimated at 15 million.[13]

Other notable series include Grierson's "Canada Carries On" (1939–50) and "The World in Action" (1940–45) as well as England's "This Modern Age" (1946–50). Close to matching the popularity and influence of the "March of Time" series was "This Is America" (1942–51). In 1933, Frederic Ullman Jr. and Gilbert Seldes produced *This Is America*, a feature film that took as its subject the evolution of American society and culture from 1917 to 1933. The film was promoted as an objective record of American life in the twentieth century, but according to Richard Meran Barsam, "its underlying purpose seems to have been the presentation of an optimistic, enthusiastic view of the future."[14] A decade later, in 1942, Ullman developed the "This Is America" series, which one of its writers described as an effort to "relate the small cog to the big wheel instead of showing the big wheel as 'The March of Time' did."[15] Over the next ten years, 112 documentary shorts, averaging seventeen minutes in length, reassured American audiences that they had good reason to be optimistic about their future.[16]

Hollywood director Frank Capra began his military career with training films but was quickly reassigned from the military's Morale Branch to the Information-Education Branch. There he took up the cause of rallying support for America's involvement in the war among the civilian population.[17] The seven-part "Why We Fight" series was intended for military audiences only but was "ultimately shown to general audiences in theaters around the country at President Roosevelt's behest."[18]

Government filmmaking continued after the war. In 1953, the Eisenhower administration created the United States Information Agency, which produced films to be released abroad to shape foreign perceptions of the United States.[19] Other government agencies, such as the Department of Defense and the Department of Agriculture, became major producers of instructional and propaganda films directed at selected audiences. Most developed nations use film to shape public opinion on both sides of their borders.

The Anti-establishment Tradition

Documentary filmmakers have not always supported those in power. Since the inception of the medium, a "political avant-garde" has worked mostly on the margins of both society and the film industry to challenge the social structures that seem to oppress the many for the benefit of the few.[20] In the 1920s and 1930s, the Workers' Film and Photo Leagues "produced information about strikes and other topical issues from the perspective of the working class."[21] Filmmakers working within nearly every political system used documentary to question authority and promote change. Unlike Dziga Vertov, Grierson, Riefenstahl, Capra, Ford, and others, these artists were activists, rallying sentiment against their governments. After World War II, the anti-establishment documentary tradition flourished around the world and in the United States. In the tradition of agitprop, and owing some debt to the film noir movement, which adopted and popularized many documentary conventions, the cinema of social and political change took up causes from civil rights to the feminist movement, from Communism to Vietnam.

The Old Political Documentary

Much of the history of documentary film can be regarded as "political" on some level. But ever since *William McKinley at Home*, there has been a subgenre of explicitly political films—films concerned not merely with political issues but with specific politicians, political parties, and political processes. In the United States, the WWII documentaries were political in the sense that they depicted the nobility of the war effort, the bravery of the troops, the assistance of allied nations, and the threat of the enemy. Presidents, parties, and elections were not their concern. After the war, the social documentary blossomed again, and other filmmakers were enlisted to support explicitly political agendas sponsored by candidates or interests.

The end of the war roughly coincided with a number of technological advances that changed the art of filmmaking. The development of lightweight synchronous-sound equipment gave rise to the cinema verité and direct cinema movements of the 1950s, 1960s, and 1970s. These new technologies permitted unprecedented behind-the-scenes views of political events, as in *Primary* (1960) and *Crisis: Behind a Presidential Commitment* (1963), and brought a wide range of social and cultural issues into public debate.[22]

Public television in the United States contributed significantly to the development of the long-form social documentary, featuring the works of such filmmakers as Frederick Wiseman and Ken Burns and long-running documentary series such as *Frontline* (1983–present) and *Now* (2002–present). These films and series have altered discussion of public institutions and political issues ranging from the Cold War to the war on terror, Vietnam and Watergate to 9/11 and Iraq, domestic spying and international prisons, and political ties to big oil, big media, and the big money contributions of lobbyists.

The presidential campaign film has been a predictable and stable form of political documentary. Mixing stock photos and film footage, talking-head interviews, emotionally rousing and often patriotic music and voice-over narration, campaign films were made throughout the twentieth century. Appearing during election years and typically shown during nominating conventions, these films "provide the fullest visual portrait of a candidate available in one package during an election," according to Joanne Morreale.[23] Morreale argues that early films such as *William McKinley at Home, The Life of Calvin Coolidge*

(1923), and *The Dewey Story* (1948) anticipated the genre but that the era of the "classical presidential campaign film" did not get underway until 1952 with the Dwight Eisenhower and Adlai Stevenson campaigns.[24]

Ronald Reagan's 1984 reelection campaign film, alternately referred to as *It's Morning in America Again* and *A New Beginning*, was broadcast on most television networks without interruption, running for nearly twenty minutes, and was so moving that challenger Walter Mondale's campaign headquarters reportedly indicated that it brought his staff to tears.[25] In 1992 and 1996, Arkansas-natives-turned-Hollywood-producers Harry Thomason and Linda Bloodworth-Thomason helped to elect and reelect Bill Clinton with *The Man from Hope* (1992) and *A Place Called America* (1996). The press has come to regard campaign films as both a force in the campaign and a sign of its health. Michael Dukakis's 1988 film and Al Gore's film in 2000 were remarkably ineffective, and the weakness of the films was read by the press as a sign of trouble in the candidates and campaigns. No serious presidential candidate can accept his or her party's nomination without a documentary film that assures its audience that the party has chosen wisely.

Another staple of the late twentieth century has been the behind-the-scenes campaign film produced outside the campaign. These films follow the candidate on the campaign trail from announcement speech to Election Day, along the way offering an inside look at the campaign and the candidate. Unlike the new political documentary, these films are usually released after the election and are typically less partisan, if not less polemical, in tone. The behind-the-scenes documentaries of the direct cinema movement, especially when they featured major political figures, contributed to the developing sensibility that much of the real political action was taking place backstage and that the politicians were presenting the public with a contrived facade. In the spirit of such books as *The Making of the President 1960*, *The Boys on the Bus*, *What It Takes*, and *The Girls in the Van*, films like *Primary*, *The War Room* (1993), *Journeys with George* (2002), and *Diary of a Political Tourist* (2004) have turned the backstage into political spectacle. These documentaries—and fictional films such as *The Candidate* (1972), pseudo-fictions like *Primary Colors* (1998), and pseudo-documentaries like *Bob Roberts* (1992)—have changed the way we imagine campaigns, leading campaigns to reframe their own narratives.

The New Political Documentary

The history of documentary provides a loosely evolving and diverse rhetoric that the new political documentary draws on and to which it appeals for authorization. But nothing in the history of documentary entirely prepared the voters or the campaigns for what they encountered in 2004.

The rhetoric of the new political documentary is in many ways distinctive. The films of 2004 were typically shot with relatively low budgets, in video rather than film, making use of interviews and stock footage rather than observation of uncontrolled behavior. The quality was often good enough and interest sufficiently intense that the films were shown in theaters and on television, which provided legitimacy and visibility, before quickly being released on DVD and VHS, in which form they could be marketed rapidly on the Internet. Sometimes they were also shown directly on the Internet. The films were highly partisan but typically independent—at least ostensibly—from political parties. Though they were relatively cheap, the films were by no means homemade—these are professional productions, of varying technical quality and political professionalism. The economies of production and distribution, at least in this round of the new political documentary, focused attention on national issues and the national campaigns, though in principle they could be emulated by citizen-filmmakers at more local levels in the future. Usually, the films were closely linked to attacking or defending the character of a candidate or engaged in historical exposé. Issues of policy, when debated, usually were framed within the narrative of a person, party, or administration rather than concentrated on prudential discussion of future decision-making in the realm of policy.

The films experimented with a wide range of rhetorics, from the personal mix of comic disparagement and earnest confrontation of Michael Moore to various emulations of traditional news and documentary voices. *Fahrenheit 9/11* is dominated by Moore's personal indictment of the Bush administration. Its most popular rejoinder, *Fahrenhype 9/11*, invests as much energy in attacking Moore as it does in defending Bush, an inherently risky refutational stance, since it elevates Moore at the same time that it attacks him and cannot match his complex wit. In films like *Fahrenhype 9/11*, *Celsius 41.11*, or *George W. Bush: Faith in the White House*, the directors' names appear on the films and have not been hidden in any way, yet the mode of address is "corporate" rather than "personal." Both voices, personal and corporate, are able to claim implicitly, and sometimes explicitly, that they are not connected to any candidate or party, which allows them a wide latitude of tone, style, and content that an acknowledged campaign message might not be able to achieve—even in the climate of recurrently negative campaigning of recent years.

It is not known, of course, whether the new documentary films of 2004 had a major influence on the results of the election, primarily because so few of the films were seen by audiences not already predisposed to agree with them, by professional partisans eager to refute them, or by journalists reporting on this novel wave of controversy. It is clear that the new political documentary shaped the discourse of the campaign and that there would be more such films in the next election cycles. Moore himself vowed to make a sequel to *Fahrenheit 9/11*, and a chorus of conservative voices quickly began rehearsing its response.[26] Whatever happens in 2008 and beyond, the new political documentaries of 2004 are significant in their own right as a window into the politics of our post-9/11 world and as important texts of American political rhetoric. This book is addressed to citizens, scholars, and the press as a rhetorical history and criticism of the new political documentaries of 2004 and as an attempt to develop tools for understanding their role and their potential in the national debate.

Shawn J. and Trevor Parry-Giles argue that *Fahrenheit 9/11* engages in both deliberative and campaign rhetoric, which, they point out, is an especially difficult task in a time of war, when a president may use a variety of means to delegitimize dissent, and in the context of a campaign, when it can be charged that deliberative rhetoric is actually campaign rhetoric in disguise. The deliberative rhetoric of the film is further complicated, and perhaps undermined, argue the authors, by the peculiar mix of humor and earnestness, of political idealism and mass media commodification, of insistence on authenticity and appeal to the virtual spectacle of hyperreality; the film's pleasures are those of spectatorship rather than grounded participation in the political community. The film was an enormous success as a commercial entertainment and influenced the rhetoric of the whole campaign, but its influence on the election itself or on larger, collective social change is dubious, argue Parry-Giles and Parry-Giles. Their chapter illustrates with precision that, however disappointing the film may have been in generating deliberation, it is a brilliant piece of filmmaking and marketing and a significant marker of the conditions of our national discourse.

Jennifer L. Borda considers two films that were promoted as direct refutations of *Fahrenheit 9/11*. Both *Fahrenhype 9/11* and *Celsius 41.11* implicitly acknowledge the importance of Moore's film by making it the subject of refutation, and they commit themselves to a level of discourse that they are unable to deliver. The films are both tightly edited direct-address expositions of opposition to Moore's film, using interview sound bites with conservative pundits and activists who speak to the camera. Where non-interview material is used, it is typically stock footage used to illustrate points made on the sound track. The mode of address is so direct and so partisan, argues Borda, that the films are likely to appeal only to those already converted. The films do not do what they claim to do—provide a point-by-point argument refuting Moore's claims—but they may well serve to motivate partisans already committed to the cause, to provide them with talking points, and to move them to action. The films are not, in substance, rational arguments, though they are presented as a series of claims and charges, which undermines the claims they make for themselves and limits their utility as models of how feature-length documentaries might "debate" each other for the public good. That may be an inherent limit of the documentary mode or its expository subgenre; it may be a limitation imposed by the difficulty of trying to respond to Moore's peculiar combination of mockery and exposé; or it may simply be a product of the limits of these filmmakers. In any case, it is a nuanced indicator of the tone of the 2004 presidential campaign and its fragmented partisanship.

In "Vietnam Flashbacks," Roger Stahl examines two films that present opposing narratives of John Kerry's Vietnam War record—a record that the candidate presented as part of his own claim that he was qualified for the presidency. In the Vietnam War, Kerry served as a navy lieutenant in command of a Swift Boat patrolling the rivers of Vietnam. He was wounded three times and won several decorations for bravery. In the context of a campaign designed by the Bush forces as a story of character, the Kerry campaign responded with the story of Kerry's war record—which might have seemed a promising gambit, given the Kerry record, the wars in Iraq and Afghanistan, and reports that President Bush had himself ducked service in Vietnam with an appointment to the Air National Guard arranged by family friends. There were reports that Bush had been derelict in fulfilling the obligations of even this assignment. But the Kerry war record was attacked by a third-party group calling itself the Swift Boat Veterans for Truth, which released *Stolen Honor: Wounds That Never Heal* in September 2004. *Stolen Honor* claims that Kerry lied about his war service and that he dishonored his country in opposing the Vietnam War after he had been honorably discharged from the navy. A competing narrative of Kerry's war service is told in *Going Upriver: The Long War of John Kerry,* which was released to theaters in early October and was soon available on DVD. Stahl's close reading of these two films reveals competing but quite different formal and thematic rhetorics, but he also finds that they have in common a deep and agonized concern to come to terms with the memory of war and the uses of American military power.

Martin J. Medhurst considers the film *George W. Bush: Faith in the White House* as an appeal to orthodox evangelical Christians. To understand the film, he argues, we must take into account that it is a carefully targeted message to a particular subgroup in a religious topography that is still obscure to many Americans. Medhurst estimates that 30 to 50 million Americans can now be properly identified as evangelicals. The film identifies itself as being made by evangelicals and for evangelicals and as being about faith rather than politics. The film's rhetoric is based on a dialectical narrative structure, testimonial, historical analogy, representative anecdote, and historical reconstruction.

Medhurst, who identifies himself as an evangelical Christian who twice voted for Bush, calls the film a "rousing success" as rhetoric, but he has reservations about it as theology. His reflections on the way the film mixes religion with politics pose challenges for all Americans concerned with what faith does with politics and what politics does with faith.

Robert E. Terrill examines the rhetoric of *Unprecedented: The 2000 Presidential Election*, produced by Robert Greenwald and Earl Katz. The film, argues Terrill, does a good job of laying out the evidence for its claims that Florida unjustly excluded African American Democrats from the election, that the vote recount was fraudulent, that the Supreme Court decision to award the election to George W. Bush was unjust, and that had the vote recount been conducted properly, Al Gore would have won the election. But, writes Terrill, though the film presents itself as a call to action, it does not live up to its full potential in mobilizing citizens, largely because of a failed conception of the rhetorical potential of the committed documentary. Terrill theorizes that such mobilization might be brought about not so much by an emotional arousal that parallels the intellectual convictions established by the film's arguments and evidence but rather by employing documentary's capacity to illustrate desirable modes of action that a willing audience could imitate, a mode of rhetorical aesthetics that Terrill terms "political mimesis."

Susan Mackey-Kallis examines Robert Greenwald's *Uncovered: The War on Iraq*, released in October 2004. Mackey-Kallis finds that Greenwald makes effective use of familiar rhetorical forms, employing tightly edited talking-head interviews with leading Washington insiders to refute the Bush administration's case for war and to advance the alternate case that the administration took the country into war with false claims about Iraqi links to terrorism and weapons of mass destruction, then resorted to character assassination and the cloak of patriotism in time of war to silence its opponents and critics. The interviewees, and the film itself, are offered as models for a more robust version of the duties of patriotism in time of war. Mackey-Kallis considers the film's production history in the context of the changing opportunities for the production of high-quality, low-budget alternative media that are transforming political communication but observes that dominant patterns of corporate media ownership may limit the potentially important role of the new political documentary in the public sphere.

Ronald V. Bettig and Jeanne Lynn Hall write about Greenwald's *Outfoxed: Rupert Murdoch's War on Journalism*. Their chapter is a detailed reading of the rhetoric of that documentary and an analysis of the political economy of American communication, which is the context of Greenwald's film. Bettig and Hall's description of the concentration of American media ownership, with its power to filter political news and construct political knowledge, provides a compelling case for the potential importance of the new political documentary, which is able to use the existing media system against itself—up to a point. Bettig and Hall describe not only the rhetoric of *Outfoxed* but also the rhetoric of Fox News itself and what they call the "Fox effect," as other major news outlets imitate Fox's rhetoric of sensationalism, blurring of news and political commentary, aggressive graphics and editing, and displays of patriotism. They conclude that "a truly democratic communications system cannot exist as long as culture, knowledge, and audiences are treated as commodities, produced primarily for their exchange value in the media marketplace."

The new political documentaries of the 2004 election cycle were a significant part of the larger rhetoric of the campaign. Drawing on traditional forms of documentary, news, and political advertising, producers made innovative uses of new developments in digital media technology to produce and distribute a wide range of political discourses. The documentaries themselves became the subject of campaign rhetoric and entered into the vernacular of political talk. It is hoped that the critical analyses in this book will contribute to understanding the rhetoric of these documentaries and their implications for democratic discourse.

In 1964, Arthur M. Schlesinger Jr. observed that "one of the most questionable words in the vocabulary of film is 'documentary.' It seems an honest, weatherbeaten word, conveying the feeling that here, at last, there is no nonsense, no faking, only the plain facts. . . . [T]he line between the documentary and the fiction film is tenuous indeed. Both are artifacts; both are contrivances. Both are created by editing and selection. Both, wittingly or not, embody a viewpoint."[27] The new political documentaries addressed in the present book would almost certainly not be mistaken by any viewer for purely objective observations of naturally occurring reality, and yet there is a lingering rhetorical aura about documentary as an idea that does suggest a sort of seriousness, a special claim on truth-telling, however tenuous. The independent political documentaries of the 2004 election cycle draw on the power of the documentary tradition as a rhetoric that shapes the films themselves, as a complex rhetoric of reading practices exercised by their audiences in the American electorate, and as an aspiration to truth-telling and speaking out as ideals against which the films may be measured.

Using a variety of approaches adapted to each case, the contributors to this book offer a composite history and criticism of what we have called the new political documentary—a group of films and feature-length videos released in the months before the 2004 American presidential election. The critics in this book describe how the films draw upon and appeal to the documentary idea, and they also hold the films accountable to the standards implied by that appeal—standards that are implicit in the conduct of controversy in a democratic society and that themselves reach far back in the history of the rhetorical tradition. While they find that the films often fall short of the best implied standards of documentary and of democratic rhetoric, they also find in every case both important news about the temper of the 2004 election and the potential of documentary to contribute to civic debate in the age of the Internet, the war on terror, and the new century.

President Bush was reelected in a bruising campaign against his Democratic opponent, Senator Kerry. Wars raged in Afghanistan and Iraq. The war on terror continued at home and abroad. Saddam Hussein remained in jail, but Osama bin Laden remained at large. Evidence about prisoner abuse and even torture surfaced and spread. The economy improved slightly, though the gap between the rich and the poor widened and the middle class lost ground. Manufacturing jobs left the United States, often replaced, if at all, with lower paying jobs in the service economy. Millions of Americans were without health care. State appropriations for higher education slipped and tuition rose, burdening graduates with huge personal debts and threatening America's economic advantage in science, engineering, and innovation. Gas and oil prices rose dramatically. The federal government swelled to a record size, as did the national deficit. Social security reform, health care, prescription drug plans, No Child Left Behind, the USA PATRIOT Act, global warming, stem cell research, alleged media bias, corporate accounting scandals, and same-sex marriage were among the issues that dominated the national agenda and defined the election.

The political documentaries of 2004 explored some of these issues in depth while ignoring others altogether. The character and background of the presidential candidates, the war in Iraq, media bias, electoral fraud, and the relationship between national security and civil liberties were addressed directly and repeatedly by documentary filmmakers. Social security reform, education reform, and global warming—all issues that were talked about in other forms of campaign rhetoric, including speeches, debates, and television advertisements—were hardly mentioned in the leading political documentaries that most assertively linked themselves to the election campaign. On the other hand, the new political documentary does not exhaust the range of documentary material of all sorts, much of it related to social and political issues and regularly produced by public, network, and cable television and by independent producers. Our focus in this study has been on that peculiar group of highly visible independent documentaries that emerged in and were directly related to the presidential campaign.

The Facts

Perhaps the most consistent criticism offered by the contributors to this book is that the political documentaries of 2004 distorted the facts. Whether it was the inclusion of outright lies, the promotion of unsubstantiated conspiracy theories, the subtle revision of the historical record, or just sloppy research, inaccuracy is the charge leveled against many of these films. In other cases, it was not that the films were inaccurate in their claims so much as that they provided insufficient context for understanding those claims. For example, even as Bettig and Hall appear to side with the makers of *Outfoxed* in that film's critique of Rupert Murdoch's News Corp. and the Fox News channel, their own thorough examination of the causes and consequences of corporate media ownership demonstrates just how much the viewer of *Outfoxed* does not learn from the film about this central issue.

On the other hand, Mackey-Kallis argues that *Uncovered: The War on Iraq* avoided the temptation to treat factual matters too lightly. "Greenwald's film, methodically and consistently constructed from talking heads and archival footage, provides an important historical record not only of what a number of officials both inside and outside the Bush administration were saying and thinking but of what twenty-six different experts, from the intelligence community service to the diplomatic corps, were saying and thinking about America's war against Iraq in 2003. Maybe it is possible for talking heads to 'rock the house.'"

Mackey-Kallis concedes that Greenwald's talking-heads approach may not be as entertaining as the style and tone of other political documentaries, but she admires its commitment to examining the full depth and breadth of the issues.

Audience Analysis and Citizen Action

In her essay on *Fahrenhype 9/11* and *Celsius 41.11,* two films designed to refute Moore's *Fahrenheit 9/11,* Borda recognizes the inherent double bind in films that respond directly to other documentaries. "If the films are to craft their responses using the impassioned discourse and emotional appeals that contemporary viewers have come to expect from a documentary . . . , they risk speaking only to those audiences already sympathetic to their political views." When they take this approach, warns Borda, the films do little to educate their own most partisan viewers and offer no sensible appeal to the neutral or skeptical viewer. Medhurst echoes this criticism in his analysis of *George W. Bush: Faith in the White House,* "a film made by evangelicals, addressed primarily to evangelicals, and designed in large measure to meet the ego-needs of evangelicals at the beginning of the twenty-first century." Preaching to the converted may have its value in getting voters to the polls, but it does little to improve the quality of political debate in a polarized country.

Most of the films analyzed in this book were made by and for partisans predisposed to agree with their assertions long before anything resembling proof was offered. Documentary film is an argumentative art form, and it does not seem that neutrality is what these critics are recommending. Rather, claims should be supported by evidence that audiences of all political perspectives might find compelling. On the most pragmatic grounds, multiple perspectives should be considered, even if all but one are eventually discarded. Sufficient context should be provided so that viewers are able to make informed decisions about what they are seeing and hearing. Few if any of the films analyzed in this book meet this basic standard for rational discourse, but the goal is attainable, even in circumstances of passionate advocacy.

Spectacle and Distraction

Nearly all of the essays in this volume criticize the new political documentary for resorting too often to negative personal attacks and spectacular imagery and not often enough to reasoned debate and critical evaluation. Stahl writes that "*Stolen Honor* relies heavily on a discourse of pain." Parry-Giles and Parry-Giles argue that *Fahrenheit 9/11* "takes the media spectacle to new levels of virtual reality and emotionality as a cinematic extravaganza. Murray Edelman contends that art can contribute to politics by 'excit[ing] minds and feelings as everyday experiences ordinarily do not[;] it is a provocation, an incentive to mental and emotional alertness. Its creation of new realities means that it can intrude upon passive acceptance of conventional ideas and banal responses to political clichés.'" Documentary is capable both of generating that excitement and of moving past mere stimulation to the clash of contending perspectives.

Calls to Action

Only one essay in this book faulted the film it examined for failing to offer a clearer and more specific call to action. In his critique of *Unprecedented: The 2000 Presidential Election*, Terrill notes that the film "expends its energy in the presentation of evidence rather than in a call to action." Here we find that the presentation of evidence, said to be so thoroughly lacking in some of the other documentaries, is regarded as only the first step toward effecting positive social change. Why would *Unprecedented* be judged differently? Perhaps it is because the call to act is implicit in most of the other films: to vote for or against a specific candidate. *Unprecedented* does not tell its viewers how to vote. Instead, it calls into question the reliability of the voting process itself. Does this make the film a special case? Perhaps not, since the negativity and spectacle of many of these films might as easily contribute to passivity or alienation as to mobilization.

Entertaining Citizens

If political documentaries were more reasonable, balanced, and complex in their evidence and calls to action, would the films be interesting and entertaining enough to attract an audience? In his essay on *George W. Bush: Faith in the White House*, Medhurst reminds us that "Cicero said that the purposes of rhetoric are three—to teach, to delight, and to move." Collectively, these films certainly delighted partisan audiences, and they may have moved them as well, but did they teach them anything they did not already believe? If they had tried to do so, would they have attracted an audience?

Concluding their analysis of the most critically and financially successful of the new political documentaries, *Fahrenheit 9/11*, Parry-Giles and Parry-Giles note that, "In the end, commodified media spectacles have limited force as deliberative or campaign discourse because their persuasive power rests in the need to 'experience' the film, ensuring their value as commercially marketed entertainment but restricting their capacity to motivate and sustain meaningful political change." The future of the political documentary film may depend on its ability to inform voters and to encourage them to active citizenship even as it entertains them.

It might be argued that the passages in this book most critical of some of the political documentaries of 2004 are themselves a predictable response by academic critics, who, whatever their politics, can be expected to favor a broadly liberal vision of civic optimism based on reasonable debate of decisive issues in a public sphere that offers rationality, access, engagement, reciprocity, responsibility, and shared power. Such critics—that is, the editors of and contributors to this book—might be accused of a utopianism composed of pedagogical pieties and theoretical formalism that have little to do with the actual world of contemporary democratic politics. Such an objection would then go on to point out that the new political documentaries are and ought to be partisan, provocative, even a little paranoid, because that is what the circumstances demand and what they can do best. If this causes civic pessimism, perhaps that is preferable, such a position would argue, to a loyal enthusiasm for the misguided status quo. If this condition prompts partisan action, so much the better. If it does only part of the job of political persuasion, others are welcome to take the debate the rest of the way by whatever democratic means are at hand.

The films of the 2004 election campaign have already become part of the vernacular of American politics. When in November 2005 Pennsylvania congressman John Murtha called for a gradual withdrawal of American troops from Iraq, the White House accused the longtime defense hawk of having become a "Michael Moore." Rising to Murtha's defense, Senator Kerry said that Americans would not stand for the "swiftboating" of Murtha. The images of Michael Moore as an antagonist to President Bush and of the Swift Boat as code for accusations of betraying the troops had entered the language through the political documentaries of 2004, as in 1988 a prison inmate named Willie Horton and the "revolving door," featured in television ads for George H. W. Bush, became code for a loathing of liberal politics. Americans will attend to these political documentaries, and the films will shape political knowledge—and not merely because Americans seek distraction or are prone to deception. In the turmoil of democratic government, these films play their part, and so, it is hoped, do the sorts of reflection, analysis, and discussion encouraged by the contributors to this book.

It seems clear that the new political documentary has a future, though developing technologies and economic opportunities are bringing change with every election cycle. Within a year of the 2004 election, leading documentary producers were at work on a new round of films. Independent documentary producers have again found a way to bring new visions to public attention, as such independent documentarians as Robert Flaherty and Frederick Wiseman did before them. Independent political documentary itself is a broader genre than partisan political films embedded in the electoral cycle, with the regular production of such issue-oriented films as Al Gore's *An Inconvenient Truth* (2005) and such muckraking, anti-corporate exposés as Eugene Jarecki's *Why We Fight* (2006), Robert Greenwald's *Wal-Mart: The High Cost of Low Price* (2005), Janis Karpinski's *Iraq for Sale: The War Profiteers* (2006), Morgan Spurlock's *Super Size Me* (2004), and Nick and Mark Francis's *Black Gold* (2006). The production of more clearly electoral films also continues vigorously, with the release of such films as Mark Birnbaum and Jim Schermbeck's *The Big Buy: Tom Delay's Stolen Congress* (2006) in time for the 2006 congressional elections, which returned both houses of Congress to control by the Democrats.

The rapid development of technology now makes it possible for a citizen with a camcorder, a laptop, and a Web site to produce and distribute political documentaries at minimal cost. At the other end of the scale, the continued intensity of partisan commitments in presidential elections, and the revenues at stake, attract major producers such as Moore, Greenwald, and others. The changing mix of local, citizen documentary and citizen journalism and of fully mounted professional, independent documentary production is creating a new world for documentary. It would be a mistake for any citizen to suppose that these independent documentaries, large and small, could or should drive existing news and public television documentaries off the page; in fact, they might help set new agendas for mainstream television documentaries. In raising issues otherwise not discussed, in offering skeptical reassessment of settled politics, in sustaining collective memory that reaches beyond the hourly news cycles, and in bringing otherwise silenced voices to the public sphere, the new political documentary, for all its faults, has an important role to play in the larger array of political discourse.

The films studied in this book were all formally independent of the political parties and candidates, though in some cases there were networks of overlapping interest, money, or personnel. The independence of the films brought them the power and the limits of that independence. They were partisan, passionate, and often directed to fragments of the public. They could be impudent, presenting information and attitudes often not cultivated in the campaigns or in mainstream journalism. When candidates or campaigns speaks for themselves, they are in effect committing themselves to a point of view and, however vaguely, to an agenda. The independent documentaries could not create any such obligation, which is a necessary price of their freedom to say what candidates might not say. The new political documentary is not a cure for whatever might ail the democratic process, but the films of the 2004 season have shown that these films can play a useful role in the larger mix of political discourse.

In an essay published in 1942, in the midst of World War II, Grierson wrote that "in the authoritarian state you have powers of compulsion and powers of repression, physical and mental, which in part at least take the place of persuasion. Not so in a democracy. It is your democrat who most needs and demands guidance from his leaders. It is the democratic leader who must give it. If only for the sake of quick decision and common action, it is democracy for which propaganda is the more urgent necessity."[28] Grierson understood that his audience in the Western democracies would find his statement paradoxical or repugnant. And yet the paradox of democratic propaganda did not alarm so much as inspire Grierson, who insisted that even in a crisis, the democratic citizen in a modern liberal state "demands as of right—of human right—that he come in only of his own free will."[29] Grierson's longing for "common action" led by a benevolent elite now sounds remote and outdated, but his depiction of the demand for leadership and of the insistence on free will exercised after consideration of public persuasion seems to survive as an expectation of democracy, and the political documentary will play a part in that persuasion.

In 1942, Grierson wrote, "The materials of citizenship today are different and the perspectives wider and more difficult; but we have, as ever, the duty of exploring them and of waking the heart and will in regard to them. That duty is what documentary is about."[30] That duty is what this book is about.

Notes

1. Paul Farhi and James V. Grimaldi, "GOP Won with Accent on Rural and Traditional," *Washington Post*, November 3, 2004.

2. "The Revolution Will Be Posted," *New York Times*, November 2, 2004.

3. Grierson's review appeared in the *New York Sun*, February 28, 1926. The term "documentary" rapidly took on the meaning of "factual, realistic, applied esp. to a film or literary work, etc., based on real events or circumstances and intended primarily for instruction or record purposes" (*Oxford English Dictionary*, 2nd ed.). The *OED* notes that the French may earlier have used the term to apply to travelogues. Soon, the genre went far beyond the limits of "instruction or record."

4. It did not take long for filmmakers to discover an audience for narrative films more sophisticated than these early documentary films. Georges Melies's *A Trip to Moon* (1902) is an early example of the popularity of narrative film. By 1906, narrative had become the dominant form of American film.

5. For a catalog of Lincoln portrayals in the America cinema, see Mark S. Reinhart, *Abraham Lincoln on the Screen: A Filmography of Dramas and Documentaries Including Television, 1903–1998* (Jefferson, N.C.: McFarland, 1999). See also Cara A. Finnegan, "Recognizing Lincoln: Image Vernaculars in Nineteenth Century Visual Culture," *Rhetoric and Public Affairs* 8 (2005): 31–58.

6. Bill Nichols, *Introduction to Documentary* (Bloomington: Indiana University Press, 2001), 98.

7. Forsyth Hardy, ed., *Grierson on Documentary* (London: Faber and Faber, 1979), 11; Erik Barnouw, *Documentary: A History of the Non-fiction Film* (New York: Oxford University Press, 1974), 85.

8. See Robert L. Snyder, *Pare Lorentz and the Documentary Film* (Norman: University of Oklahoma Press, 1973).

9. *The City* was sponsored by the American Institute of Planners. For a rhetorical analysis of the film, see Martin J. Medhurst and Thomas W. Benson, "*The City*: The Rhetoric of Rhythm," *Communication Monographs* 48 (1981): 54–72.

10. David A. Cook, *A History of Narrative Film*, 4th ed. (New York: W. W. Norton, 2004), 368.

11. Quoted in John Grierson, "The Nature of Propaganda," in *Grierson on Documentary*, ed. Forsyth Hardy (London: Faber and Faber, 1946), reprinted in *Nonfiction Film Theory and Criticism*, ed. Richard Meran Barsam (New York: E. P. Dutton, 1976), 32.

12. Quoted in David Weinberg, "Approaches to the Study of Film in the Third Reich: A Critical Appraisal," *Journal of Contemporary History* 19 (1984): 105.

13. Robert T. Elson, "Time Marches on the Screen," in *Time Inc.: An Intimate History of a Publishing Enterprise, 1923–1941* (New York: Atheneum, 1973), 237–40.

14. Richard Meran Barsam, "'This Is America': Documentaries for Theaters, 1942–1951," in *Nonfiction Film Theory and Criticism*, ed. Richard Meran Barsam (New York: E. P. Dutton, 1976), 116.

15. Quoted in ibid., 117.

16. Ibid., 116.

17. Richard Dyer MacCann, *The People's Films: A Political History of U.S. Government Motion Pictures* (New York: Hastings House, 1973), 153–59.

18. Cook, *A History of Narrative Film,* 286.

19. MacCann, *The People's Films,* 173–200.

20. Nichols, *Introduction to Documentary,* 148.

21. Ibid.

22. See Garth E. Pauley, "Documentary Desegregation: A Rhetorical Analysis of *Crisis: Behind a Presidential Commitment*," *Southern Communication Journal* 64 (1999): 123–42; and Jeanne Hall, "Realism as a Style in Cinema Verite: A Critical Analysis of *Primary*," *Cinema Journal* 30, no. 4 (1991): 24–50. See also Stephen Mamber, *Cinema Verite in America: Studies in Uncontrolled Documentary* (Cambridge, Mass.: MIT University Press, 1974); P. J. O'Connell, *Robert Drew and the Development of Cinema Verite in America* (Carbondale: Southern Illinois University Press, 1992); and Thomas W. Benson and Carolyn Anderson, *Reality Fictions*, 2nd ed. (Carbondale: Southern Illinois University Press, 2002).

23. Joanne Morreale, *The Presidential Campaign Film: A Critical History* (Westport, Conn.: Praeger, 1993), 3.

24. Ibid., 45–67.

25. Susan Mackey-Kallis, "Spectator Desire and Narrative Closure: The Reagan 18-Minute Political Film," *Southern Communication Journal* 56 (1991): 308.

26. "Moore Crafting 'Fahrenheit' Sequel," *CBSNews.com*, November 11, 2004, http://www.cbsnews.com/stories/2004/11/11/entertainment/main655200.shtml.

27. Arthur M. Schlesinger Jr., "The Fiction of Fact—and the Fact of Fiction," in *The Documentary Tradition*, ed. Lewis Jacobs, 2nd ed. (New York: W. W. Norton, 1979), 383. Originally published in *Show* magazine, 1964.

28. Grierson, "The Nature of Propaganda," 39.

29. Ibid.

30. John Grierson, "The Documentary Idea," in *Nonfiction Film Theory and Criticism*, ed. Richard Meran Barsam (New York: E. P. Dutton, 1976), 86.

2

Shawn J. Parry-Giles and
Trevor Parry-Giles

Virtual Realism and the Limits of Commodified Dissent in *Fahrenheit 9/11*

The U.S. Constitution sought to "provide for the general welfare" and to "secure the blessings of liberty" for a new nation in 1789, even as it created a delicately balanced and at times inherently contradictory governmental scheme. The Constitution simultaneously grants war powers to both the Congress, with its exclusive power to declare war, and to the executive, in his or her capacity as commander-in-chief of the armed forces. The divided constitutional war powers have been a source of discord for much of the nation's history, especially during the Vietnam era. In the midst of that conflict, in an effort to reassert its constitutional prerogative to "declare war,"[1] Congress passed the War Powers Act of 1973, designed to "fulfill the intent of the framers of the Constitution . . . and insure the collective judgment of both the Congress and the President" during wartime.[2]

Although presidents have generally taken great care to seek congressional consent for any military intervention since 1973, U.S. commanders-in-chief are still given considerable authority to place troops in harm's way, with often minimal opposition from Congress and the broader public.[3] Presidents work to limit domestic dissent in times of military conflict and to secure their dominance over war-making institutions and policies. For much of the nation's history, wartime dissent violated the ideological bases for war and often was sanctioned harshly by those striving for national unification. The Alien and Sedition Acts (1798) actually sought to suppress speech that opposed the incumbent party's power during the quasi-war with France, and the Espionage

Acts of 1917 helped suppress domestic opposition to U.S. involvement in World War I. The Cold War witnessed a return to government-inspired sanctions for anti-(cold) war sentiments. Stephen J. Whitfield contends, "Since dissent seemed to slide so uncomfortably close to disloyalty, since controversy had become a code word for trouble . . . official views were rarely and insufficiently challenged on television."[4]

The national reluctance to challenge presidential wartime policies was renewed after September 11, 2001. President George W. Bush received nearly unanimous congressional support for his war resolution against the Taliban government in Afghanistan.[5] Although CNN reported that a "small but vocal group of lawmakers" led a "spirited debate" about the breadth and timing of the impending military actions in Iraq, the Senate voted 77–23 to authorize the president to attack Iraq if Saddam Hussein did not turn over weapons of mass destruction. The House backed the same resolution by a vote of 296–133. CNN concluded, "The outcome of the vote was never in doubt."[6] Addressing this lack of meaningful dissent, Victor Navasky argues, "In the aftermath of September 11 the national media have confused the questioning of official policy with disloyalty."[7] Following the Senate's vote to authorize war against Iraq, President Bush declared triumphantly, "America speaks with one voice."[8]

Despite such claims of unity, others outside of Congress began an audible and continuous drumbeat of wartime inquiry—they began the task of *deliberating* wartime necessity and progress. Perhaps the most noteworthy antiwar interrogation came in the form of a political documentary titled *Fahrenheit 9/11* (hereafter *F9/11*). Dubbed "the most successful documentary ever,"[9] Michael Moore's film grossed over $119 million domestically, more than any other documentary to date, winning the grand prize at the 2004 Cannes Film Festival, the Palme d'Or award.[10] *F9/11* and other anti–Iraq war films like *Why We Fight, WMD: Weapons of Mass Deception,* and *Hijacking Catastrophe: 9/11, Fear and the Selling of American Empire* are credited with offering "alternative explanations for the war in Iraq and the news coverage of it."[11]

Yet, as everyone who sees the film understands, *F9/11* is more than a deliberative text that debates the justification for war and its strategies of engagement. Its debut during the 2004 presidential election combined with its vehement attack on President Bush to position the film as a campaign text. The nature and timing of the film, for example, encouraged the conservative group Citizens United to charge that its release violated the McCain-Feingold campaign finance laws because the film was advertised thirty days prior to the party conventions.[12] *Time* magazine labeled Moore a "popular agitator" and credited the film with providing a "nationwide rally[ing] point for Bush opponents" and with becoming a "potential factor in the '04 presidential race."[13]

In this chapter, we interrogate the persuasive strategies at work in *F9/11*—a political text that conjoins the characteristics of deliberative (policy-centered) and campaign (character-centered) discourse. *F9/11* advances two prominent arguments, either explicitly or enthymematically. First, the film suggests the immorality and illegitimacy of the U.S. wars in Afghanistan and especially Iraq because neither achieved the thresholds for a legitimate and just war (deliberative ends). Second, the film demonstrates the illegitimacy of the Bush presidency because of the questions surrounding his election, his military experiences, and his performance as commander-in-chief (campaign ends).

In arguing its point, the film displays numerous markers of authenticity that enhance the film's realism as Moore takes the viewer "behind the scenes" of the Bush administration and its march to war. Film is uniquely capable, as a medium, to achieve such illusory realism—as Joel Snyder remarks, the camera "has taken on the status of natural machine—the giver of 'the image of nature.'"[14] In *F9/11*, the audience is *virtually* situated in political spaces often off-limits, enhancing the potential power of mediated deliberative and campaign moments over the spoken word. The camera work of *F9/11* helps situate us vicariously within the spectacle of the film, particularly by reliving the 9/11 terrorist attacks, experiencing combat in Iraq, and grieving over the impact of the war on one U.S. family—moments of virtual reality that encourage intense emotional responses.

Despite such moves toward authenticity, the content, timing, and production characteristics of the film subvert the power of its realism. Moore relies on conspiracy theories in his attempt to unmask the "reality" of the Bush administration's policies. Conspiracy theories have a contested history in U.S. political culture—they are subject to intense levels of scrutiny and suspicion, and Moore's are no exception. Moore's use of humor, which helps destabilize Bush's image as a strong commander-in-chief, also challenges the seriousness of his message and reminds viewers of the film's entertainment value. And even though Moore condemns President Bush for manufacturing the apparent necessity for war, Moore himself is guilty of his own image creations. His moments of virtual reality, while a powerful component of the film's experiential power and pathetic force, may likewise heighten anxieties about the film's truthfulness, especially as it critiques Bush's veracity during a presidential campaign.

F9/11 is a unique deliberative and campaign text, but it shares many other similarities with deliberative and campaign discourse, particularly in relation to matters of commodification. The film helped mobilize and give voice to disaffected leftists proud to call themselves liberals, even as its radical message helped mask its place as a commodity-marketed discourse that raised millions for its parent companies and the filmmaker. In the end, commodified media spectacles have limited force as deliberative or campaign discourse because their persuasive power rests in the need to "experience" the film, ensuring their value as commercially marketed entertainment but restricting their capacity to motivate and sustain meaningful political change.

Envisioning the Realism of War and the Illegitimacy of a President

As the film's writer, producer, and director, Michael Moore is focused on unmasking the image-making strategies of war and of a wartime presidential candidate. Such a move is common in contemporary political, mediated discourse, giving consumers of such texts a vision of what Joshua Meyrowitz calls "backstage behavior" that projects the appearance of being "more 'real' or honest than front region behavior."[15] *F9/11* suggests that we are being taken behind the scenes, showcasing documents and video moments seldom circulated in the public political sphere. In his foreword to Moore's official reader on the film, John Berger concludes that Moore succeeded in "interrupting the prepared, prevaricating statements of politicians" and in intervening "into immediate world politics."[16] Early in the film, for example, we are given glimpses into seldom-seen moments of Bush cabinet officials primping for media interviews, as they ostensibly prepared to sell the notion of war against Iraq. We are offered the opportunity to gaze into the eyes of Secretary of Defense Donald Rumsfeld as we hear him worry in a hushed voice over the facts of war: "Do you suppose he's pretty confident on those numbers on Iraqi security forces?"[17] Makeup—a marker of artificiality—is applied to the faces of Vice President Dick Cheney, National Security Advisor Condoleezza Rice, and Secretary of State Colin Powell. The president's hair is combed as he looks into the camera; Assistant Secretary of Defense Paul Wolfowitz spits on his comb as he styles his hair before an interview. At the close of the film, many of these same individuals remove earpieces and exit their interviews—suggesting that moviegoers were offered a glimpse into the image creations of the Bush administration.

Such visual and verbal cues function in part as markers of political authenticity. Imants Barušs defines the "authentic" as "that which is true to its own nature." Such authenticity is concerned with questions of truth, morality, and culture and has been a public (and private) preoccupation within communities since antiquity of those troubled with discerning the genuine from the fake.[18] On a political level, the preoccupation with distinguishing the real in the United States took on added fervor in the post–Vietnam, Watergate, Iran-Contra, and Clinton impeachment age as journalists became self-anointed watchdogs of political image-making, turning "questions of authenticity" into "questions of authority."[19] Or, as Margaret Morse explains, "The news [and the documentary, presumably] is a privileged discourse, invested with a special relation to the Real."[20]

This quest for authenticity, this search for the real, leads to mediated texts that are ultimately virtual in their depiction of "reality" even as they invite us to lose sight of their mediation and become more active participants in the mediated spectacle—experiencing the emotion in what feels like real time. We become virtually situated in the virtual spaces and are beckoned to see this virtuality as real, as an authentic rendition of its referent. In *F9/11*, Moore transports us to a virtual world of wartime planning and the backstage imaging of the Bush administration. Although Kevin Robins contends that "virtual reality" often represents a "utopian order," reflecting the ideal found only in dreams,[21] Moore's reality epitomizes a national nightmare where the truths of war planning and preparation as well as presidential credibility are shattered on the big screen when we relive the moments of horror from 9/11.

The first virtual reality moment in *F9/11* depicts the panic experienced when the planes hit the World Trade Center (WTC). In these mediated moments that last some two minutes and forty-five seconds, we become more than witnesses of the destruction; we are transported virtually into the spaces of terror. The sequence, in the words of one critic, is a "moment of poetry," where Moore eschews the conventional news footage available to him, opting instead for a "black screen" and a "muted soundtrack of panicked screams and street sounds" that powerfully evoke the tragedy of the 9/11 attacks.[22]

As we sit before the darkened screen for sixty-five seconds, we hear what appears to be the sound of the first plane hitting the WTC, followed by chaos—people screaming "Oh my God" and the sounds of sirens. After sitting in the dark for another twenty seconds, we hear a second explosion, representing, seemingly, the second plane hitting the second tower. The lack of visual imagery is starkly powerful as our mediated memories fill in the missing pictures for us.

The virtual reality moment continues when we hear a third explosion—perhaps the sounds of buildings beginning to collapse. When the images reappear on the screen, it is as if our eyes open for the first time after the horror. We do not see the buildings crash but instead see others looking skyward with expressions of horror and disbelief. The camera is jostling from the chaos, adding to constructed authenticity, and we see other people crying, praying, and sitting, dazed by the unthinkable engulfing them. We see the feet of those running away from the danger—our vantage point is from the ground, as if we are lying amid the ashes unable to move, frozen in fear. Such sounds and images transport us viscerally to those real-time moments—we transform from witness to virtual participant. One viewer of *F9/11* proclaimed, "When you showed the footage of the people in New York on 9/11 . . . I got chills and I cried. . . . I think everyone in the theater was crying."[23] Joel Black explains this transformation best when he asserts that memorable cinematic experiences are so intense and capture such sublime, extreme viscerality that "after the film is over, the world no longer looks the same because you see it differently."[24] Moore appreciates this capacity of film and presents other virtual reality moments in *F9/11*, particularly as he interrogates the Bush administration's war policies and transports us to the Iraqi battlefield.

The Illegitimate War

Moore delegitimizes the U.S. war effort in Afghanistan and especially in Iraq. He depicts personal relationships between the Bush family and the Saudis, particular the bin Laden family. He attends to the realities of war as experienced directly from the Iraqi battlefields, moving us once again to these virtual spaces of ideological dispute. In many instances, Moore himself does not offer explicit arguments against the war. Rather, he features first-person testimony from others who oppose the war. In addition, he explicates his arguments through visual imagery. Film theorist Rudolf Arnheim remarks that "every visual pattern . . . can be considered a proposition which, more or less successfully, makes a declaration about the nature of human existence."[25] Moore manifests this argumentative capacity of film when he creates visual enthymemes that require the audience to supply the implied and missing conclusions.

In his treatment of Afghanistan, Moore features news and congressional statements by Richard Clarke, the State Department and National Security Council official who was a well-known and outspoken critic of the Bush administration's handling of the war on terrorism. Clarke's national security ethos and first-person testimony add to the credibility of the claims he made on *Good Morning America*: "Basically the President botched the response to 9/11. He should have gone right after bin Laden." For Moore's part, he suggests that "Bush really didn't do much," leading him to wonder whether "Afghanistan [was] really about something else."

Throughout the film, Moore constructs that "something else" as the business relationships that the Bush family and friends allegedly formed with representatives of various Saudi Arabian oil conglomerates. Moore claims to have first suspected these connections and their influence with the news that in the hours and days following the 9/11 attacks, 24 members of Osama bin Laden's family and other Saudis totaling some 142 individuals were allowed to fly out of the United States, even though most planes were grounded. Moore also highlights connections between President Bush and the Taliban government or members of the bin Laden family and their mutual ties to Unocal, the

Carlyle Group, and Halliburton—the company where Vice President Cheney served as CEO. According to Moore, "The Saudi Royals and their associates have given the Bush family, their friends, and their related businesses" some $1.4 billion over the past "three decades." The film also features an interview with Dr. Sam Kubba of the American Iraqi Chamber of Commerce, who concludes: "If it wasn't for the oil, nobody would be there."

The film expends considerable time showcasing images of former president George Herbert Walker Bush and other cabinet officials with members of the Saudi government. Such camera placement creates a sense of intimacy and omniscience.[26] The intimacy is further reified through the presentation of sixteen photographs and video clips that are framed as a Bush "family album," implying a private glimpse into the personal lives of the Bushes and their Saudi business partners and "friends." The photos are depicted as snapshots, situated against a black backdrop. The music humorously reasserts the feel of intimacy as the chorus regales, "Shiny, happy people holding hands." In this Bush "family album," we see President George W. Bush holding hands with a Saudi male. The camera zooms in for a close-up of the hand-holding, evidencing the intimacy of the two while simultaneously de-masculinizing the president in the process. As this picture is replaced by a series of new visuals, we see other images of either the president or his father engaged in positive exchanges with Saudi males. The volume of images, which often situate us within the interpersonal exchanges through the camera's placement, functions as the visual proof of an intimate and thus inappropriate relationship with "the enemy." Such visuality suggests that even though political leaders attempt to control their own mediation, image busters like Moore offer competing "images of those parts of society most distant from the lives of the majority," taking us into a world off-limits to most.[27]

Deborah Willis reminds us that the "visual terrain" represents "contested political space." Regardless of the motives of the original photographer, photos can be used in multiple political ways, which exhibits a "logic of appropriation."[28] This is clearly evident in F9/11's depiction of Prince Bandar bin Sultan bin Abdul Aziz al-Saud, ambassador to the United States from the kingdom of Saudi Arabia. Moore notes that Bandar "was so close to the Bushes, they considered him a member of the family" and nicknamed him "Bandar Bush." One memorable photograph from the film implies a coziness between Bush and Bandar as it captures a look of close friends conversing privately. In it, we see President Bush meeting with the prince in a casual setting. Bush is lounging in a chair that is close to Bandar; Bush's legs are crossed, and he is wearing cowboy boots. Bandar sits on the side of the couch, leaning toward the president as the two are engaged in what appears as a serious conversation. There is no sense of context to the photograph, no placement in time or history, but the implication is clear and the association plain concerning the photo's relevance in the post-9/11 environment. Rather than make explicit conspiracy claims, though, Moore instead asks a series of questions for *F9/11*'s audience to ponder as we see an image of closeness between the two leaders: "What were they talking about? . . . Why would Bandar's government block American investigators from talking to the relatives of fifteen hijackers? Why would Saudi Arabia become reluctant to freeze the hijacker's assets?" Moore wonders aloud whether "Bush told Prince Bandar not to worry because he already had a plan." Moore answers his own questions by transitioning to a new section of the film, which features Iraq war preparations.

With the Iraq war, Moore takes us to the actual battlefield, where we see the ravages of war from the perspective of the Iraqi people and U.S. soldiers. Moreover, we experience the impact of war at home, particularly through the personal story of one mother who moves from being a war supporter to a grieved opponent of the war after the death of her son in a Blackhawk helicopter crash. In various ways, these moments become instances of virtual reality as we too experience vicariously, virtually, the emotionality and brutality of war.

In contrast to the restrictive news media coverage, where displaying the "coffins coming home" is prohibited, Moore's *F9/11* offers us a behind-the-scenes sense of the war that breaks the facade of the government's tight control over imagery and narrative emanating from Iraq. The entire segment is told through the use of direct address, where the subjects of the camera's gaze look back into the camera. The use of this filming technique is significant, as Paul Messaris notes when he reflects on the power of direct address, where "one or more characters look directly 'out' of the image into the *space* of the spectator."[29] Such direct address helps accentuate the feel of virtual reality as the subject hails us and draws us into the spaces of contestation—we become implicated in the war itself rather than remain bystanders distanced by time and place. The subject and audience, thus, meet in this shared space of virtual experience.

From the viewpoint of *F9/11*, the U.S. war against Iraq is unjust and immoral—contentions that are articulated predominantly through first-person narratives and hypergraphic visual images. As Bush prepares to deliver his March 19, 2003, speech that announces the beginning of the Iraqi war, we see his pre-speech antics, where he plays eye games with the camera. These odd eye movements periodically appear throughout the early stages of the film: the president is shown moving his eyes in unusual, playful ways; in one instance, he moves his eyes from left to right quickly as he smiles at the camera. As he prepares to speak, we finally realize that such nonverbal eye games are part of his prewar address preparations. Not only does such gesturing seem inappropriate given the gravity of the wartime situation, it also appears irreverent because he is looking at us and we are looking back at him; such behavior in an interpersonal encounter suggests he does not care that we are looking on. Messaris suggests that we typically rely on the same kind of "interpersonal processes" used in everyday conversation to assess visual imagery, particularly involving the camera's placement.[30] Even though such moments are private ones not meant to be part of the public record, they become part of the spectacle of war preparation given their placement in *F9/11*—they function to give us a glimpse into the private world of George W. Bush. And because these scenes make public that which would be normally private or unseen, they undermine the gravity of Bush's speech and indicate an artificiality to his presidency and his war against Iraq.

Following Bush's eye antics, Moore offers images of life in Baghdad before and after the bombing. Given that the typical images of Iraq focus on violence and chaos, the tranquil images seem incongruent with the mediated world we regularly see in the Middle East. We first see the words "ICE CREAM" on a sign that accompanies Arabic lettering—the discursive marker of other. Even as the familiar othering of Arabs is apparent, though, Moore still presents imagery that invites our identification with the people we see in the film. A boy happily jumps up and down before the camera as he works to gain our attention. Women walk by us, glancing back in a quick moment of direct address—we see them and they see us. A boy gets his hair cut, and two other boys ride a bike as one of them holds up what looks like a peace sign, smiling as they go by. Boys run with a kite toward an intact apartment dwelling. As these children run and play, we hear the president's voice inform us that "coalition forces have begun striking selected targets of military importance."

In an image reminiscent of Lyndon B. Johnson's (in)famous 1964 "Daisy" advertisement, we see a young girl sliding down a playground slide as the scene changes to an explosion of immense proportions. The juxtaposition of tranquillity and "normal" life in Iraq with the sights and sounds of the American invasion is compelling. Mitchell Stephens explains that "moving images with sound can make such leaps through time and space particularly persuasive and compelling"; the images that fill the screen in *F9/11* and the accompanying sounds are overwhelming.[31] Moore provides a total of eleven separate frames of nighttime explosions, either from the perspective of the recipient or from the sender, as we also experience the moment at which the missiles leave the ships or airplanes. We hear the whistle of missiles arriving just before the explosion erupts, and we hear the rumblings of buildings falling and sirens wailing to warn the Iraqi populace to take cover. The successive explosions are unnerving—much louder than on the television news—creating visceral moments of living in the war zone. In the next visual moments, we are transported to the rubble of death and destruction. Close-up images of dead children, badly burned, fill the screen, forcing us to comprehend such violence closer than most have ever experienced.

These images give us insight into the violence against the Iraqi people that is exhibited in *F9/11* and, as such, function argumentatively to indict the war. At the same time, they also demonstrate the depth of the virtual reality contained in the film. The viewer is taken directly into the war zone to see, to gaze upon, scenes that are unfamiliar and jarring in their difference from more conventional depictions of the war. This discourse reflects the concept that Fatimah Tobing Rony characterizes as the "third eye," where "we turn to the movies to find images of ourselves and find ourselves reflected in the eyes of others."[32] In the process, Meenakshi Gigi Durham contends, "the gaze that the object of ethnographic spectacle turns back on the viewer" represents "a gaze that marks the viewer and reconstitutes him from the viewpoint of the objectified other."[33]

Although we might expect that glimpses into the work of the U.S. military will help alleviate some of our anguish over the war, Moore refuses to allow such solace as we witness the lack of humanity expressed by certain U.S. soldiers. *F9/11* features first-person narratives with many soldiers speaking directly into the camera in interview fashion. The candor seems unusual given that such interviews are rarely carried on broadcast news, exhibiting once again the feel of behind-the-scenes discourse. Many who speak seem quite young, and some appear to enjoy the violence of war. In one unforgettable scene, a U.S. soldier talks about getting "pumped up" and "ready to go" into battle. Other soldiers begin one of their favorite battle songs. As we see images of Baghdad on fire, we hear a soldier sing, "We don't need no water, let the motherfucker burn, burn motherfucker burn." The song "Let the Bodies Hit the Floor" now plays as part of the film's musical score—it too is loud—and we see more images of death and destruction. Such images of violence show the virtual reality of war as a man runs toward us with a boy in his arms—we are situated in the war zones once again. The boy's body is lifeless and his pants are stained from urine—sights seldom displayed in conventional news coverage of this war.

These images question the rightness of the U.S. war against Iraq from a different perspective—one that invites the viewer to experience the war virtually, to hear directly from the people involved, to feel its consequences and its traumas. Moore's interrogation of the Bush administration's war motives combines with the grotesque images of war and the callousness of U.S. soldiers toward death to draw the viewer toward enthymematic conclusions that the war in Iraq constitutes an immoral and thus unjust war. Moore's use of these images and testimonials confirms a fundamental tenet of what Richard J. Regan identifies as "just war" principles: namely that "citizens are the ultimate interpreters of a democratic constitution," which means that "legal authority in a constitutional democracy will ultimately reflect the will of the people."[34]

Moore also features the testimony of a military mother forced to face the firsthand effects of war through the death of her son. Virtually, we too grieve over the death of her son as we are transported to her space of grief and as we witness the personification of her emotion, her loss. With this portrayal, Sarah L. Rasmusson argues, "Moore seems to exploit . . . feminine grief."[35] Such exploitation is not unique to Moore—Nira Yuval-Davis notes that women, serving as moral barometers for the nation, "often symbolize the collective unity, honour and the *raison d'être* of specific national and ethnic projects, like going to war."[36] Miriam Cooke and Angela Woollacott also contend more specifically that "[w]ar transforms motherhood from a social to a political factor."[37]

When we first meet Lila Lipscomb, executive assistant to Career Alliance in Flint, Michigan, she is a strong proponent of military service, especially for her own children: "The military is a good option. I can't afford to have you go to college, I cannot pay your way." Lipscomb also conveys hostility toward war protesters, charging that their actions are "a slap in my face," even as she recognizes that they were protesting the idea of war rather than condemning her children. It is not long, though, before we learn that Lila's son, Sergeant Michael Pedersen, died in a helicopter crash in Iraq. As Lila is surrounded by her husband, Howard, and family, she discloses that her son "didn't want to go to Iraq" because he was "really scared." Lila embodies a good republican mother by encouraging her son to fulfill his civic obligations.[38] Lila reports how she told Michael that "sometimes some fear is healthy because it keeps our senses about us." As Lila shares the events of Michael's death, we are situated through the camera's placement in the living spaces of the Lipscomb-Pedersen grief. Lila cries as she reads the last letter from their son. She ends the letter expressing Michael's love for "all of you guys"; her crying now prevents her from speaking for a moment. Eventually, she gives voice to the ultimate agony for any parent: "I want him to be alive. And I can't make him alive. But your flesh just aches. You want your child. It's out of sync. A parent is not supposed to bury their child."

The raw emotion that we experience in the living room scene becomes even more pronounced as we accompany Lila to the White House to see the place where war decisions are made. As she approaches the presidential residence, she encounters an Iraq war protester and expresses solidarity for her cause. We are positioned behind her as she engages the protester, who calls the president "a terrorist." At that moment, another woman walks up beside Lila and says, "No he isn't. . . . This is all staged." After a brief exchange, Lila walks toward the White House and the woman yells, "Blame al-Qaeda." As Lila gets closer, she begins to break down in tears—she is now sobbing in a way that creates a sense of consubstantiality between us and Lila, a visceral moment where we are one emotionally with this anguished mother.[39] We experience her grief as she bends down, gasping for air: "I need my son." When she bends over, the camera goes with her, and we can see her face, at least momentarily. We are thus in her space of grief. In an e-mail to Moore, "Michael H." expresses the sense of virtual reality captured in this poignant moment of perceived authenticity: "Hearing Mrs. Lipscomb speak at the end of the film about her son and nearly collapse on the sidewalks of D.C. from the grief brought the war home to me. Images on TV don't do that. On TV, the war is a place getting leveled by bombs. In life, it's something much more: people. Your film . . . changed me more than I thought possible."[40]

Moore thus situates us in the private spaces of grief and the behind-the-scenes ravages of war to motivate us to deliberate over the rightness of this war. Such graphic imagery targets our emotions, which Ann Marie Seward Barry contends are the "primary means of influencing attitudes before critical thought is engaged."[41] Moore tells us explicitly, in *F9/11*, that this war is unjust because the Bush administration "invaded a sovereign nation . . . that had never attacked . . . or threatened to attack the United States"—common *topoi* used historically in justifying war. Through markers of authenticity and virtual reality steeped in emotion, however, we are constituted as the ultimate decision-makers in assessing the evidence we *experience* throughout the film. James Jasinski suggests that political narratives enact the "ongoing project of communal (re)constitution: a continual process of shaping and reshaping our possibilities for collective action."[42] The discourse of the film thus can be understood as constituting the audience as the decision-makers in the public spaces of deliberation. One avenue for such collective action, *F9/11* suggests, is to remove President Bush from office on November 2, 2004, serving the elective as well as deliberative ends of the film. After all, before his death, Michael Pedersen tells his parents in his last letter home: "Do not reelect that fool, honestly."

The Imposter President

Moore's film displays many markers of authenticity. The filmmaker, though, also devotes considerable time to (in)authenticating George W. Bush's presidential image. Of course, Congress, the Democratic leadership, and the news media do not escape Moore's wrath. Moore emphasizes how no U.S. senator, for example, supported House claims of misconduct in suppressing voter turnout in the 2000 election. Congressman John Conyers (D-Mich.) admits in the film that few Democrats even read the USA PATRIOT Act. And Moore showcases a series of statements by news media figures like Ted Koppel of ABC's *Nightline*, who calls the U.S. military "an awesome synchronized killing machine," and Katie Couric of NBC's *Today*, who quips, "I think Navy SEALS rock!" In spite of such critiques, the bulk of Moore's criticism targets Bush as an illegitimate commander-in-chief.

From the opening of the film, Bush's presidency is contested. Moore reviews the events of the 2000 election in a lighthearted manner, wondering "Was it all just a dream?" Moore answers the question at the end of the opening segment: "It turns out none of this was a dream. It's what really happened." Grounding Bush's election in the "reality" of misconduct, where a person can be elected president "as long as your daddy's friends on the Supreme Court vote the right way," Moore devotes much of the film to discrediting the Bush presidency.

In a segment on Bush's service in the Texas Air National Guard, Moore suggests a conspiratorial cover-up as he showcases secret documents revealing that Bush and his friend James Reynolds Bath failed to take a physical exam on the date required. This segment reminds the audience of Bush's alleged drug use. In one quick moment, as Moore narrates that Bush and Bath were "suspended for failing to take their medical examination," we hear a brief but loud bar from the song "Cocaine." This very fast moving musical enthymeme suggests that Bush did not take his medical exam because of his illegal drug use—a contention debated during the 2000 and 2004 campaigns. Rather than make the claim explicitly, though, Moore instead implies it with this humorous musical reference, which requires background knowledge of Bush's alleged past. This kind of humor and much of the other humor targeting the president reflects what Mary Douglas calls the "subversive" notion of "a victorious tilting of uncontrol against control." In other words, "it is an image of the levelling of hierarchy, the triumph of intimacy over formality, of unofficial values over official ones."[43] For Moore, humor is a key component in trying to subvert the Bush imaginary.

Moore also uses humor to attack Bush for ignoring key documents that forewarned of the 9/11 attack because he spent too much time on vacation. Moore cites a *Washington Post* article indicating Bush was on vacation 42 percent of the time during his first year in office. Moore then offers a series of humorous vignettes where we see Bush taking his numerous working vacations accompanied by The Go-Go's lyrics "Vacation, all I ever wanted / Vacation, had to get away." Moore accentuates the notion that "George Bush spent the rest of August at the ranch" where "life was less complicated" and ignored a "security briefing that was given to him on August 6, 2001," which allegedly warned of the September 11 terrorist attack. Addressing the use of humor in relation to serious matters, Jeffrey P. Jones concludes, "Publics can express their disillusionment with the social hierarchies and farcical elite arrogance."[44] In *F9/11*, such humor unmasks what Moore suggests is a fraudulent image of President Bush as a strong commander-in-chief.

Moore's attack on Bush's commander-in-chief image is the focus when *F9/11* highlights the president's behavior in the elementary school classroom as he hears the news of the second plane crash into the World Trade Center. Even though Bush knew of the first attack, he "decided to go ahead with this photo opportunity," insinuating once again that Bush's public image is inauthentic. We watch the period of nonverbal anxiety as Bush sits with young children. We are situated on the same level with the press cameras filming the event as we witness Bush's indecision. At times, the president is in the moment, reading with the children and offering smiles and nods of encouragement to them. At other times, especially after Chief of Staff Andrew Card enters the room to tell him that "this nation is under attack," Bush's attention is diverted. He glances toward us more and looks nervously around the room. Moore features the different faces of Bush during this moment of crisis, and the focus on these seven minutes of indecision diminishes Bush's credibility as commander-in-chief. Rather than taking charge, "Mr. Bush just sat there and continued to read *My Pet Goat* with the children," seemingly "not knowing what to do."

Bush's positioning in the room in comparison to our own advances the diminutive image of the president put forth in *F9/11*. Because Bush is sitting with the children, the camera looks down on him—situating us above him and diminishing him in stature. We are positioned with the other adults in the room—the news media, serving as assessors of the truth—bearing witness to the president's actions in the heat of battle. We see him reading with children rather than acting courageously to protect our nation. The context and the camera location destabilize his authority, de-masculinizing him in the process. Alexander DeConde contends that U.S. political culture tends to "celebrate the activist, virile, strong leaders who magnified the powers of the executive office through military action."[45] In this one moment when the country needed the president most, he was not visibly and gallantly protecting the nation, Moore suggests. Instead, he was participating in a "photo opportunity" with schoolchildren and exhibiting acute indecision. Such scenes suggest that the *real* George W. Bush is exposed in that moment with "no one telling him what to do." The implicit conclusion is that President Bush is not fit to lead the United States through another four years of the war on terrorism.

In talking about the role of documentaries and politics, Terry Christensen notes that people often turn to television documentaries when they are "in search of strong political content." Because audiences "demand slick enter-tainment" when they "go to the cinema . . . American audiences tend to avoid them," Christensen concludes.[46] Part of the attraction for *F9/11* is that it combines politics with "slick entertainment," also offering audiences what many crave in this postmodern context where the real is often difficult to discern. Yet, many of those same authenticating strategies that enhance the film's veracity also undermine its credibility and its connections to the political reality it depicts and open the film up to charges of propaganda.

The Limits of Realism in a Postmodern World of Media Spectacle

Discussing issues of visuality, place, and memory, Victor Burgin reminds us that *"representations cannot be simply tested against reality, as reality is itself constituted through the agency of representations."*[47] Our mission throughout this chapter is not to discern the real from the unreal or the authentic from the inauthentic. Rather, our goal is to interrogate the strategies of authenticating the real at work in the film, which operate, at least partially, at an unconscious level not only for the viewers but also for the producers of the film. Even as such strategies are woven throughout the film, these same strategies help disrupt the film's claims to authenticity, particularly in relation to the conspiracy logics in the film, the political attacks leveled at President Bush during an election campaign, and the mixed messages linked with the use of humor.

The Limits of Conspiracy Theories

Richard Hofstadter once wrote: "When conspiracies do not exist it is necessary for those who think in this fashion to invent them."[48] Benjamin McArthur defines conspiracy as "a belief held by a sizable number of people that there are influential and malevolent groups seeking more power for themselves and/or harm to others."[49] Conspiracy theories are often "met with dismay and alarm from some social commentators" and are assumed to be "distorted."[50] These presuppositions about conspiracy theories work to undermine Moore's realism. *Time* postulated that, "whereas [Oliver Stone's] *JFK* merely spun conspiracy theories about a dead President, *Fahrenheit 9/11* goes after a sitting one with the explicit goals of unmasking his supposed crimes and removing him from office."[51]

Conspiracy rhetorics are most prevalent in *F9/11* when Moore talks about Bush's election in 2000 and his covert oil connections with the Saudis. Moore depicts how Florida (and thus the election) was called for Al Gore. He discusses how the first call was retracted and how the projection was changed when Florida's electoral votes were awarded to Bush, initially by the conservative Fox News channel. Moore informs us that "what most people don't know is that the man who was in charge of the decision desk at FOX that night, the man who called it for Bush, was none other than Bush's first cousin John Ellis. How does someone like Bush get away with this?" Moore again answers his own question and turns his attention to Florida and Jeb Bush—the governor of the state and brother to the presidential candidate. Moore fuels the conspiracy notion by airing a remark from George Bush as he sat on a plane with his brother at his side: "You know something, we are going to win in Florida. Mark my words. You can write it down." Moore also draws connections between the Supreme Court's final decision in the ballot debacle and Bush's "daddy's friends"—referring to George Herbert Walker Bush's own Supreme Court nominees. Such arguments reflect what Shane Miller calls an "argumentative role" of conspiracy theories, where people believe that "some powerful entity is engaged in a grand scheme to control or deceive the masses."[52] These narratives are a common feature in Hollywood films, notes John Nelson, where films expose conspiracy theories that have "shadowy bosses who communicate behind the scenes to pull the world's strings."[53] That Moore opts for such a common Hollywood thematic further underscores the entertainment value of the film—its capacity to function and succeed alongside more typical entertainment fare.

Moore suggests another "grand scheme" relating to Bush's connection with James Bath as well as to the covert connections between the Bushes and Saudi oil. Accentuating the economic motives for such ties, Moore ponders, "Okay, so let's say one group of people, like the American people, pay you $400,000 a year to be President of the United States, but then another group of people invest in you, your friends, and their related businesses $1.4 billion over a number of years . . . who are you gonna like? Who's your daddy? Because that's how much the Saudi Royals and their associates have given the Bush family, their friends, and their related businesses in the past three decades." Moore shows a White House Secret Service agent approaching him as he films outside the Saudi Arabian embassy. After being questioned on film, Moore tells the officer, "I didn't realize the Secret Service guards foreign embassies." The agent responds, "Uh, not usually. No sir." Moore explains to us that "Bandar is perhaps the best protected ambassador in the U.S. . . . with a six-man security detail."

Moore offers what some would consider compelling evidence (video support and government documents) when establishing the connections between Bush, Bath, and the bin Ladens. Such evidence, Miller suggests, can help citizens "reasonably engage in the argument itself" and aid in their "critique" of those in positions of "power." In the end, though, Miller concludes that in spite of empowering citizens, such conspiratorial arguments are limited because the label "remains pejorative" and easily dismissed, especially by the news media.[54]

Brian L. Keeley argues that one of the biggest constraints with conspiracy theories is "a problem with the *theorists* themselves, and not a feature of the theories they produce."[55] Speaking of contemporary conspiracy mongers, Gordon S. Wood claims that many embody a "paranoid style symptomatic of psychological disturbance" and are "marginal people, perhaps, removed from the centers of power."[56] Much of the criticism of this film centered on the filmmaker as political activist or propagandist, demonstrating another obstacle to Moore's claims of credibility and the connections of his film to reality and raising doubts about his ultimate motives that were often dismissed as politically motivated.

The Limits of Partisanship

Moore's ethos as a radical leftist combined with the debut of the film in the heat of the 2004 presidential contest to cast doubt on the accuracy of the film for many, especially those predisposed to reject the film on partisan grounds. Such timing and Moore's propensity for attacking businesses and political officials in power led opponents to brand the film as yet one more act of propaganda by the controversial filmmaker. The political activities of Moore and the production companies provided even more support for their opponents. At the turn of the twenty-first century, any agent of change with a hint of political leaning is often dismissed and debased, evidencing the changing pejorative use of the concept "propaganda."[57]

Even before the film debuted, Moore and his documentary were critiqued and dismissed by persons on the Right. Given these declarations, the news media and Democratic Party leaders were cautious in their discussions of the film. The film, however, helped excite those on the Left, eager to find someone other than Howard Dean (whose quixotic campaign for president ended in March, two months prior to the opening of *F9/11*) who would boldly take on the president and his war on terrorism. Labeling Moore "a lightning rod for hyperbolic praise and disgust," Richard Porton of *Cineaste* observes that Moore was "hailed by the left as the new Tom Paine" yet "denounced by his right-wing opponents as the incarnation of Joseph Goebbels," the famed Nazi propagandist.[58] Even Steve Grossman—the former chair of the Democratic National Committee—suggests that the movie seemed like "out-and-out propaganda."[59] In documentaries, the filmmaker's own credibility and views either enhance or detract from a film's authenticity. In Moore's case, his ethos accomplishes both.

The publicity and controversy surrounding *F9/11* began in May when the Walt Disney Company decided that its subsidiary Miramax Films could not distribute the film after all. From that moment, the film attracted almost constant attention from the press. Judy Bachrach of *Vanity Fair* explains that former Bill Clinton campaign staffers Mark Fabiani and Chris Lehane helped market the film, seeking, in Lehane's words, to "create news" almost "every day" in order to "drive the coverage in a way that defined the movie on our terms."[60] Moore's agent, Ari Emanuel, is the brother of former Clinton advisor Rahm Emanuel, who was elected to Congress (D-Ill.) in 2002.[61] With strategies reminiscent of political campaigns, Moore, through *F9/11* and his marketing apparatus, became a central voice in the battle for the presidency, politicizing the film's role in the election contest.

Moore also served other public roles for progressive political contenders. He campaigned for Howard Dean's 2004 bid to be the Democratic nominee in New Hampshire and Iowa and later, after Dean's bid failed, endorsed General Wesley Clark. Moore was highly visible during the Democratic National Convention of 2004 and was featured on *Nightline* and on the covers of *Time* and *Entertainment Weekly*. He attended the Republican National Convention as a "journalist," creating considerable attention and ire, particularly on the convention's first night when Arizona senator John McCain referred to him from the podium as a "disingenuous filmmaker . . . who would have us believe that Saddam's Iraq was an oasis of peace."[62] McCain's comments provoked boos aimed at Moore and chants of "Four more years," to which Moore replied from his perch in the press gallery, "Two more months."[63] Moore believes that his political actions and his film made a difference in the 2004 campaign, telling *Vanity Fair*: "What I did, what MoveOn did, what Bruce Springsteen did—we prevented a Bush landslide." Political commentators like Grossman of the DNC concluded that the film as well as Moore's omnipresence may have created "unintended consequences" by helping galvanize the Right as much as it did the Left: "The other side would not allow their president to be trashed by Michael Moore."[64]

Moore was not the only one associated with the film who had clear connections to Democratic candidates. Once Disney and Miramax pulled out, the film was distributed by Lionsgate Films, IFC Films, the Fellowship Adventure Group, Dog Eat Dog Films, Sony Pictures Entertainment, and Columbia TriStar Home Entertainment. Dog Eat Dog Films is Moore's production company. Harvey Weinstein and Bob Weinstein formed the Fellowship Adventure Group to distribute *F9/11*. These two brothers, who head Miramax, worked independently from Miramax to help distribute the documentary with IFC Films and Lionsgate Films.[65] Since 1980, Harvey Weinstein has reportedly donated $361,567 to political campaigns and groups—85 percent to Democratic candidates, $55,000 to special interest groups like MoveOn and their 2004 Voter Fund, which received $50,000, and $250 to Republican candidates. He supported such candidates as Hillary Rodham Clinton,

John Kerry, and Howard Dean, while Bob Weinstein donated funds to the campaigns of Barbara Boxer and Charles Schumer. Since 1990, Moore has reportedly donated $4,500 to political campaigns, including Democrats Hillary Clinton and Harvey Gantt. Some 72 percent of Lionsgate Entertainment's campaign donations have targeted Democratic candidates.[66] Donations of this kind bolster the case by Republicans that Moore and the Weinstein brothers produced and distributed *F9/11* primarily for political aims.

At the turn of the twenty-first century, anyone connected to partisan politics in any way is suspect, and the assertion that such partisans can uncover any sense of political abuse is summarily rejected. Nuance is lost, and the result is that nothing in *F9/11* warrants serious attention. For instance, conservative commentator Jonah Goldberg, writing in the *National Review's* on-line edition, concluded that he had no intention of seeing *F9/11*, calling Moore a "liar, a propagandist, a crafty fool" who does not make arguments and only offers claims, assertions, and "visual innuendo."[67] In Goldberg's formulation, the concept of propaganda has transformed from a government-sponsored activity to one practiced by foreign *and* domestic enemies who are unjustly targeting the U.S. government, irresponsibly spreading malicious falsehoods. The result is that *F9/11* is dubbed a partisan screed, and any claims it makes to deliberative authority or meaningful political debate are lost.

The Limits of Humor

Moore's arguments in *F9/11* clearly reflect the gravity of the wartime context and seek to spur reflection about the legitimacy of the war and those who execute it. Yet his use of humor also raises questions about his seriousness, exhibiting the same kind of mixed messaging that Moore finds troubling in the Bush administration's rhetoric. On the one hand, Moore stresses how the administration warned us to be very scared after the terrorist attacks of 2001. Bush himself argued, "The world has changed after September 11th. It's changed because we're no longer safe." Conversely, Moore features Bush suggesting that we should not change our lives because of the terrorist threats: "Fly and enjoy America's great destination spots"; "Take your families and enjoy life"; and "Get down to Disney World in Florida." Moore's use of humor employs similar kinds of mixed messages. While the humor enhances the film's entertainment value and may have served a subversive role in disrupting dominant sources of power, it also raises doubt about the severity of the issues that Moore explores. After all, if the Bush administration is as corrupt as Moore suggests, what could possibly be so funny?

In many instances, Moore's humor is designed to further the notion of Bush as an illegitimate president, portraying him in ways that suggest his absurdity. One such instance involves the "Mission Accomplished" moment in which President Bush declared the fighting over in Iraq as he landed on an aircraft carrier in a flight suit by way of a Navy S-3B Viking aircraft. As we see still images and video footage of Bush surrounded by military personnel in brightly colored fighter suits, the president is smiling from ear to ear with his arms around these crowds of men. While such images are familiar to us, Moore frames the images with humorous music, making Bush look more like the "village idiot," especially since the mission was not accomplished. Featuring the president with exaggerated smiles, the music plays:

> Look at what's happened to me.
> I can't believe it myself.
> Suddenly I'm on top of the world . . .
> Who could it be?
> Believe it or not, it's just me.

Jerry Palmer notes that "a social function can be parodied by showing it being performed by someone who is inadequate to the function in question."[68] Moore's framing of the photo opportunity suggests that Bush is a parody of himself. Because such humor is degrading, it disrupts Moore's more serious arguments of presidential wrongdoing in the war against terrorism.

More confusing are the mixed messages that Moore sends about the seriousness of the issues he interrogates. As Moore discusses the allegation that Saudi officials and members of the bin Laden family were allowed to fly out of the United States in the days following 9/11, he begins the segment with the musical cue "We've got to get out of this place, / If it's the last thing we ever do." Moore talks with Senator Byron Dorgan (D-N.D.) and Craig Unger (author of *House of Bush, House of Saud*) about the law enforcement irregularities of not interviewing the bin Laden family members before they left the country. At the end of the segment, Moore inserts clips from the 1960s television show *Dragnet,* where the humorously serious Joe Friday interrogates a witness. Although providing a respite from the accumulating evidence against the Bush administration, such humor raises questions about the seriousness of the allegations.

Moore's use of humor here emphasizes the contradictions of White House actions as family members of a terrorist leader were allowed to leave the country at the moment when the United States needed to elevate its war against terrorism. If, in fact, the White House authorized such individuals to leave the country without being questioned, such charges warrant further exploration. Yet Moore's humor creates ambiguity over the solemnity of the situation. John Evan Seery cautions that "irony is so risky, so unstable, so covert, its 'successes' cannot be considered inevitable."[69] James S. Ettema and Theodore L. Glasser offer a similar warning: "Even as irony promises to be a mode of thought that is genuinely enlightened, it casts doubt on any effort to capture the truth of things in language."[70] The humor enhances confusion about the film's truth claims, elevating the entertainment features of the film over its deliberative and campaign ends.

The Limits of Virtual Reality

Virtual reality depends on visuals that when spliced together from image to image provide seamlessness, even if the shots were "taken at widely separate times and places."[71] Barbie Zelizer contends that "composite images can be made to appear natural," reflecting the power of virtual reality.[72] At the same time, however, the notion of virtual reality can heighten the anxiety of the U.S. public, which is becoming increasingly aware of the technological manipulation of mediated images. Stephens explains, "We are beginning to accept the idea that the world can be distorted, reimagined, that it can be made to collide with alternative visions of itself."[73] Steven Jones concludes, "Virtual reality calls into question our very notions of authenticity."[74]

Documentary film, in particular, splices together visual images that participate in the narration of the filmmaker. In films like *F9/11*, the result can be the appearance of reality, of a true, real picture of worldly phenomena. Yet, virtual reality is a "mechanistic" process,[75] reflecting the hyperreality of media spectacles in the postmodern age, "grounded in ambiguity, confusion, and irony."[76] We argue elsewhere that "the spectacle is the currency of postmodern politics, where visuality predominates."[77] In many ways, the Bush administration's war against terrorism reflects these media spectacles—from the president's standing on the rubble of the WTC with a bull horn to his landing on the deck of an aircraft carrier to his campaign, which relied on such wartime images. The role of embedded journalism in the Iraq war reflects these same hyperreal spectacles where the distinctions between the "real" and the representational collapse,[78] imploding "the binary concepts of reality and representation into a single concept" and merging "'the copy' with the 'original,' the 'image' with its 'referent.'"[79]

F9/11, like Bush's war against terrorism, reflects these same hyperreal characteristics of the media spectacle. Even though much of *F9/11* is based on the assumption that the Bush administration *created* the rationale for war "based on a lie" for ulterior economic motives, Moore too manufactures images in the creation of his case against the Bush administration. In one obvious example, the representation of 9/11 does not reflect the real-time moment that it portrayed, as the planes hit the towers twenty seconds apart in the film rather than the seventeen minutes on that fateful morning. Within this 9/11 reenactment, Gary Rizzo, the sound editor for the film, also talks about how the makers of the film used archival sound footage from the attack in *F9/11*'s reconstruction of those frightful moments. Because some of the audio that accompanied the visual images contained "really bad sound," they inserted "another source for the same piece of audio," all of which came from the 9/11 terrorist attacks. In certain instances, however, alternative sounds were not available, so "other elaborate audio restoration actions had to be taken." The goal throughout was to "make it real"[80]—or, rather, hyperreal. As films attempt to move us closer and closer to the real, the "real" becomes that which is manufactured in the editing studios, made to "look better than nature."[81]

The power of such hyperreal images is driven in part by the emotionality of these reenactments, these moments of virtual reality. Moore is critical of the Bush administration for using fear as a means of persuasion. As Congressman Jim McDermott (D-Wash.), a psychiatrist and member of Congress, expressed, "You can make people do anything if they're afraid." And because they were "afraid," Moore concludes, "they turned to their leader to protect them." Moore's media spectacles, however, are also motivated by the force of emotion; the most vivid moments of the film (the attacks on the WTC, the war footage, the death of a soldier-son) evoke strong feelings of anger, sadness, anguish, and grief that linger beyond the film's end. Barry cautions that such "political images can affect emotional response before critical analytical abilities are invoked" or can "bypass cognitive processing" altogether.[82] Offering a critique of the "televisual age," J. Michael Hogan complains that a common strategy of political actors "both in and outside of the political mainstream" involves routinely substituting "storytelling for argument, images and emotions for information and ideas."[83]

Our goal is less about rejecting the use of such media spectacles than about understanding how meaning is created through such mediated moments and the speculative consequences of such mediation. The pervasiveness of the media spectacle designed to depict the real, we believe, also serves in the end to accentuate ambivalence and uncertainty surrounding authenticity in U.S. political culture. The competition among such mediated spectacles that portend alternative truths leaves the U.S. public skeptical about most of what they consume, recognizing that "seeing is no longer believing."[84] Ron Burnett insists that "at no point do media spectacles freeze viewers into positions that they cannot control or change."[85] Black makes similar claims of the audience's power to challenge such spectacles in his discussion about documentaries and realism: "There will always be some viewers who question such filmed evidence and who doubt visual documentation of historical occurrence"[86]—the legacy of living in a hyperreal, postmodern age. Put differently, as virtual reality heightens the emotional and the visceral power of postmodern discourse, it simultaneously evokes its own argumentative, deliberative limits.

Media Spectacle as Political Discourse

At the beginning of *F9/11,* Columbia TriStar Home Entertainment and Sony Pictures Entertainment provide the following disclaimer: "The following Interviews and Commentaries are for entertainment only." At the end, Moore dedicates the film to Michael Pederson, Brett Petriken, and "all the soldiers from the Flint area who have died in the Iraq War." The film also is also dedicated to "Bill Weems and the 2,973 who died on 9/11/01 and the countless thousands who have died in Afghanistan and Iraq as a result of our actions." In between, Moore takes us through the complexities of war and the performance of a wartime president to suggest the illegitimacies of both. As he does so, he undermines the corporate disclaimers from the film's beginning.

F9/11 both reflects and contradicts features of deliberative and campaign discourse. Like all texts centered on policy or the election of a public official, *F9/11* enters the "constant struggle to articulate . . . identities, a battle that is, in one incarnation, fought over the claim to 'represent' those competing identities," seeking the "authority to speak for the people." [87] *F9/11*, like other deliberative and campaign discourse, contests matters of production and the influence of institutional and corporate forces on the underlying motives of discourse. Except in length and depth, *F9/11* also resembles negative campaign ads that depend on visuality, aurality, and implied argument that are often dismissed as partisan propaganda. As with political ads, political professionals are employed to market the film.

Unlike most deliberative texts, though, *F9/11* also demonstrates a heightened dependence on the media spectacle, attracting unusual attention as a political documentary commenting on a war still in progress and alleging presidential improprieties about a controversial commander-in-chief still in office. *F9/11* takes the media spectacle to new levels of virtual reality and emotionality as a cinematic extravaganza. Murray Edelman contends that art can contribute to politics by "excit[ing] minds and feelings as everyday experiences ordinarily do not[;] it is a provocation, an incentive to mental and emotional alertness. Its creation of new realities means that it can intrude upon passive acceptance of conventional ideas and banal responses to political clichés." In the end, texts like *F9/11* can help "foster a reflective public" on matters related to war and the presidency. [88]

The limits of virtual reality spectacles restrict and retard their deliberative or even campaign ends. As emotion drives the power of virtual reality, such moments are meant to be *experienced*, restricting their ability to effect significant change. While the experience of media spectacles may help inspire a counter-movement, for that oppositional force to alter U.S. political culture—to stop a war or to remove a president—participants require the substance of argument that can chain out from political activist to political activist. Because the virtual reality of *F9/11* must be experienced by each individual to achieve its full impact, the film moves the true believers into the theater to live the moments vicariously more than it propels them into the political spaces as a collectivity to debate the issues. One fan-inspired banner suggests, as it trails behind an airplane flying along the beaches of Delaware and Maryland: "GET YOUR HEAD OUT OF THE SAND—SEE FAHRENHEIT 9/11."[89] Real politics requires more than drawing people into the theater time and time again for a virtual experience and the rush of emotion. Referencing the "Simulated Actor," Roderick P. Hart notes how television (and presumably other media) encourages "viewers [to] respond by watching the political system rather than working for it."[90] The rhetorical power of *F9/11* is less about ending a war or unseating a president than it is about entertainment, celebrity, and profit. Politics as entertainment may be democratizing—it may attract and excite more citizens, more consumers to the political spectacle. But virtual realism, humor, and conspiracy theories are limited in activating substantive social reform. *F9/11* and similar examples of commodified dissent, while emotionally and virtually powerful, ultimately have a restricted capacity for collective social change.

Notes

1. Although article 1, section 8, of the Constitution gives Congress the power to "declare war," article 2, section 2, identifies the president as "commander in chief of the Army and Navy of the United States."

2. *War Powers Resolution*, Public Law 93-148, H.J. Res. 542, 93rd Congress, 1st sess., November 7, 1973.

3. There are exceptions. Congress forced President Reagan to pull the troops out of Lebanon and refused to give him support to fund the Contras in Nicaragua. President Clinton met with resistance for his military actions in Haiti and in the Balkans.

4. Stephen J. Whitfield, *The Culture of the Cold War*, 2nd ed. (Baltimore, Md.: Johns Hopkins University Press, 1996), 154–55.

5. Representative Barbara Lee (D-Calif.) represented the lone vote of opposition to House Joint Resolution 64 that authorized the use of force "against those responsible for the recent attacks launched against the United States." See *Authorization for Use of Military Force*, H.J. Res. 64, 107th Cong., 1st sess., September 14, 2001, *Library of Congress: Thomas*, http://thomas.loc.gov/.

6. "Senate Approves Iraq War Resolution: Administration Applauds Vote," *CNN.com*, October 11, 2002, http://archives.cnn.com/2002/ALLPOLITICS/10/11/iraq.us/. Twenty-three senators voted against the resolution, including notable Democrats Edward Kennedy, Barbara Boxer, Patrick Leahy, and Paul Wellstone. Only one Republican, Rhode Island's Lincoln Chaffee, voted no. Twenty-nine Democrats voted yes, including Hillary Clinton, John Kerry, and John Edwards.

7. Victor Navasky, "Foreword," in *Journalism after September 11*, ed. Barbie Zelizer and Stuart Allan (London: Routledge, 2002), xvi.

8. George W. Bush, "President's Statement on Senate Vote," October 11, 2002, *The White House: George W. Bush*, http://www.whitehouse.gov/news/releases/2002/10/print/20021011.html.

9. Daniel Fierman, "The Passion of Michael Moore," *Entertainment Weekly*, July 9, 2004, 30, on-line at *LexisNexis Academic*, http://www.lexisnexis.com/ (accessed August 8, 2005).

10. "Movies of 2004," *The Movie Times*, http://www.the-movie-times.com/thrsdir/moviesofyear.mv?moviesof2004+ByTGross (accessed August 8, 2005). See also John Berger, "Foreword: 'The Work of a Patriot,'" in *Fahrenheit 9/11: The Official Reader*, ed. Michael Moore (New York: Simon and Schuster, 2004), ix.

11. Lorie Conway, "Iraq War Documentaries Fill a Press Vacuum," *Nieman Reports* 59, no. 1 (2005): 106–7.

12. Jessica E. Vascellaro, "Movie Tests Campaign Rule," *Boston Globe*, June 27, 2004, on-line at *LexisNexis Academic*, http://www.lexisnexis.com/ (accessed August 8, 2005).

13. "The World According to Michael," *Time*, July 12, 2004, on-line at *LexisNexis Academic*, http://www.lexisnexis.com/ (accessed August 8, 2005).

14. Joel Snyder, "Picturing Vision," in *The Language of Images*, ed. W. J. T. Mitchell (Chicago: University of Chicago Press, 1980), 230. Ann Marie Seward Barry reinforces this view when she notes that "words represent an artificially imposed intellectual system removed from primal feeling; images plunge us into the depth of experience itself." See Ann Marie Seward Barry, *Visual Intelligence: Perception, Image, and Manipulation in Visual Communication* (Albany: State University of New York Press, 1997), 75.

15. Joshua Meyrowitz, "New Sense of Politics: How Television Changes the Political Drama," *Research in Political Sociology* 7 (1995): 122.

16. Berger, "Foreword," ix.

17. All quotations from the film are taken from the screenplay of *F9/11* that Moore published in his companion book after the film was completed. See Michael Moore, *Fahrenheit 9/11: The Official Reader* (New York: Simon and Schuster, 2004).

18. Imants Barušs, *Authentic Knowing: The Convergence of Science and Spiritual Aspiration* (West Lafayette, Ind.: Purdue University Press, 1996), 152. See also Alexander Nehamas, *Virtues of Authenticity* (Princeton, N.J.: Princeton University Press, 1999). For a more extensive discussion of political authenticity, see Shawn J. Parry-Giles, "Political Authenticity, Television News, and Hillary Rodham Clinton," in *Politics, Discourse, and American Society: New Agendas*, ed. Roderick P. Hart and Bartholomew H. Sparrow (Lanham, Md.: Rowman and Littlefield, 2001), 211–27.

19. Hanno Hardt, "Authenticity, Communication, and Critical Theory," *Critical Studies in Mass Communication* 10 (1993): 59. See also Miles Orvell, *The Real Thing: Imitation and Authenticity in American Culture, 1880–1940* (Chapel Hill: University of North Carolina Press, 1989).

20. Margaret Morse, "The Television News Personality and Credibility: Reflections on the News in Transition," in *Studies in Entertainment: Critical Approaches to Mass Culture*, ed. Tania Modleski (Bloomington: Indiana University Press, 1986), 55.

21. Kevin Robins, *Into the Image: Culture and Politics in the Field of Vision* (London: Routledge, 1996), 16–17.

22. Lynn A. Higgins, "Documentary in an Age of Terror," *South Central Review* 22 (2005): 32.

23. E-mail from Andrew J. Marsico to Michael Moore, July 2, 2004, in Moore, *The Official Reader*, 208.

24. Joel Black, *The Reality Effect: Film Culture and the Graphic Imperative* (New York: Routledge, 2002), 60.

25. Rudolf Arnheim, *Visual Thinking* (Berkeley: University of California Press, 1969), 296.

26. Jamieson concludes that visual placement such as the techniques used by Moore "lures us into believing that we know the people." Kathleen Hall Jamieson, *Beyond the Double Bind: Women and Leadership* (New York: Oxford University Press, 1995), 145.

27. Larry Gross, John Stuart Katz, and Jay Ruby, "Introduction: A Moral Pause," in *Image Ethics: The Moral Rights of Subjects in Photographs, Film, and Television*, ed. Larry Gross, John Stuart Katz, and Jay Ruby (New York: Oxford University Press, 1988), 27.

28. Deborah Willis, *Picturing Us: African American Identity in Photography* (New York: New Press, 1994), 187.

29. Paul Messaris, "Visual 'Manipulation': Visual Means of Affecting Responses to Images," *Communication* 13 (1992): 187 (emphasis added).

30. Paul Messaris, *Visual "Literacy": Image, Mind, and Reality* (Boulder: Westview Press, 1994), 42.

31. Mitchell Stephens, *The Rise of the Image, the Fall of the Word* (New York: Oxford University Press, 1998), 126.

32. Fatimah Tobing Rony, *The Third Eye: Race, Cinema, and Ethnographic Spectacle* (Durham, N.C.: Duke University Press, 1996), 4.

33. Meenakshi Gigi Durham, "Displaced Persons: Symbols of South Asian Femininity and the Returned Gaze in U.S. Media Culture," *Communication Theory* 11 (2001): 209.

34. Richard J. Regan, *Just War: Principles and Cases* (Washington, D.C.: Catholic University of America Press, 1996), 22.

35. Sarah L. Rasmusson, "Masculinity and *Fahrenheit 9/11*," *International Feminist Journal of Politics* 7 (2005): 140.

36. Nira Yuval-Davis, *Nation and Gender* (London: Sage, 1997), 47.

37. Miriam Cooke and Angela Woollacott, eds., *Gendering War Talk* (Princeton, N.J.: Princeton University Press, 1993), xii.

38. For an in-depth discussion of republican motherhood, see Linda K. Kerber, *Women of the Republic: Intellect and Ideology in Revolutionary America* (Chapel Hill: University of North Carolina Press, 1980).

39. See Kenneth Burke, *A Grammar of Motives* (Berkeley: University of California Press, 1969).

40. E-mail from Michael H. to Michael Moore, July 22, 2004, in Moore, *The Official Reader*, 211.

41. Barry, *Visual Intelligence*, 255.

42. James Jasinski, "(Re)constituting Community through Narrative Argument: *Eros* and *Philia* in *The Big Chill*," *Quarterly Journal of Speech* 79 (1993): 480.

43. Mary Douglas, "Jokes," in *Rethinking Popular Culture: Contemporary Perspectives in Cultural Studies,* ed. Chandra Mukerji and Michael Schudson (Berkeley: University of California Press, 1991), 297.

44. Jeffrey P. Jones, *Entertaining Politics: New Political Television and Civic Culture* (Lanham, Md.: Rowman and Littlefield, 2005), 139.

45. Alexander DeConde, *Presidential Machismo: Executive Authority, Military Intervention, and Foreign Relations* (Boston: Northeastern University Press, 2000), 6.

46. Terry Christensen, *Reel Politics: American Political Movies from Birth of a Nation to Platoon* (New York: Basil Books, 1987), 220.

47. Victor Burgin, *In/Different Spaces: Place and Memory in Visual Culture* (Berkeley: University of California Press, 1996), 238 (emphasis in original).

48. Richard Hofstadter, *The Age of Reform* (New York: Vintage Books, 1955), 72.

49. Benjamin McArthur, "'They're Out to Get Us': Another Look at Our Paranoid Tradition," *History Teacher* 29 (1995): 38.

50. Anita M. Waters, "Conspiracy Theories as Ethnosociologies: Explanation and Intention in African American Political Culture," *Journal of Black Studies* 28 (1997): 112–13.

51. "The World According to Michael."

52. Shane Miller, "Conspiracy Theories: Public Arguments as Coded Social Critiques: A Rhetorical Analysis of the TWA Flight 800 Conspiracy Theories," *Argumentation and Advocacy* 39 (2002): 41.

53. John Nelson, "Conspiracy as a Hollywood Trope for System," *Political Communication* 20 (2003): 499.

54. Miller, "Conspiracy Theories," 53–55.

55. Brian L. Keeley, "Of Conspiracy Theories," *Journal of Philosophy* 96 (1999): 126.

56. Gordon S. Wood, "Conspiracy and the Paranoid Style: Causality and Deceit in the Eighteenth Century," *William and Mary Quarterly* 39 (1982): 441.

57. For a discussion of the differences between propaganda and documentary in *F9/11*, see Eric Langenbacher, "The Degeneration of American Political Culture and the Documentary Film in *Fahrenheit 9/11*," *Forum* 2 (2004): article 10.

58. Richard Porton, "Weapon of Mass Instruction: Michael Moore's *Fahrenheit 9/11*," *Cineaste* 29 (Fall 2004): 3.

59. See Grossman's statement in Judy Bachrach, "Moore's War," *Vanity Fair,* March 2005, on-line at *LexisNexis Academic,* http://www.lexisnexis.com/ (accessed August 8, 2005).

60. Ibid.

61. Michael Finnegan, "Film and Election Politics Cross in *Fahrenheit 9/11*," *Los Angeles Times,* June 11, 2004, on-line at *LexisNexis Academic,* http://www.lexisnexis.com/ (accessed August 8, 2005).

62. "Text: Remarks by Sen. McCain to the Republican National Convention," *Washington Post,* August 30, 2004, available at http://www.washingtonpost.com/wp-dyn/articles/A47237–2004Aug30.html.

63. See Chris Smith, "Moore, Less," *New York,* August 31, 2004, available at http://nymetro.com/nymetro/news/rnc/9732/.

64. Bachrach, "Moore's War."

65. "*Fahrenheit 9/11,* to Open Nationally on June 25th" *Business Wire,* June 2, 2004, on-line at *LexisNexis Academic,* http://www.lexisnexis.com/ (accessed August 8, 2005).

66. See "Michael Moore," *NewsMeat*, available at http://www.newsmeat.com/celebrity_political_donations/Michael_Moore.php (accessed August 8, 2005); and "The List of Companies Giving Under 55% to Republicans," *2205Blue.com*, available at http://www.2005blue.com/?template=list&sql=&sort=&sl=1 (accessed August 8, 2005).

67. Jonah Goldberg, "Moore Politics," *National Review*, June 28, 2004, available at http://www.nationalreview.com/goldberg/goldberg200406280944.asp.

68. Jerry Palmer, *Taking Humour Seriously* (London: Routledge, 1994), 48.

69. John Evan Seery, *Political Returns: Irony in Politics and Theory from Plato to the Antinuclear Movement* (Boulder: Westview Press, 1990), 201.

70. James S. Ettema and Theodore L. Glasser, *Custodians of Conscience: Investigative Journalism and Public Virtue* (New York: Columbia University Press, 1998), 88. Some commentators praise Moore's ability to balance the news and entertainment functions in *F9/11*. Carol Wilder concludes that Moore is a "wily communicator who knows how to speak the cinematic language of popular culture where the elision between news and entertainment is complete, and further yet a culture where the production values of entertainment have prevailed." See Carol Wilder, "Separated at Birth: Argument by Irony in *Hearts and Minds* and *Fahrenheit 9/11*," *Atlantic Journal of Communication* 13 (2005): 70–71.

71. Messaris, *Visual "Literacy,"* 35.

72. Barbie Zelizer, *Remembering to Forget: Holocaust Memory through the Camera's Eye* (Chicago: University of Chicago Press, 1998), 6–7.

73. Stephens, *The Rise of the Image*, 195.

74. Steven Jones, "A Sense of Space: Virtual Reality, Authenticity, and the Aural," *Critical Studies in Mass Communication* 10 (1993): 238.

75. Ibid., 250.

76. Steven E. Schier, "Introduction: A Unique Presidency," in *The Postmodern Presidency: Bill Clinton's Legacy in U.S. Politics*, ed. Steven E. Schier (Pittsburgh University of Pittsburgh Press, 2000), 1.

77. Shawn J. Parry-Giles and Trevor Parry-Giles, *Constructing Clinton: Hyperreality and Presidential Image-Making in Postmodern Politics* (New York: Peter Lang, 2002), 5.

78. See Jean Baudrillard, *Simulations,* trans. Paul Foss, Paul Patton, and Philip Beitchman (New York: Semiotext(e), 1983).

79. John Fiske, *Media Matters: Everyday Culture and Political Change* (Minneapolis: University of Minnesota Press, 1996), 2.

80. "Headlines: Gary Rizzo Making *Fahrenheit 9/11*," *Full Sail*, available at http://www.fullsail.com/index.cfm/fa/news.story/con_id/1845/Gary_Rizzo_Mixing_Fa%5C (accessed August 8, 2005).

81. Stephens, *The Rise of the Image,* 126.

82. Barry, *Visual Intelligence,* 66, 19.

83. J. Michael Hogan, *The Nuclear Freeze Campaign: Rhetoric and Foreign Policy in the Telepolitical Age* (East Lansing: Michigan State University Press, 1994), vii–viii.

84. Parry-Giles and Parry-Giles, *Constructing Clinton,* 191.

85. Ron Burnett, *Cultures of Vision: Images, Media, and the Imaginary* (Bloomington: Indiana University Press, 1995), 6.

86. Black, *The Reality Effect,* 112.

87. John Street, *Politics and Popular Culture* (Philadelphia: Temple University Press, 1997), 22, 20.

88. Murray Edelman, *From Art to Politics: How Artistic Creations Shape Political Conceptions* (Chicago: University of Chicago Press, 1995), 143.

89. Moore, *The Official Reader,* 56–57.

90. Roderick P. Hart, *Seducing America: How Television Charms the Modern Voter* (New York: Oxford University Press, 1994), 104, 120–21.

3

Jennifer L. Borda

Documentary Dialectics or Dogmatism?

Fahrenhype 9/11, *Celsius 41.11*, and the
New Politics of Documentary Film

Sir Isaac Newton's third law of motion states that for every action, there is an equal and opposite reaction. This observation also may be used to describe the landscape of political documentaries during the 2004 presidential election season. The initial action was the release of Michael Moore's much anticipated, much hyped award-winning and unapologetically outspoken film *Fahrenheit 9/11* in June 2004. Grossing more than $119 million in the United States and $220 million worldwide, Moore's film broke documentary box office records, and its opening weekend showing on 868 screens (which alone grossed more than $23 million) made national headlines.[1] However, the unprecedented public interest in Moore's manifestly political film—and the subsequent publicity it generated—was met by an equally impassioned response from those on the opposite end of the political spectrum.

Even before its release, *Fahrenheit 9/11* had become a target of both mainstream and conservative critics' attempts to discredit the film, Michael Moore, and his alleged polemicist tactics. Critical reaction to the film became an industry all its own. Several books intending to discount Moore's allegations and produce counter-publicity were published in the summer and fall of 2004, including *Fahrenheit 9-12: Rebuttal to Fahrenheit 9/11* by Aaron I. Reichel, Esq., which claims to replace "'ad hominem' discord with rational discourse";[2] and *Michael Moore Is a Big Fat Stupid White Man* by David T. Hardy and Jason Clark. Countless Web loggers also were moved to deconstruct

Moore's propaganda in an effort to reveal him as a fraud and manipulator of American audiences. One of the most ambitious of these was an on-line article titled "Fifty-nine Deceits in *Fahrenheit 9/11*," which David Koppel, research director of the Independence Institute, published on his Web site with a preface that urged readers to photocopy it as often as they would like as long as they gave it away for free. Other Web sites devoted to Moore-bashing include Findoutmoore.com, Moorewatch.com, Mooreexposed.com, Moorelies.com, and Fahrenheit 411 (f411.com). Some critics chose to respond to Moore via his modus operandi: the documentary film. However, because of these conservative-political-pundits-turned-filmmakers' lack of Hollywood industry connections and clout (and often relatively small budgets), the films became the projects of little-known directors and achieved either a very limited theatrical release or went straight to video. Two of these documentaries were produced during the summer of 2004 in an effort to capitalize on the publicity that Moore and his film had received and also as an entry into the political debates that had begun to define the 2004 presidential election. *Fahrenhype 9/11* went direct to video on October 5, 2004 (coordinated to coincide with the DVD release of *Fahrenheit 9/11*), and *Celsius 41.11: The Temperature at Which the Brain Begins to Die* was released in a small number of theaters on October 22, then quickly released in DVD format just a few weeks later.

Both *Fahrenhype 9/11* and *Celsius 41.11* were billed as explicit, point-by-point rebuttals that would function as a cinematic counterstrike to Moore's film. With taglines such as "Unraveling the truth about *Fahrenheit 9/11* and Michael Moore," "You knew it was a lie . . . and now you'll know why," and "The truth behind the lies of *Fahrenheit 9/11*," *Fahrenhype 9/11* and *Celsius 41.11* were marketed as nonfiction films intending to set the record straight and refute the allegedly fictionalized and propagandistic accounts in Moore's film. Neither film, however, achieves the level of rational debate it claims; instead, both films fall victim to the same dogmatic tactics of which they accuse Moore. These films, in relation to Moore's precedent, provide a case study of how political documentary recently has evolved as a rhetorical form and pose the question of whether this medium is capable of meeting the rhetorical challenge of political dialogue in a participatory democracy.

This chapter examines the 2004 documentary films *Fahrenhype 9/11* and *Celsius 41.11* as models of conservative American agitprop (or in *Time* film critic Richard Corliss's words, "agit-doc") cinema.[3] These recent examples of a rapidly emerging subgenre appropriate documentary filmmaking convention—the construction of visible evidence—in an effort to deconstruct the claims of Moore, *Fahrenheit 9/11*, and the political arguments he espouses. The very terms of this documentary debate create a double bind, however. If the films are to craft their responses using the impassioned discourse and emotional appeals that contemporary viewers have come to expect from a documentary (a precedent established by the popular success of Moore's films), they risk speaking only to those audiences already sympathetic to their political views. That is, these films require an audience that is willing to accept documentary style (politically conservative personalities as "expert" talking heads, emotional appeals, and the expository form) over substance (argument backed by proof). Yet, these films are marketed on the claim that they are restoring a standard of rationality to the documentary debate by offering a dialectical engagement with *Fahrenheit 9/11* (arriving at truth by disclosing the contradictions in Moore's argument and resolving them). What the films offer, rather, is a series of assertions and attacks based on enthymematic reasoning that delimits the audiences' rational judgment and the films' rhetorical potential only to those viewers who already support a conservative ideology. This strategy blurs the distinction between documentary realism and political advertising, overrides political argument with political dogma, and consequently misses an opportunity to engage with a diverse audience who may represent a range of political views.

Documentary Heritage and the New Political Film

Documentary filmmaking in the United States has long been the purview of leftist filmmakers. Documentary reached its political zenith in the 1960s, when the confluence of new developments in film technology (including lightweight, mobile equipment), the potential of television as a medium for distribution, the emergence of direct cinema, and an increasingly independent system of film production revitalized the nonfiction film.[4] Filmmakers began to use documentary to raise consciousness, recruit new members to their movements, challenge power relations, and present new perspectives on cultural issues such as race, gender, and class inequality.[5] Yet by the 1980s, as the ideological liberalism of the previous two decades gave way to a widespread conservatism, some began to predict the demise of liberation filmmaking. Rather, throughout the 1980s and into the 1990s, the art and function of nonfiction film was reaffirmed, "and the social documentary, in particular, reclaimed its role as advocate—the Griersonian heritage—in shaping thought and discussion on the major issues of our time."[6] *Fahrenhype 9/11*, *Celsius 41.11*, and a slate of other political documentaries produced in recent years have extended this heritage into the twenty-first century by contributing to the partisan discourse and issues of debate surrounding the 2004 presidential election.

As a form of commentary on our social and political mores, documentaries have become akin to what film scholar Bill Nichols refers to as "discourses of sobriety." He writes that such discourses are "sobering because they regard their relation to the real as direct, immediate, transparent. Through them power exerts itself. Through them things are made to happen. They are the vehicles of domination and conscience, power and knowledge, desire and will."[7] Similar observations regarding documentary's legitimate purpose of serious social analysis have been repeated by many scholars. For example, in his historical treatment of the documentary tradition, Lewis Jacobs writes, "The documentary film came to be identifiable as a special kind of picture with a clear social purpose, dealing with real people and real events, as opposed to staged scenes of imaginary character and fictional stories of the studio-made pictures."[8] Paula Rabinowitz explains that often these films go beyond commentary on social politics to function as a call to action: "The representation of politics practiced by documentary address is also about the politics of representation, as objects of inspection become subjects of action."[9] Similarly, Carl R. Plantinga, in arguing for the rhetorical potential of nonfiction film, writes that such films "perform distinct social functions."[10] All of these observations about documentary film speak to its rhetorical nature: the way it asserts claims and implies attitudes rather than merely provides an objective reflection of our social realities.

Traditionally, documentaries have acted as a sort of social conscience, often against those in power. *Fahrenhype 9/11* and *Celsius 41.11* represent a departure from this tradition in that the party in power (or those representing or supporting that political party) has chosen to bear the burden of response to a film critiquing the status quo. Although these films do not follow the progressive and liberationist nature of many films within the documentary tradition, which generally provide a critique of dominant institutions, they do indeed provide a social analysis from a conservative standpoint on the current political landscape, contemporary events, and situations. They employ what Nichols refers to as "documentary logic" through "argument about the world, or representation in the sense of placing evidence before others in order to convey a particular viewpoint."[11] In the rhetorical logic of these films, *what* the films have to say about contemporary political issues "can never be separated from *how* they say it, how this saying moves and affects us, how we engage with a work."[12] Nichols categorizes four different approaches used by filmmakers: expository, observational, interactive, and reflexive. *Fahrenhype 9/11* and *Celsius 41.11* are primarily examples of the expository mode but have overtones of the interactive mode as well. Nichols characterizes expository texts as those that address the viewer directly, making an argument about the historical world, and those that "take shape around commentary directed toward the viewer; images serve as illustration or counterpoint."[13] Consequently, the mode "emphasizes the impression of objectivity and of well-substantiated argument."[14] Both *Fahrenhype 9/11* and *Celsius 41.11* develop their overarching structure through a systematic disputation of points made in Moore's film, including topics such as George W. Bush's victory in the contested election of 2000 and the reality of terrorist threats and weapons of mass destruction, which, for the most part, take the form of various commentators' assertions (in favor of Bush and his administration's policies). As such, the films also utilize the characteristic function of the interactive mode in which "textual authority shifts toward the social actors recruited: their comments and responses provide a central part of the film's argument. Various forms of monologue and dialogue (real or apparent) predominate."[15] The films are edited in the traditional expository form, offering "an economy of analysis, allowing points to be made succinctly and emphatically, partly by eliminating reference to the process by which knowledge is produced, organized, and regulated so that it, too, is subject to the historical and ideological processes of which the film speaks."[16]

Given these documentaries' predilection for, in Nichols's terms, "a subordinated logic," in which "persuasive effect tends to override the adherence to the strictest standards of reasoning," and combined with their overtly partisan subject, the rhetoric of *Fahrenhype 9/11* and *Celsius 41.11* functions more like a feature-length political advertisement than straightforward documentary.[17] That is, the films consist of impassioned discourse in the form of brief sound bites accompanied by visceral imagery, which advance the films' overarching message. Both films establish a logic of visible evidence for spectators through their formal style and structure, namely the way they present an abundance of edited statements by various commentators that act as a building-up of proof for the case being presented. For the most part, this results in a fairly dry presentation of statements and sheer accumulation of observations by a legion of mostly self-proclaimed experts. While *Fahrenhype 9/11* uses a panel of mostly unidentified but recognizable political pundits to add a sense of affect and passion to the film's assertions (most of the commentators are emphatic and are portrayed in casual settings as if they are chatting with friends—political consultant Dick Morris sits at a table with a cup of coffee, Democratic senator Zell Miller is working on his farm, and actor Ron Silver often speaks to the camera while driving through Manhattan in his convertible), *Celsius 41.11* strictly adheres to the traditional documentary staple of the "talking-head" expert. Each commentator is clearly identified by name and professional title, and the identification is repeated at least two or three times throughout the film. The commentators are all shown in close-up shots against a black background. The panel of experts includes Fred Thompson, a former U.S. senator; Barbara Comstock, former director of public affairs for the Department of

Justice; and Michael Barone, senior reporter for *U.S. News and World Report*. However, those who contribute most to the film are identified more vaguely, such as Charles Krauthammer, "Pulitzer-Prize Winning Syndicated Columnist"; Mansoon Ijaz, "Terrorism Expert"; Michael Medved, "Radio Talk Show Host/Author"; and Joshua Muravchik, "Resident Scholar American Enterprise Institute."[18] As in *Fahrenhype 9/11*, long sequences of edited and redundant remarks from these experts form the proof for *Celsius 41.11*. Within these films, brief sound bites from various commentators create the "logic" of the text, or organizational backbone, which lends conceptual coherence to the kinds of arguments the films wish to advance rather than reasoned arguments as to *why* their particular view makes logical sense. The arguments produced in these documentaries take the form of generalities and ideological positions, such as American exceptionalism as justification enough for all actions and the means behind the decision to go to war (protecting Americans' safety at all costs) justifies the ends (unilateral and preemptive strike against and current occupation of Iraq). However, while these brief statements and flashing images may effectively assert the filmmakers' ideological commentary and stir emotions in like-minded viewers, these rhetorical devices amount to stylistic assertion rather than substantive debate.

Blurring the Boundaries between Documentary Politics and Partisan Political Ad

In an op-ed column for the *New York Times* published a week after the release of *Fahrenheit 9/11*, Paul Krugman noted, "There has been much tut-tutting by pundits who complain that the movie, though it has yet to be caught in any major factual errors, uses association and innuendo to create false impressions."[19] Yet, this critique also may be applied to the numerous clearly partisan documentaries inspired by or in reaction to Moore's film that were produced during the 2004 presidential race, most of which use the same organizing structure—a feature that was not lost on many reviewers of these films. Michael Atkinson, film critic for the *Village Voice*, calls *Celsius 41.11* "in effect a feature-length Bush campaign commercial." Philip Kennicott, in a review for the *Washington Post*, questions whether the film is "an overlong attack ad on John Kerry, or an earnest effort at ideological argument with Michael Moore," and concludes that "there's really nothing more here than you can find watching dreadful political advertisements." *Variety* film critic Robert Koehler asserts that the film "plays as a virtual feature-length political ad for George W. Bush, defending him against critics while castigating Democratic opponent, Sen. John Kerry."[20] Similarly, an on-line film reviewer of *Fahrenhype 9/11* refers to the film as "little more than an infomercial for conservative thinking."[21]

Writing for the *Washington Post*, William Booth remarks that films such as these "tend toward the obvious" and appeal to audiences on the same level as political pamphlets, bumper stickers, or ninety-second attack ads so commonly seen during any presidential campaign. Booth cites political scientist Art English, who dubs such projects "reinforcement films," or partisan films funded by partisan groups and made for partisan audiences.[22]

While some reviewers emphasized the partisan nature of these films, others remarked on the documentaries' preoccupation with stylistics and spectacle rather than serious, substantive engagement with political issues. Several reviewers observed that "this film spends way too much time preaching. There are far too many sentimental moments, too many speeches about American solidarity and appeals to patriotism. In this respect, the rhetoric kills the film," and "I couldn't help but notice that much of the film is style over substance."[23] *New York Times* critic Manohla Dargis notes that *Celsius 41.11* spends relatively little time going after Michael Moore; instead, what the filmmakers "want to do with their movie is make you afraid, very, very afraid," and as a result, "the film presents a vision of the world verging on the apocalyptic."[24] In fact, many reviews seemed to focus on the preponderance of "talking heads, static images . . . soaring music and unabashed idolatry of the Great Leader," which is a consequence of the films' design as media spectacle rather than thoughtful, reasoned discourse and debate.[25]

According to Douglas Kellner, media spectacles are "those phenomena of media culture that embody contemporary society's basic values, serve to initiate individuals into its way of life, and dramatize its controversies and struggles, as well as its modes of conflict resolution," which are characteristic of our current era of "media sensationalism, political scandal and contestation, seemingly unending cultural war, and the new phenomenon of Terror War."[26] However, spectacle does more than reflect the culture; it also has the rhetorical power to produce meaning. Thomas B. Farrell writes, "Spectacle becomes a form of knowledge insofar as it presents us with something more and something new to know. And in this novelty, the appeal to sight appears to erase the need for the inconvenient particularities of argument and inference."[27] Kellner notes that current political discourse has devolved into "a mode of spectacle in which the codes of media culture determine the form, style, and appearance of presidential politics, and party politics in turn becomes more cinematic and spectacular."[28] As a result, in films such as *Fahrenhype 9/11* and *Celsius 41.11*, the terms of political debate have been taken from the contemporary media culture, in which image conveys ideology and discourse consists of reinforcing the intuitive knowledge of an established constituency. When the norms of politics are reduced to such codes of media spectacle, as Kathleen Hall Jamieson notes in her book *Dirty Politics*, those producing political discourse begin to "treat assertion as if it constitutes argument, while the strategy perspective that pervades campaign coverage deprives the public of an ability to judge the legitimacy of candidate discourse"; engaged political discourse becomes the equivalent of "calculated strategies of distraction."[29]

In analyzing the dissolution of political argument and democratic engagement into deception and distraction in the last four decades, Jamieson notes that, over the course of two centuries of political speech, public norms for appropriate political discourse and the ideals to which it should aspire have developed. These include the assumption that both sides have a right to be heard and that those who are attacked have a right to reply, argument should be backed by proof, fairness and accuracy of evidence should be subjected to scrutiny, the context from which evidence emerges should not be distorted, and those making the claims should be held responsible for them.[30] *Fahrenhype 9/11* and *Celsius 41.11* take their agenda from the first principle (discourse should emerge from both sides and those attacked are warranted a rebuttal), but they disregard the remainder of these norms and do not exemplify the ideals that assume "that those on opposing sides will grant the good will and integrity of their opponents" or "that those involved in the discussion will not be swayed by specious claims or attacks that appeal to prejudice rather than reason."[31] For example, about midway through *Fahrenhype 9/11*, Dick Morris comments, "So add up these facts any way you want politically. Add them up to vote for Bush, add them up to vote for Kerry, stay undecided. That's not what this is about. Know the facts, that's what this is about." Yet, despite this assurance that the film seeks only to reestablish the ideals of fairness and factual accuracy to this debate, the majority of the film encourages spectators to reject Moore's political views through repeated examples of faulty reasoning, such as ad hominem and false analogies, as when David T. Hardy remarks that Moore's film is "not a documentary—it's a lie. Moore is un-American—he isn't British, he must be French." Similarly, in *Celsius 41.11* soon after the opening credits, a deep-voiced narrator informs viewers: "We begin from the premise that John Kerry is a decent man with a distinguished record of public service, as is George W. Bush, a president dedicated to leading America to victory in the struggle against terrorists determined to destroy us. So, how is it we have people comparing our president to Adolph Hitler and screaming 'anybody but Bush'?" In this opening statement, the film suggests that it is operating from a standard of rationality that seeks to engage this debate honestly by granting those who do not share the filmmakers' political stance a right to their conflicting views. The wording of this remark reveals the film's prejudice, however, as the narrator's premise asserts that Kerry's decency and public service will be compared to Bush's dedication and heroism as an undaunted leader in the war on terror, thus setting the terms of the debate based on unparallel claims. After spending the majority of the film defending Bush and the leadership decisions he has made in the face of terrorist threats, *Celsius 41.11* then devotes the last third of the film to challenging Kerry's record of war service and thus his political leadership.

Jamieson further notes that contemporary political spectacle—taking its form for the most part from sound bites and political advertising—very often falls short of these norms/ideals and instead falls prey to assertion over argument, which over time "reinforces the notion that politics is about visceral identification and apposition, not complex problems and their solutions."[32] The spectacle employed by *Fahrenhype 9/11* and *Celsius 41.11* reflects this dissolution of decorum and the ideal of appropriate discourse and instead focuses much more on *what* those opposed to Michael Moore believe but very little about *why*. What is overlooked by the films, and lost for viewers, is "a clear relationship between the appealing claim and its public policy incarnation."[33] The films, then, result in not much more than political pandering for their favored candidate using the same tactic employed in the grand media spectacle of political campaigns and advertising: argument and engagement on issues are reduced to assertion on behalf of the favored candidate and attack on the opposition. The basic logic and structure of both films is assertion in favor of George W. Bush and his political agenda and attack against Michael Moore and other Bush detractors. The films' stylistic choices operate within the realm of the visual and the visceral and engage in assertion and attack rather than reasonable argument, which would more fully constitute an invitation to rational response from spectators on both sides of the political debate.[34]

The New Politics of the Political Documentary

More than two dozen political documentaries were released over just a few months during the presidential election campaign in 2004. According to documentary film scholar Michael Renov, "Their premium is on timeliness. They want to have direct impact on the elections. It doesn't have to be a great film. It's all about the audience and its political impact, first and foremost, with artistry and creativity playing a secondary role."[35] This new style of political film, the point-counterpoint documentary, has been facilitated by new technologies that allow for rapid turnaround. Bryan Preston notes that digital filmmaking systems like Avid XPress Pro and Unity allowed *Fahrenhype 9/11* to become "one of the first documentaries to refute another documentary in as close to real time as current technology and the human mind will allow."[36] Many of the new political documentaries spent little time in theaters, instead moving quickly into the DVD market, for as Corliss notes, "theatrical release is just the gravy for agit-docs; DVD is the meat."[37] After all, people are used to watching their political ads on television, not in the theater.

Fahrenhype 9/11 took advantage of the new opportunities for political films. The project began production in August 2004 and was finished just thirty-two days later on a budget of $500,000. The film went straight to DVD, was sold exclusively at Overstock.com, and was available at video rental stores and has grossed $3 million to date. The film was financed by Jeff Hayes, veteran producer of numerous television movies and miniseries, and directed by freelance filmmaker Alan Peterson. Peterson admits that, before 9/11, he had considered himself an intellectual liberal, but after watching the planes crash into the World Trade Center, he realized how "stupid he had been."[38] The script was co-written by Eileen McGann and Dick Morris, a former political consultant for Bill Clinton and current TV talk-show political pundit. The film is narrated by actor Ron Silver, who turned to the Republican Party after the 9/11 attacks on his native New York, and features commentary from Democratic senator Zell Miller of Georgia, former New York City Democratic mayor Ed Koch, and political commentators Ann Coulter and David Frum, among others.

Celsius 41.11 was funded by Citizens United, a conservative nonprofit organization formed in 1988 whose stated mission is to "reassert the traditional American values of limited government, freedom of enterprise, strong families, and national sovereignty and security."[39] The organization is headed by David Bossie, who also executive-produced the film and is best known as the chief investigator for the Whitewater hearings during the Clinton administration and, most recently, as author of the books *Intelligence Failure: How Clinton's National Security Policy Set the Stage for 9/11* and *The Many Faces of John Kerry*, on which *Celsius 41.11* was based. The film was written and produced by Lionel Chetwynd, the Christian libertarian director of the film *The Hanoi Hilton*, which dramatized the torture of American POWs in Vietnam, and Ted Steinberg, a veteran television producer. The film's director, Kevin Knoblock, also comes from television, as a director of numerous History Channel documentaries such as "The History of the Gun" and "Plantations."[40] *Celsius 41.11* generated $93,000 in revenue during its short run and extremely limited release at a few independent theaters on both the East and West Coasts, then was released to DVD less than two weeks later. Copies were sold exclusively through the film's official Web site.

Fahrenhype 9/11 launches its attack against Michael Moore in the first thirty seconds of the film. The documentary opens with what appears to be a television clip of Moore speaking to an audience at a lecture or press conference, although the location is never revealed. Moore is shown in a medium shot against a dark blue velvet curtain; he is wearing a black T-shirt, which makes the scene appear dark and sinister. He states, "There is no terrorist threat," then the clip is quickly replayed, and he appears to repeat the phrase. Moore then goes on to explain, "Yes, there have been horrific acts of terrorism, and yes there will be acts of terrorism again. But that does not mean that there is some massive terrorist threat." The crude editing is obvious in this short scene, and it is clear that the statements are cobbled together out of sequence and that Moore's remarks are taken out of their original context. At the end of the statement, the scene turns to black and white and flickers like a horror film, and there is a sound reminiscent of a gunshot.

A voice-over acts as a transition into the next scene. A woman's voice says, "I remember where I was when King was assassinated. I remember where I was when Kennedy was assassinated. I remember the space shuttle. You can pinpoint a place in time. How many people will be able to say, on 9/11, I was in the company of the president?" The scene begins with a black-and-white shot of the presidential motorcade, then cuts to the front of Emma F. Booker Elementary School, and finally ends on a framed photograph of George W. Bush in the Florida classroom taken on the morning of 9/11. The woman speaking is not identified as she summarizes what happened that morning, making clear that the president was not reading to the children but that the children were reading *My Pet Goat* to the president (perhaps a rebuttal to the Osama bin Laden tape in which the terrorist mastermind accused the president of reading a children's book while the attacks were happening). The woman then assures the audience that the president was not holding the book upside down, as members of the media had claimed, and that a journalist had contacted her after the event to question whether she believed the president should have done something sooner after hearing the news of the attack (a reference to an early scene in Moore's film that shows the president sitting in the classroom for seven minutes after getting word of the attack on New York). She answers, "Got up and done what?" Later on in the scene, she explains that she was pleased by how the president reacted; she had not voted for him, but in that moment she could have because he looked "presidential." She believes he handled the situation well because he chose "to stop, and think, and respond, rather than react to the terrorism."

The film next offers testimonials from several unidentified people who also conclude that there was nothing the president could have done at that moment. The film cuts to the president speaking at a national press conference from the second-grade classroom after the attack. He assures the nation:

> Ladies and gentleman, this is a difficult moment for America. . . .
> Today we've had a national tragedy. Two airplanes have crashed
> into the World Trade Center in an apparent terrorist attack on our

country. . . . I've ordered that the full resources of the federal government go to help the victims and their families and to conduct a full-scale investigation to hunt down and to find those folks who committed this act. Terrorism against our nation will not stand. And now if you'll join me in a moment of silence. May God bless the victims, their families, and America.

The screen fades to black and the *Fahrenhype 9/11* logo appears. The film is established as both an answer to Moore's absurdist claims and a reminder that 9/11 serves as proof that the terrorist threat could not be more real.

Celsius 41.11 begins with similar allusions to 9/11. A folksy song begins in the background over the opening credits with the lyrics "Do you believe in anything strongly enough to stick to your guns when the going gets rough?" The song ends as a freeze-frame halts the second plane's flight toward the south tower of the World Trade Center, heightening the suspense, and then the soundtrack falls silent and the plane crashes soundlessly into the tower, which explodes into a large ball of flames upon impact. This is followed by many quickly edited shots of the buildings collapsing, the Manhattan streets filled with debris, and the horrified looks of bystanders.

The scene then cuts abruptly to a montage of sound bites made by President Bush after the attacks intercut with scenes of soldiers in Iraq, of the 9/11 hijackers and Saddam Hussein, and of a military burial. Seamlessly, Bush's short phrases are edited together into a coherent statement regarding America's stance on terrorism:

> War has been waged against us by stealth and deceit and murder. This nation is peaceful, but fierce when stirred to anger. Whether we bring our enemies to justice or bring justice to our enemies, justice will be done. The men and women of our armed forces have delivered a message now clear to every enemy of the United States, even seven thousand miles away, across oceans and continents, on mountaintops and in caves: you will not escape the justice of this nation. Steadfast in our purpose, we now press on; we have known freedom's price, we have shown freedom's power, and in this great conflict, my fellow Americans, we will see freedom's victory.

The scene cuts to a protester holding up his middle finger and yelling, "Fuck you, asshole," which is juxtaposed with a shot of Michael Moore at what appears to be a film screening for *Fahrenheit 9/11*, as he is seen in a suit and tie standing with Lila Lipscomb, one of the stars of his documentary. In a voice-over, we hear him say, "These words need to be said somewhere on national TV: There is no terrorist threat, there is no great terrorist threat."

In *Celsius 41.11*, the organizational logic used to order the film, although never explicitly stated, is a systematic rebuttal to five points Moore's *Fahrenheit 9/11* raises. The narrator instructs the film's audience that people are clamoring for "anybody but Bush" because they believe that (1) Bush stole Florida; (2) Bush didn't do enough to stop 9/11; (3) Bush is stealing our civil liberties; (4) Bush lied about weapons of mass destruction; and (5) the Bush doctrine inflames Islamists. All but the last correspond directly to points Moore makes in *Fahrenheit 9/11* regarding the 2000 election, Bush's vacation time before 9/11, the problematic nature of the USA PATRIOT Act, and his ties to Saudi Arabia and the oil industry. *Celsius 41.11* spends more than half the film disputing these notions one by one in a straightforward and methodical manner, unlike *Fahrenhype 9/11*, which uses similar subject points but often strays off-topic. The last third of *Celsius 41.11* then offers perspectives on why Bush is the only choice in the 2004 presidential election, namely because John Kerry would be such a poor one.

The openings of these two documentaries parallel one another: both films begin with references to the terror threat against America and invoke strong memories of 9/11. That tragic moment in our nation's history is established as the foundational perspective for both films, and the nation's response to the terrorist threat becomes the basis of every assertion that the films put forward. The films also quickly set up a duality, an us-versus-them view of the post-9/11 world. In *Celsius 41.11*, Bush is announced as the hero and protector of the nation, and the antagonists are Bush's hostile and vitriolic detractors, to whom Moore is linked both visually and aurally. In *Fahrenhype 9/11*, Moore is clearly the adversary of Bush supporters everywhere, and his opening remarks serve to initiate spectators to the structure of the film; what will follow is a rebuttal to Moore's false claims.

Both films also establish Moore as the principal target of their ad hominem attacks early on, and the various statements he has made become counterpoints for the films' own assertions. In *Celsius 41.11*, for example, between various segments in which the film refutes arguments presented in *Fahrenheit 9/11*, a shot of Moore giving his Academy Award speech is shown, over which various quotes are superimposed in white lettering. In the first one, viewers read a quote that states, "[Americans] are possibly the dumbest people on the planet. . . . Our stupidity is embarrassing." A later quote reveals Moore comparing the USA PATRIOT Act to *Mein Kampf*. The film does not provide a context for these remarks; rather, they are merely used as transitional elements within the structure of the film. To an even greater degree than in *Celsius 41.11*, criticism of Moore is threaded through every aspect of *Fahrenhype 9/11*. For example, after that film's opening title appears on the screen, the camera zooms in on a photograph featuring a head shot of Moore, and in voice-over we hear the film's narrator, Ron Silver, ask: "Was it all just a dream? That's the question Michael Moore asks at the opening moments of *Fahrenheit 9/11*. Was it all just a dream? There is no terrorist threat in this country. It's a lie. Is that just a dream?" He continues:

> Michael, I know why you're so upset. You worked for Nader; Nader cost Gore the election. I understand, but the first recount went to Bush; the second recount went to Bush. What are you waiting for, the Supreme Court? They agreed, Bush won. A six-month study in 2001 by news organizations, including the *New York Times*, the *Washington Post*, and CNN, verified it. Come on, Michael. I worked for Gore in 2000, while you were working for Nader. I've accepted it; Al Gore's accepted it. It's time to move on. Stop dreaming. Wake up.

These voice-overs represent Silver's ongoing—albeit one-sided—dialogue with Moore and reoccur as transitional elements between the film's major segments.

While the films purport to address Moore's film directly and to provide a clear rebuttal to his arguments, many of the points they offer hastily dismiss largely tangential claims made in Moore's film without offering an opposing perspective or argument. For example, an early segment in *Fahrenhype 9/11* titled "The Pantagraph" begins with remarks by David Koppel, author of "Fifty-nine Deceits in *Fahrenheit 9/11*," which Silver remarks is "the most comprehensive rebuttal" to Moore's film. This segment also features David T. Hardy and Jason Clark, authors of *Michael Moore Is a Big Fat Stupid White Man*. The commentators accuse Moore of quickly panning over some headlines regarding the recount for the 2000 election and allege that he blew up the headline on a letter to the editor from a newspaper called *The Pantagraph* and presented it as "objective news." At the conclusion of this brief segment, Silver makes this accusatory yet nonsensical statement directed at Moore: "When you can make fun of people, why waste time lying about anything else, like Truth?" The commentators never offer a rebuttal to Moore's claim that Bush stole the Florida election; they merely focus on an extremely brief segment of his film to challenge the legitimacy of his methods.

Another point *Fahrenhype 9/11* addresses in depth is Moore's claim that Bush took more vacation time in his first eight months in office than any other president. Silver notes, "*Fahrenheit 9/11* wants us to believe that President Bush vacationed more than he worked and that he'd rather enrich his oil buddies than do his job. Wake up, Michael." Clark concludes that the 42 percent vacation time figure reported in the *Washington Post* wrongly included weekends and travel time (which implies that the president of the United States should take weekends off). Hardy adds that this time also included thirty-eight days spent at Camp David, which is a fully equipped presidential headquarters. Hardy asserts that there is a distinction between time away and an actual vacation and that in 2004, while Bush spent time away in Crawford, Texas; Kennebunkport, Maine; or the White House retreat at Camp David, "this is just time he wasn't in the White House." To further build up evidence, Silver states, "Let's just review a week and see how a president vacations"; while the days of the week from Sunday, August 19, to Sunday, August 26, count down on a small graphic, descriptions of Bush's work on any given day scrolls by too quickly to read. There are roughly three activities listed per day, and when the DVD is viewed in slow motion, it is revealed that these include many vague descriptions, such as "Met with Karen Hughes, Condi Rice, and Josh Bolten, and other staff," "Briefly spoke with the press," and "Issued a statement regarding the retirement of Sen. Jesse Helms." The film spends a considerable amount of time refuting a claim that in Moore's film was a brief source of humor or affect rather than addressing the more poignant accusation by Moore that during that vacation month, Bush and his administration ignored security briefs warning of a bin Laden attack on the United States. Similarly, *Fahrenhype 9/11* fails to seriously engage a number of the prominent arguments in *Fahrenheit 9/11*, such as the claim Moore makes about Bush and his business associates' close ties to Saudi Arabia and their major economic interest in the machinery of war. In response to this assertion, *Fahrenhype 9/11* merely reveals the names of a few Democratic contributors who also have been associated with the Carlyle Group (a conglomeration that Moore fingers as a leader in the war industry) and accuses Moore of overexaggerating the percentage of Saudi foreign interest in the U.S. economy.

The films also address assertions made by *Fahrenheit 9/11* only to redirect attention to other nonrelated issues. For example, in *Fahrenhype 9/11*, on the topic of the Afghan pipeline (which Hardy and Clark contend was "all a lie from start to finish"), the film makes the accusation that the French, Russians, and Germans (who wouldn't give Bush the United Nations mandate) were promised oil fields by Iraq in exchange for opposing sanctions on the country. Dick Morris claims that France was promised 10 million barrels of oil at ten dollars a barrel and that bribes were made to the prime minister of Russia and all party candidates. Hardy ultimately surmises that "for the movie, Moore just changes conspiracy theories. . . .Where one conspiracy is refuted he just substitutes another one." With no apparent transition, this segment launches accusations against Bill Clinton, arguing that little was done in terms of national security during his administration. After discussing various intelligence-gathering procedures that Clinton vetoed (wrongly, in Morris's opinion) because he believed they infringed on civil liberties, Morris remarks that Bush may rightly deserve some blame for eight months of security failure, but Clinton deserves eight years of blame. Similarly, in *Celsius 41.11*, Mansoon Ijaz comments that "when 9/11 happened, I think that the entire burden of that argument lies on the shoulders of the cumulative failures that were taking place during eight years where Bill Clinton did not get on top of this problem. It's not that they didn't want to, it's that they were just sittin' on the wrong railroad tracks." The film goes on to cite Clinton's weakening of the intelligence community, which consequently was dumbed down over the years to the point where Bush had no access to the information he needed before 9/11.

Fahrenhype 9/11 makes further points that claim Moore misrepresents information on the evacuation of Saudi nationals; misconstrues comments by the state police officer interviewed in *Fahrenheit 9/11* about state budget cutbacks and their connection to security lapses (which the officer claims were taken out of context in Moore's film); and slanders politicians such as John Ashcroft and Paul Wolfowitz. In these segments, *Fahrenhype 9/11* criticizes Moore for using misleading cinematic strategies to present his views but never takes the opportunity to counter Moore's overarching arguments, such as his allegations that Saudi nationals were not interviewed using established intelligence-gathering procedures upon their evacuation immediately after 9/11 and that local police, fire, and emergency rescue funding has been cut in many municipalities in the name of "national security." Commenting on Moore's negative associations, innuendo, and false allegations in the film, Silver concludes, "You give me enough footage of Michael Moore in enough situations, I can make him look like an anorexic right-winger." However, both *Fahrenhype 9/11* and *Celsius 41.11* employ these same cinematic techniques when necessary. For example, about midway through *Celsius 41.11*, a montage begins with brief clips of Bush and Prime Minister Tony Blair of England commenting on the faulty intelligence that convinced them to invade Iraq, followed by edited testimony from John Edwards, Madeleine Albright (secretary of state under Clinton), Hillary Clinton, and John Kerry that is summarized into an argument that Saddam Hussein, an international outlaw, and his regime represent a clear threat to the United States and to the values of freedom and democracy due to Iraq's possession of weapons of mass destruction, and the time has come for decisive action. Charles Krauthammer then comments that only after Bush's approval ratings had dropped and everyone was "in a questioning mood" did "the guns come out a-blazin'," and the film shows a montage of Kerry, Ted Kennedy, Howard Dean, and others during the 2004 election campaign criticizing

Bush for misleading us into war based on false intelligence. By eliminating all historical context between the statements compiled in the first montage and those referenced in the second, the juxtaposition of these two segments portrays these Democratic politicians as "flip-floppers" seeking political gain by manipulating the facts as they see fit.

Both documentaries also emphasize visceral, crude emotion rather than reasoned logic, which is often achieved through the visual. Prominent visuals used in both films are the now iconic images of 9/11 and its aftereffects in New York City. To the tune of "Amazing Grace," *Fahrenheit 9/11* lingers over images of photographs taken of the Twin Towers on fire, Ground Zero, and various memorials to the New York rescue workers, while *Celsius 41.11* initiates several scenes of the film with images of the smoking towers. Both films make sweeping claims that since 9/11, America is under constant threat of attack and that we have been spared the destruction of another 9/11 only because of the federal mandates pushed forward by George W. Bush. This is where the films make their most convincing claims to those who are already inclined to believe that the war on terror was justification for the war in Iraq. In *Fahrenhype 9/11*, for example, Dick Morris runs through a list of terror threats on New York as proof the terrorist threat Moore denies is, in fact, real: "Eight blocks up that way is the City Corp. Center, which they were casing, and forty blocks down that way is the New York City Stock Exchange they were casing, and forty-five blocks that way is the Brooklyn Bridge that a guy actually tried to knock down and blow up. . . ." He lists numerous other planned attacks foiled in New York, Las Vegas, and Virginia and concludes, "They are targeting every one of us," but he provides no sources for his information. *Celsius 41.11* similarly uses a visual montage of terrorist incidents beginning with the Iranian revolution in 1979. As pictures of burned-out buildings, dead bodies, and various incarnations of wreckage quickly flash past, the names and dates of dozens of other attacks worldwide are superimposed in white and scroll by just as quickly, all leading up to the latest attacks on four American airliners in September 2001. Yet, the geopolitical context for these attacks is never referenced, nor are the various groups these terrorists represent identified. The attacks are never differentiated according to sources or distinguished from one another with regard to the various political situations that produced them; instead, they are all equated with 9/11, whether the result of Islamic jihad or stemming from the Israeli-Palestine conflict, and they all serve as an accumulation of evidence that the terror threat to the United States is real. *Celsius 41.11* also frequently cuts to brief images of Middle Eastern children and women in burqas undergoing extreme torture, including fingers being severed and a public execution by gunfire. The time or place of these atrocities is never cited, nor is the context in which the acts took place and toward whom, but the assumption is that they are the ruthless acts of Saddam Hussein.

Of all the counterpoints that *Fahrenhype 9/11* asserts, it devotes the most time to the defense of Bush's invasion of Iraq. At one point, Silver explains in voice-over, "Here's the hard truth. After 9/11, our world was changed. Far-off tyrants like Saddam Hussein suddenly felt very close to home. *Fahrenheit 9/11* spoke to this. *Fahrenheit 9/11* took great pains to convince us that Saddam's regime was, in Michael Moore's words, a nation that had never attacked the United States, a nation that had never murdered a single American citizen." Images of Saddam waving and kneeling in worship are the accompanying visuals, yet the film never directly refutes Moore's claims that Iraq had never attacked the United States or its citizens. Instead, the next scene begins with Bush's Iraq ultimatum delivered to Congress: "But let there be no misunderstanding, if Saddam Hussein does not fully disarm, for the safety of our people and for the peace of the world, we will lead a coalition to disarm him." Following this speech, commentator Frank Gaffney, former assistant secretary of defense to Ronald Reagan, states, "I think the image and the thesis that underpin the film, that President Bush was only too happy to provoke a war with Iraq and wanted more than anything in the world to go to war, and seized upon the pretext of 9/11 to have the war that he wanted to have, is simply a fabrication." The next shot is an extreme close-up of David Frum, former Bush speechwriter, who comments with clear outrage, "The theory that it was done solely for the purpose of enriching Bush's business cronies is just preposterous; it is both impressively stupid and impressively and maliciously, arrogantly mean-spirited." The scene then cuts to commentator Ann Coulter, who asks, "Gas has gone up [laughs], how about that? When are they going to explain that to us? Why are gas prices so high if we went to war for oil?" Next, Dick Morris further asserts that the war-for-oil equation alleged by Bush detractors is simply untrue based on the following logic: "Number one, we support Israel that doesn't have any oil and we oppose the Arabs who have it all; number two, we don't buy Iranian oil, we're the only country in the world that boycotts Iranian oil; and number three, for fifteen years we opposed letting Iraq pump oil." These statements do not directly dispute Moore's claim, however, but rather form a distraction from the question at hand—namely, was there any proven justification for the invasion of Iraq?

Rather than address Moore's question explicitly, the films justify the decision to go to war by shifting the debate: the issue is not whether Iraq threatened us in the past but whether that country constitutes a threat to the United States in the future. For example, *Fahrenhype 9/11* addresses Bush's decision to go to war without the approval of the United Nations with an anecdote by Zell Miller:

I was working in my backyard cleaning out some old stacked rocks, some steps that had been there years ago . . . and I came across a nest of copperhead snakes. . . . When I came across them, I did not go before the city council and ask for a resolution; I didn't call Shirley, my wife, like I do on everything else that comes up; I didn't call any of my neighbors; I just took a hoe and chopped their heads off. Now, you might call that preemptive action or unilateral action. But, those things were dangerous; they could kill my grandchildren; they could kill my great-grandchildren; they play around those steps all the time. I had to do something about their safety. And that's kind of how I see this situation right now: we're in a fight with a bunch of snakes, a bunch of vipers, and we've got to get to them and fight it out in their neck of the woods instead of them fighting it out in our neighborhood.

Directly after Miller's story, the film cuts to Gaffney, who concludes, "The strategy of waiting for people to hurt us was simply irresponsible." This statement is followed by Morris interviewing Koch, in which he sincerely asks the former mayor of New York City, "If you knew there would be no WMDs, would you still have supported us going to war?" Koch responds: "We had a responsibility to go in and prevent this tyrant from killing—murdering—his own people, gouging out eyes, cutting off limbs. We have found more than 300,000 bodies. They expect to find a million bodies. You can't walk away from that anymore. I thought if I were a congressman, I would definitely have voted to declare war against Iraq, even if I knew there were no weapons of mass destruction." This statement is followed immediately by Coulter's remarks, "I'll pay $1,000 for any liberal who will mention the Kurds—that never passes their lips," in which she makes a false analogy between preemptive action and sanctioned genocide. In *Celsius 41.11*, Joshua Muravchik of the American Enterprise Institute claims, "That we could get Russia and France and Germany and all these others to do it with us on our side is just demagogic nonsense," which is immediately followed by *U.S. News and World Report* senior reporter Michael Barone's statement that "you continually hear that [phrase] 'without allies,' it's almost as if you repeat something long enough—a big lie—people are going to start believing it." All of these statements add up to the films' presumptions that the United States had no choice but to enter Iraq (despite not having the support of the United Nations) in order to remove an evil tyrant who may possibly have become a threat to our own security.

Both films also use the proof of the mounting terrorist threats they establish to defend Bush's decisions since 9/11, and in particular his institution of the USA PATRIOT Act. *Fahrenhype 9/11* includes an elaborate recounting by Dick Morris outlining how he believes the PATRIOT Act allowed federal intelligence to prevent terrorists from blowing up the Brooklyn Bridge, while Ed Koch states emphatically, "I thank God we have the PATRIOT Act, and when I ask many of these people with whom I discuss it, 'What don't you like about the PATRIOT Act?,' most of them don't know what's in the PATRIOT Act." In *Celsius 41.11* the PATRIOT Act is compared to the tools law enforcement had used for years to go after the mob and drug dealers and is now merely being employed to go after terrorists; it is described as a bill "whose time had come," given what was going on in the world and the country at the time.

Both films conclude by summarizing their overarching claims with strong patriotic overtones, impassioned support for George W. Bush as our sovereign leader, and a clear repudiation of anyone who might disagree, namely Michael Moore. *Fahrenhype 9/11* concludes with Silver in a monologue inspired by his experience with Moore's film:

> Was it a dream? For some, *Fahrenheit 9/11* was entertaining; it's always fun to poke at our leaders. For others, it was maddening, divisive—we should support our country in a difficult time. Was it a documentary, was it propaganda, or was it just a dream? Our nation is deeply divided over what's best for our future. We can learn from 9/11 about the value of uniting in purpose. If we want to have peace in the world, we need peace at home. So, let's have the debate, let's make the peace, and that is the dream that should carry the day.

This is followed by testimonials from every commentator on why they love America and why we need to remember 9/11 before we determine who needs to lead us and before we vote our conscience on Election Day. The film ends on a silhouette of the Statue of Liberty at sunset overlooking New York Harbor. *Celsius 41.11* concludes on a similar tone, providing a statement on the real question for Americans. Thompson states, "We have got to get to a place in this world where we understand, the good people of this world understand, we're in a battle between the forces of order and the forces of disorder, the forces of anarchy against the rule of law. I think that's what's at stake here this year." Images of Bush are juxtaposed with images of Lincoln, Robert and John Kennedy, and Ronald Reagan, which then fade into a rapidly edited montage of American soldiers, children in caps and gowns, children in Little League outfits, children smiling and playing and getting a haircut. There are also flashing images of flags and shots of a diversity of Americans at work and at play. Over this we hear the end of Bush's acceptance speech at the 2004 Republican

National Convention, in which he reminds the audience what the election really is about: "This moment in the life of our country will be remembered. Generations will know if we kept our faith and kept our word. Generations will know if we seized this moment and used it to build a future of safety and peace. The freedom of many and the future security of our nation now depend on us. My fellow Americans, I ask you to stand with me." As he accepts the nomination in a voice-over, a slow-motion replay of Bush throwing the first pitch at Yankee Stadium during the World Series shortly after 9/11 is shown, and the film fades out on a shot of him waving to the crowd.

Spectator Politics and Political Documentary

According to Kellner, the biggest drawback of the turn to spectator politics, "in which viewer/citizens contemplate political spectacles," is that it ultimately "undermines a participatory democracy in which individuals actively engage in political movements and struggles."[41] The lack of rational discourse in the political documentaries *Fahrenhype 9/11* and *Celsius 41.11*, I believe, exemplifies this problem. Given the unprecedented popularity of Moore's *Fahrenheit 9/11*, these films had an opportunity to address a mass audience by creating a reasoned dialogue, or dialectical engagement, with Moore by responding to his arguments on their own terms. Rather, these films capitalize on the media attention that Moore's documentary garnered to address their constituency, choosing to forgo the opportunity to seriously engage Moore on the issues in any substantive manner and thus delimiting the films' rhetorical potential by appealing only to those already agreeable to a conservative perspective. In many ways, Moore's film just becomes a convenient excuse for more of the same liberal bashing that the pundits featured in *Fahrenhype 9/11* and *Celsius 41.11* engaged in weekly on *Meet the Press* and *This Week with George Stephanopoulos* in the months before the election. In the films, Moore becomes a stand-in for the Democratic Party as a whole, but given the filmmaker's reputation for controversy (with those across the political spectrum), the filmmakers of *Fahrenhype 9/11* and *Celsius 41.11* may have viewed him as a more obvious target than an entire segment of the voting public. Only at the end of *Fahrenhype 9/11* are liberals mentioned by name: Zell Miller addresses "the long-toothed liberals" who are still fighting over the Vietnam War specifically, and the film warns viewers that "Michael Moore is mistaken and [the liberals] misunderstand history."

In a film review for the *Washington Post*, Phillip Kennicott summarizes what he believes is the difference in terms of these films' distinct appeals to pathos: "Moore's film not only preaches to the choir but also makes a creative effort to stir new emotions; [*Celsius 41.11*] presumes the emotional state of [its] audience going in—fear of terrorists, anger at the left—and limits itself to stoking more of the same."[42] Indeed, both *Fahrenhype 9/11* and *Celsius 41.11* situate their appeals in the realm of affect rather than argument, attack rather than discourse, but this is merely a cue that they take from the appeals made in Moore's film. The media spectacle of each of these films relies on fear appeals and inflammatory remarks based in an us-versus-them, you're-either-with-us-or-against-us view of the world. This is a consequence of documentary's conflicting role as a "discourse of sobriety"; because documentary films must function within and meet expectations established by the imagistic cinematic medium—and the contemporary media culture—they must appeal to spectators accustomed to affect, media sensationalism, and scandal while still striving to critique the society that has created these expectations. Nichols notes, "Instead of directly confronting an issue or problem, the discourse must ricochet off this image-based, illusionistic medium of entertainment."[43] Documentary film's very existence within the realm of contemporary media spectacle precludes anything other than politics as usual. The lesson to be learned from *Fahrenhype 9/11* and *Celsius 41.11* is that documentary dialectics merely reflect back to us the nature of politics itself in the twenty-first century: visual and dramatic style trumps rational and debatable substance, and political rancor rather than reason come to define the limits of our capacity for democratic engagement, especially when it is needed most, in the year of election.

Notes

1. *Internet Movie Database*, http://www.imdb.com/title/tt0361596/business (accessed August 25, 2005).

2. This quote is from the book description on *Amazon*, available at www.amazon.com.

3. Corliss describes the agit-doc tone as mixing "sober condemnation with japish wit." See Richard Corliss, "That Old Feeling: The Year in Docu-politics," *Time* Web exclusive, December 20, 2004, http://www.time.com/time/columnist/printout/0,8816,1010031,00.html (accessed October 9, 2005).

4. Richard M. Barsam, *Nonfiction Film: A Critical History Revised and Expanded* (Bloomington: Indiana University Press, 1992), 300.

5. Ibid., 361.

6. Ibid., 375.

7. Bill Nichols, *Representing Reality: Issues and Concepts in Documentary* (Bloomington: Indiana University Press, 1991), 4.

8. Lewis Jacobs, *The Documentary Tradition*, 2nd ed. (New York: W. W. Norton, 1979), 2.

9. Paula Rabinowitz, *They Must Be Represented: The Politics of Documentary* (New York: Verso, 1994), 219.

10. Carl R. Plantinga, *Rhetoric and Representation in Nonfiction Film* (New York: Cambridge University Press, 1997), 11.

11. Nichols, *Representing Reality*, 125.

12. Ibid., xiii.

13. Ibid., 34.

14. Ibid., 35.

15. Ibid., 44.

16. Ibid., 35.

17. Ibid.

18. More specifically, but not revealed in the film, this group consists of a former psychiatrist-turned-neo-con-columnist for the *Washington Post* (Krauthammer); a Pakistani-American investment banker with a significant economic stake in Sudanese oil (Ijaz); a politically conservative Orthodox Jewish film critic who occasionally writes op-eds for the *Wall Street Journal* (Medved); and a member of a conservative think tank who sits on the board of the Committee for the Liberation of Iraq and the Jewish Institute for National Security Affairs (Muravchik).

19. Paul Krugman, "Moore's Public Service," *New York Times*, July 2, 2004, national ed., A19.

20. Michael Atkinson, "Brain Dead: With Race Closing, Conservatives Go after *F9/11*," review of *Celsius 41.11*, *Village Voice*, October 26, 2004, http://www.villagevoice.com/generic/show_print.php?id=57871&page=atkinson5&issue= (accessed October 8, 2005); Philip Kennicott, "*Celsius 41.11* Generates Heat but No New Light," review of *Celsius 41.11*, *Washington Post*, October 22, 2004, C05; Robert Koehler, review of *Celsius 41.11*, *Variety*, October 11, 2004, http://www.variety.com/review/VE1117925214?categoryid=31&cs=1 (accessed October 6, 2005).

21. Vince Leo, review of *Fahrenhype 9/11*, *Qwipster* on-line film reviews, October 2004, http://qwipster.net/fahrenhype.htm (accessed February 14, 2005).

22. William Booth, "Docu-Trauma: For Political Films, the Box Office Is More Bombo Than Boffo," *Washington Post*, November 1, 2004, http://www.washingtonpost.com/ac2/wp-dyn/A17419–2004Nov1?language=printer (accessed October 9, 2005).

23. Aaron West, review of *Fahrenhype 9/11*, *Movie-Vault* on-line film review, October 2004, www.movie-vault.com/archive/printreview.pl?action=moviereview (accessed February 14, 2005); Scott Spicciati, review of *Fahrenhype 9/11*, *Aggressive-Voice* on-line film review, October 2004, http://aggressive-voice.com/zzz187.html (accessed February 14, 2004).

24. Manohla Dargis, "Lowering the Subtlety of Political Discourse," review

of *Celsius 41.11*, *New York Times*, October 22, 2004, http://www.nytimes.com/2004/10/22/movies/22CELS.html (accessed October 8, 2005).

25. Kennicott, "*Celsius 41.11* Generates Heat."

26. Douglas Kellner, *Media Spectacle* (New York: Routledge, 2003), 2.

27. Thomas B. Farrell, "Media Rhetoric as Social Drama: The Winter Olympics of 1984," *Critical Studies in Mass Communication* 6 (1989): 161.

28. Kellner, *Media Spectacle*, 160.

29. Kathleen Hall Jamieson, *Dirty Politics: Deception, Distraction, and Democracy* (New York: Oxford University Press, 1992), 204, 205.

30. Ibid., 218.

31. Ibid.

32. Ibid., 212.

33. Ibid., 213.

34. Ibid., 219.

35. Michael Renov cited in Booth, "Docu-Trauma."

36. Bryan Preston, "Turning Up the Heat on Moore," review of *Fahrenhype 9/11*, *National Review*, October 20, 2004, http://www.nationalreview.com/comment/preston200410200837.asp (accessed February 14, 2004).

37. Corliss, "That Old Feeling."

38. Alan Peterson cited in Preston, "Turning Up."

39. See *Citizens United*, http://www.citizensunited.org.

40. Kennicott, "*Celsius 41.11* Generates Heat."

41. Kellner, *Media Spectacle*, 177.

42. Kennicott, "*Celsius 41.11* Generates Heat."

43. Nichols, *Representing Reality*, 4.

Roger Stahl

Vietnam Flashbacks

Dueling Memories of Dissent in the 2004 Presidential Election

If war is another means of waging politics, 2004 was a year of nested battles. The political air was still thick with the dust of September 11, 2001, and President George W. Bush's subsequent christening of a "war on terror." Within this war, the nation was sharply divided regarding the wisdom of the 2003 Iraq invasion and the ongoing occupation. National security remained a central issue in the presidential election as both Bush and Democratic contender John Kerry clamored for the title of patriarch-protector. The debate quickly found a home in the question of each candidate's service in Vietnam, especially Kerry's. Documentary film would provide the weapons for this contest, and combat would take place on the symbolic field of national identity. By late 2004, the public appetite for political documentary had been whetted by a bumper crop of political documentaries mostly critical of the Bush administration, though there were also a handful of rejoinders. Documentary "broke free from its film festival ghettos," Jessica Clark of *In These Times* observed.[1] As the election approached, two films faced off to define Kerry's character. *Stolen Honor: Wounds That Never Heal* launched a salvo in late September claiming Kerry's antiwar actions after his service in Vietnam were tantamount to treason. *Going Upriver: The Long War of John Kerry* arrived on its heels, celebrating both Kerry's service and his efforts to question American involvement in Vietnam.

These films were not only about Kerry, however. In a very immediate sense, they were also about the meaning of American military power. In late 2004, Vietnam and the specter of "quagmire" seemed to haunt every conversation

VVAW, especially his allegations that American soldiers committed atrocities in Vietnam. Second, the SBVT co-chair John O'Neil questioned the legitimacy of both Kerry's Bronze Star and Silver Star and contended that Kerry's third Purple Heart was a minor, self-inflicted wound that Kerry reported in order to be discharged early.[17]

In August, the SBVT began flooding swing states with a series of nine advertisements, eventually spending $10 million in private funds on the campaign. The first ad, entitled "Any Questions?," begins with John Edwards's admonition that if we have any questions about Kerry's service, we should just ask the men who served with him. What follows is a series of fifteen short testimonials that range from vague accusations ("He lied about his record"; "When the chips were down, you could not count on John Kerry") to claims about the legitimacy of his medals ("I know John Kerry is lying about his first Purple Heart, because I treated him for that injury"; "John Kerry lied to get his Bronze Star. I know; I was there; I saw what happened") to expressions of disgust with Kerry's testimony in front of the Senate Foreign Relations Committee ("He betrayed all his shipmates; he lied before the Senate"; "He dishonored his country; he most certainly did").[18]

The ads that followed elaborated on this initial set of themes. One ad featured Stephen Gardner, the gunner on Kerry's Swift Boat, denying Kerry's claim that they spent Christmas 1968 in Cambodia.[19] Kerry had stated on several occasions that he was secretly sent into Cambodia to perform covert operations, though official U.S. policy at the time respected the border.[20] Another ad questioned the 1971 VVAW march on Washington, which ended with a ceremony where a number of veterans, including Kerry, threw their medals in protest over a makeshift barricade onto the Capitol Building steps. The ad equates the medals with "the heroes they represent" and implies that Kerry cannot be trusted because "he renounced his country's symbols."[21] The ad does not take issue with any reason Kerry gave for doing such a thing. We are left only with the impression that he did so simply because he does not like America and what it stands for. The ad campaign later took issue with Kerry's apparent equivocation of whether he threw his ribbons or his actual medals over the fence. Yet another ad compares Kerry with Jane Fonda, contending that Kerry "secretly" met with the enemy at the 1971 Paris Peace Talks before returning home and "accusing American soldiers of committing war crimes."[22] A final set of ads, aired in late September, featured the members of the SBVT, mainly reiterating the familiar charges. An exception was an ad depicting testimonials of the wives of former Vietnam prisoners of war. The line of reasoning begins with the premise that "all of the prisoners of war in North Vietnam were tortured to obtain confessions of atrocities." The ad concludes

concerning Iraq. U.S. soldier casualties continued to mount. The possibility of torture and atrocities against civilian populations once again appeared. The meaning of "patriotism" became hotly contested. A significant segment of the U.S. public again questioned the candidness of the executive branch, and peace protesters filled the streets. The memory of Vietnam thus became, among other things, an analogy through which Iraq and the public controversy at home could be understood. *Stolen Honor* and *Going Upriver* emerged to offer competing narratives for navigating the troubled waters.

This essay begins by tracing the political terrain from which the documentaries grew and on which they would eventually do battle. In this case, the two films served to elaborate on election-year sound bites already in circulation, especially those issued forth by the Swift Boat Veterans for Truth attack campaign. As such, documentary film came to provide a forum by which the campaign advertisement could break free from the ghetto of the thirty-second television spot. Feature-length documentary not only allotted time to make sustained arguments but also afforded a credibility that had yet to be fully exploited. Next, the essay examines the films themselves, paying special attention to the arguments and umbrella narratives presented. These films give us insights into a deeply contentious election and represent perennially recurring stories that animate public life in the age of American empire. Both films tell tales of power, of those who wield power and those who suffer under its boot. In the end, what is at stake is the meaning of war itself. *Stolen Honor*, I argue, locates its understanding of Vietnam through the metaphor of the "enemy within," with its byproducts of self-sabotage and pain. *Going Upriver* understands Vietnam primarily through a metaphor of alienation, an absentee leadership that produced a culture of ignorance and irresponsibility.

The Electioneering of Kerry's War

Due to an early series of negative Republican ads, the election quickly became a contest of personal character. The Republicans had had four years to fine-tune Bush's Texas cowboy persona: a straight-talking, rough-around-the-edges man of the people. In contrast, the Democratic campaign found itself contending with an image of Kerry as an indecisive, out-of-touch, blue-blooded limousine liberal.[2] One later ad represented the successful maturation of this image. The ad runs footage of Kerry windsurfing off the coast of Nantucket, a vacation that was an attempt by the Kerry campaign to display not only masculine prowess but also nonchalance in the face of the Republican National Convention.[3] The ad literally turns this image against itself, juxtaposing shots of Kerry sailing in one direction, then the other. A voice-over tells us that Kerry changed his mind regarding the legitimacy of the Iraq war, military spending, and Medi-

that since Kerry testified in front of the Senate about soldier atrocities, he gave "aid and comfort to the enemy."[23]

This final claim was to become the narrative kernel for *Stolen Honor: Wounds That Never Heal*. The documentary was not officially associated with the SBVT (who later changed their name to the Swift Vets and POWs for Truth), but many of the POWs interviewed in the film also appeared in the ads.[24] The forty-two-minute film, which cost $250,000, was produced in Harrisburg, Pennsylvania. According to the production house—Carlton Sherwood and Red, White, and Blue Productions—the money to make the film came from a dozen or so Pennsylvania veterans, but the producers declined to release the names.[25] The film was released September 10, 2004, on video and did not play in theaters. It was a film without a venue.

Stolen Honor found its venue a month later, when Sinclair Broadcasting Group, the largest owner of network affiliate stations, announced in October that it would preempt its regular programming to air the documentary in its entirety. At the time, Sinclair reached a quarter of the U.S. population and held stations in each of the crucial swing states. Sinclair had already made news in April of that year when it refused to air an edition of *Nightline* devoted to reading the names of U.S. soldiers killed in Iraq, as it would be "contrary to the public interest."[26] Before that, Sinclair had led the charge to cancel Bill Maher's *Politically Incorrect*, ordering its seven ABC affiliates to stop broadcasting the show after Maher questioned whether the 9/11 terrorists were technically "cowards." Mark Hyman, Sinclair's vice president for corporate affairs, was at the time the host of the conservative polemic *The Point* and another called *News Central,* a segment that Sinclair required to be aired during many of its affiliates' local news programs. Sinclair's affinities with the Bush administration extend further.[27] Although Sinclair offered Kerry a chance to respond after the documentary, which he declined, the decision to air *Stolen Honor* was immediately controversial. The pressure mounted not only from those who considered the forced airing to be political propaganda in its baldest sense, perhaps even violating election laws, but also from Sinclair stockholders, who witnessed sponsors pulling ads. Sinclair finally caved to the pressure and announced that it would show only parts of the documentary in the context of a special about political documentary and would air it on only forty of its sixty-two stations.[28]

Going Upriver: The Long War of John Kerry has a much less storied existence. In contrast to *Stolen Honor*'s strictly video release, *Going Upriver* is a feature-length film with a much higher production value. The film was released on October 1, 2004, near the beginning of the Sinclair controversy. It opened in 163 theaters and grossed $614,000. The film's director, George Butler, was responsible for the documentary films *Pumping Iron* (1976), which brought Arnold Schwarzenegger his first taste of fame, and *The Endurance: Shackleton's Legendary Antarctic Expedition* (2001), shown on public television. *Going Upriver* is based on the biography *Tour of Duty: John Kerry and the Vietnam War* by Douglas Brinkley, the counterpoint to John O'Neil's *Unfit for Command*. At the time, Butler was no stranger to Kerry's life, claiming to have known Kerry for forty years.[29] Butler conceived of *Going Upriver,* like *Stolen Honor,* as an election-year film and was not shy about his hope that it would influence the outcome.[30]

The film examines a similar time frame as *Stolen Honor,* roughly Kerry's years at Yale from 1966 through his protest activities in 1971. *Going Upriver* functions to lengthen the election-year sound bites that were in play in 2004. This includes telling the story of Kerry's initial idealism in his decision to enlist while at Yale and involves a detailed account of the incidents that earned him his medals. The film explores the motivations of the VVAW, contextualizing the march on Washington. It generously excerpts Kerry's testimony in front of the Senate and tells the story of the ceremonial medal-throwing from the point of view of those who participated. One film critic noted, "The film serves as a well-crafted rebuke without stooping to even acknowledge the charges."[31] The rebuke does not, however, mention Kerry's 1971 trip to the Paris Peace Talks, nor does it offer any clarification of the charge that Kerry lied about spending Christmas of 1968 in Cambodia.

Stolen Honor: The Politics of Pain

One of the reasons *Stolen Honor* would have done well on Sinclair TV is that it borrows many of the stylistic conventions of television. The film begins with a teaser, or what might function as a "bumper" between television shows, that tersely sets up the film's central theme of betrayal. We are greeted not by opening credits but by a talking head, the central voice of the program, Carlton Sherwood. Sherwood's voice in the film splits the difference between what Bill Nichols identifies as expository and interactive modes of documentary representation.[32] At times, Sherwood acts as an authoritative "voice of God" narrator in the expository mode. At other times, he injects his own experience as a marine who served in Vietnam. The resulting aesthetic is a mix of authority and personal investment in the stories of the film's subjects, mostly former POWs. The darkly lit interviews portray a sense of identification, as if the interviewees and the viewer were having a collective living room conversation.

Sherwood introduces himself first as an investigative journalist who has exposed treachery in the government, the corporate world, health care, and organized religion.[33] In this sense, the documentary positions itself as an exposé similar to the television news magazine segment whose charge is consumer advocacy or pulling back the curtain on power and corruption. Sherwood's introduction links Kerry's testimony in front of the Senate with others who had "dishonored their profession," such as "doctors who were actually ordering the starvation of handicapped children, and charlatans who preached faith from the pulpit, but who practiced greed and deception in their personal lives." He casts himself as a character in the documentary. "Only for me, it's a lot more personal. It's about a war I fought in and what I saw happening when I got back from it. It's about a treachery that was, in some ways, as frightening as the hand-to-hand combat I experienced as a young marine." This treachery was Kerry's Senate testimony, the focal point of the film.

As a documentary, the film implicitly allies itself with late-twentieth-century American political documentary, a tradition that has a reputation of functioning as an "alternative press" or underdog medium of the people, mainly, but not exclusively, for the Left and progressive causes. In this tradition, the documentary is widely viewed as a genre outside the interests and machinations of power.[34] This was especially true of the vast majority of political documentaries that appeared in 2004, an explosion that can be partly attributed to documentary's seeming credibility in a media environment of partisan corporate conglomerates. Moreover, the lineage of "Vietnam documentary" is a particularly critical one. If we were to look at the major films that enjoyed theatrical release during and since the conflict, we would find Emile de Antonio's *In the Year of the Pig* (1969) and the Academy Award–winning *Hearts and Minds* (1974), both highly critical of the motives and tactics of the U.S. government. Later came the British documentary *We Can Keep You Forever* (1987), which investigated the possibility of MIAs and POWs in Vietnam and serves as a touchstone for those who hold the government responsible for leaving soldiers behind. More recent was Errol Morris's *The Fog of War* (2003), another Academy Award–winner that, somewhat ambivalently, takes former Secretary of Defense Robert McNamara to task for his role in prosecuting the Vietnam War.[35]

Stolen Honor frames itself as both a piece of investigative journalism and a critical documentary. An implicit narrative is drafted with regard to the film's political role, which is as advocate of the powerless in the face of the powerful. This narrative depends on a mainstream narrative of Vietnam, which is retold at the beginning of the film: Vietnam was the only foreign war America has ever lost, and though we sacrificed mightily, the effort was lost at home, brought down by an unsympathetic media and politicians intimidated by an antiwar movement that extended the war, encouraged our enemies, demoralized our troops, and put our POWs at risk. The film conspicuously avoids the subject of why the United States entered Vietnam, instead referring somewhat vaguely to the reasons given by Presidents Truman, Kennedy, and Johnson. Nixon is left off the list, presumably for credibility's sake. The powerful character in this drama is the antiwar movement of the time, which crippled the nation and caused it to lose the war. The powerless in the documentary are the American Vietnam POWs, who not only suffered physically under the brutal thumb of their North Vietnamese torturers but endured psychological torment at the hands of Jane Fonda, Tom Hayden, and other activists who traveled with impunity between the United States and Vietnam, sometimes meeting with the torturers themselves. Kerry's Senate testimony is positioned at the crest of the antiwar movement, both as an opportunistic political ploy for fame and a tortuous betrayal of those still in captivity.

Stolen Honor relies heavily on a discourse of pain. To intensify the sense of victimization and thus betrayal by Kerry and others, the film privileges the suffering that the American POWs were made to endure while imprisoned. The stories of torture at the Hoa Lo Prison, known by American POWs as the "Hanoi Hilton," make up nearly a third of the forty-two-minute documentary. This section of the film relies on a memory of Vietnam largely established by the 1987 prowar drama The Hanoi Hilton. In the spirit of the passion play, The Hanoi Hilton positions the heroism of the POWs in direct proportion to their suffering. Stolen Honor, in turn, offers an abridged version of this story. Indeed, the discourse of pain functions to anchor the documentary in a space beyond rational argument, a place of unimpeachable truth.[36]

Moreover, the detailed description of torture serves as evidence for Kerry's treachery. The more horrific the suffering, the greater Kerry's guilt. This logic works through the clear Manichean dichotomy between those who supported America's efforts and those who betrayed the country. The narrative kernel here is a familiar one, summed up in the bumper sticker "Support Our Troops," which is code for "Support the War." If one does indeed support the troops but not the war, one must add the caveat "Support the Troops: Bring Them Home." The nation saw a similar line of reasoning after September 11, 2001, in which President Bush divided the globe between those who "are with us" and those "with the terrorists."[37] The film thus implies that if one wanted American withdrawal from Vietnam, one also, knowingly or not, supported the torture of American POWs.

Stolen Honor cements its indictment of Kerry largely by establishing a link between Kerry and Jane Fonda. We are first greeted with the established image of Jane Fonda as the turncoat "Hanoi Jane" as seen in the famous photo of her sitting atop an antiaircraft gun emplacement with Viet Cong soldiers, a photo that became a ready referent for those critical of the peace movement.[38] One

POW claims that Fonda "made tapes" condemning U.S. soldiers, which were played in the camps to demoralize the captives.[39] The film also claims that Fonda and other antiwar activists, at the invitation of the North Vietnamese, routinely visited the prison camps to deliver their message to the humiliated American POWs. *Stolen Honor* associates Kerry with Fonda by twice displaying a photo of Fonda at an antiwar rally with Kerry in the background.[40] The implicit conclusion is that, in this binary world, Kerry must have endorsed Fonda's actions even to the point of complicity. Indeed, through Fonda, Kerry is portrayed as acting in league with the torturers themselves.

Stolen Honor further claims that the sole purpose of the torture was the extraction of confessions that U.S. soldiers committed atrocities, confessions that were later used by the North Vietnamese for propaganda purposes. The film draws the conclusion that Kerry, in his Senate testimony of American atrocities, painlessly gave the Viet Cong the phony confession they desired, an act many POWs resisted, even under intense torture. If this were not enough, the film claims that Kerry's "willing testimony" actually emboldened the Viet Cong to step up the torture. Kerry could not plead ignorance as to the effects of his deeds, as he had been in Vietnam himself. In this way, Kerry's comfort is portrayed to be inversely proportional to the pain endured by the POWs. The conclusion is that Kerry is not only a traitor but also a sadist.

The accounts of torture dovetail with the notion that Kerry's Vietnam service was insignificant, an image cultivated by his opponents during the 2004 election. In direct contrast to those who underwent the pain and humiliation in these dank prisons, Kerry is presented in the film as serving only a "four-month tour of duty." In fact, Kerry had spent two tours in Vietnam. His first tour was aboard the *USS Gridley* off the coast of Vietnam from February 9, 1968, to November 16, 1968. His second tour, to which the documentary refers, was aboard the Swift Boat, from November 1968 to March 25, 1969, after which he was sent home for being thrice wounded. From enlistment to discharge, Kerry had spent four years in the navy during Vietnam. His record notwithstanding, the film juxtaposes Kerry's seemingly paltry sacrifice with those still languishing in POW camps. This discourse of pain is in conversation with the charges brought forth both in O'Neil's book *Unfit for Command* and the SBVT ads, which charge that Kerry's wounds were superficial and perhaps even a self-inflicted ploy to be sent home early. In short, Kerry is portrayed as having been remiss in his duties, an argument visually buttressed by images of Kerry cavorting with hirsute peace activists at home. The gulf between Kerry's pain and the pain of the POW serves as the affective scaffolding of the film's argument.

The list of accusations continues, including that Kerry urged veterans to fabricate testimony of atrocities for the Winter Soldier Hearings, even duping a grieving mother of a POW to testify.[41] The timing of Kerry's remarks, the film adds, raises more questions about Kerry's motives. Sherwood tells us, "In 1971, when Kerry delivered his 'stop the killing, end the war' manifesto, the war had all but ended. Less than half of our army remained in Vietnam. A year later, they too would be gone." The implication is that Kerry's motives were more about his personal political ambitions than stopping the war. In fact, when Kerry gave his Senate testimony, nearly 300,000 troops remained in Vietnam, and it would be another four years before the United States withdrew completely.[42]

Apart from an understanding of Kerry as an individual, at stake in the film is the *memory* of Vietnam and America's involvement. While *Stolen Honor* skirts the reasons for being there, other than "containing Communism," we do get an extended discussion of soldier atrocities. The film first excerpts a famous passage from Kerry's Senate testimony: "They had personally raped, cut off ears, cut off heads, taped wires to human genitals and turned up the power, cut off limbs, blown up bodies, randomly shot at civilians, razed villages in the manner of Genghis Kahn, shot cattle and dogs for fun, poisoned food stocks, and generally ravaged the countryside of South Vietnam." In this oft-quoted selection, Kerry appears to paint all veterans with a broad, accusatory brush. In fact, the sentence begins, "They told the stories at times they had person-ally raped . . . ," referring to the stories told at the Winter Soldier Hearings. The selective editing fosters the film's claim that the testimony was one man's wild, fabricated accusation.

The film missteps a bit in referencing Kerry's appearance on NBC's *Meet the Press* on April 28, 1971, six days after his Senate testimony. Here Kerry mentioned that he himself participated in search and destroy missions and free fire zones: "There are all kinds of atrocities and I would have to say that, yes, yes, I committed the same kind of atrocities as thousands of other soldiers have committed."[43] Based on this remark, *Stolen Honor* advances some strange "even if" arguments. As one veteran reasons, "Then [Kerry] adds on that he did it, which automatically means that he's a war criminal. If he says what he really said, he did it too. We just don't do that. We're Americans." Another crafts a similar non sequitur: "If he had actually seen these things, would he say that on television, risking the chance that somebody would say, 'Why the hell didn't you stop it?'" We know, however, that Kerry *did* say it on television and, in so doing, took that risk. Here the film finds itself in a conundrum. If Kerry lied, then he cannot be painted as a war criminal. If he told the truth, the film would have to concede that Americans committed atrocities.[44] In any case, the film cannot account for Kerry's self-incriminating remarks. In drawing attention to the remarks, the film inadvertently advances the notion that Kerry was less of an opportunist than a reluctant witness.

The film eventually settles on the foundational argument that Kerry's testimony of atrocities and the stories that issued forth from the Winter Soldier Hearings were utter fabrications designed to shock America. This argument cannot be separated from assumptions about the news media. Colonel Bud Day, a Medal of Honor winner, states: "The thing about the Kerry comments back in 1971 was that they were so sensational, they were so outrageous, that they were precisely the kind of things that a propaganda expert and the news media were looking for." Sherwood echoes this narrative of media complicity. Whereas Kerry's testimony "literally created the image of American soldiers as deranged, drug-addicted, psychopaths—baby killers," Hollywood and the news media took the ball and ran, Sherwood continues, creating films like *Apocalypse Now* (1979), *Platoon* (1986), and *Casualties of War* (1989), which continue to slander Vietnam veterans. The idea that the media—news journalism, in particular—conspired to hamper the war effort remained in both the popular imagination and the ranks of the Pentagon under the name of the "Vietnam Syndrome."[45] The notion of a media hostile to veterans helps to round out the film's narrative of power and the film's role as an antidote to powerful interests.

One burr in this smooth narrative is the January 1968 massacre of the village of My Lai, in which Charlie Company, 11th Brigade, executed some five hundred unarmed civilians, primarily elderly men and women, children, and babies. The unit was commanded to assume that anyone left in the village was a Viet Cong fighter, which amounted to a "free fire zone" policy common to U.S. practice in Vietnam. The massacre was eventually halted by two intervening U.S. soldiers, who found themselves vilified at the time as traitors. After a failed military cover-up, the story broke in the news media almost two years later, in November 1969, with the help of investigative reporter Seymour Hersh. Photos of the pile of infants and elderly became a lightning rod for the peace movement and remain to this day some of the more salient images of Vietnam.[46]

Stolen Honor's response to My Lai is a rhetoric of desystemization common to organizations accused of wrongdoing. Responsibility for the massacre is pinned on one person, platoon leader Lieutenant William Calley, who infamously turned his machine gun on a ditch filled with civilians.[47] Though Calley did not act alone in the torture, rape, and killing at My Lai, the film implies that Calley was a "bad apple."[48] To boost this contention, the film draws attention to the soldiers who halted the killing and others who "exposed the cruelties of My Lai." While it is true that one soldier from the 11th Brigade had written a letter accusing his unit of committing atrocities, he also suggested that others did so routinely. Nevertheless, the film maintains that My Lai was an isolated incident, an act of one man who was exposed by his comrades. "Wasn't John Kerry [in his Senate testimony] taking the exception and making it the rule?" asks Sherwood. In isolating Calley, the film draws blame as far away from military leadership as possible. If atrocities do persist in the public memory, the claim goes, it is the fault of the John Kerrys and a media system eager to exploit a My Lai when it does slip through the cracks.

The title, *Stolen Honor*, most directly refers to the final major claim that Kerry's antiwar efforts turned all Vietnam veterans into reviled pariahs. The claim relies on an enduring narrative of the returning Vietnam soldier. The story proceeds as such: Already yoked with the image of "baby killers," returning GIs were met with derision at home, taunted, and even spat upon by antiwar activists. It is true that many Vietnam veterans did not return to a hero's welcome, as there was significant social upheaval at home. What is notable, however, is that the narrative is a reiteration of the film's binary structure. That is, the film suggests that the peace movement (and the media complicity surrounding it) was a war on our own troops. The image of the antiwar activist spitting on the returning GI is one that Jerry Lembcke examines in his book *The Spitting Image: Myth, Memory, and the Legacy of Vietnam*. According to Lembcke, while there are plenty of newspaper accounts of prowar counter-demonstrators spitting on antiwar demonstrators, there are no actual press accounts of protesters spitting on servicemen, an event that would have very likely involved a physical altercation.[49] The myth appeared in *Rambo: First Blood* (1982) and since then, Lembcke argues, has been uncritically accepted and repeated as fact.[50] *Stolen Honor* blames Kerry for the initial vilification of the returning GI. While the story reiterates the familiar binary structure, insofar as the spat-upon soldier walks away scorned, the story is also about power. Kerry and the peace movement are the powerful aggressors. The tortured POWs and the returning soldiers are the powerless martyrs and victims of this aggression.

Going Upriver: A Reluctant Hero's Passage

As a rejoinder, *Going Upriver: The Long War of John Kerry* is far less argumentative in the traditional sense. The film does not lay out a clear opponent. Rather, it attempts to tell Kerry's story in the tradition of the hero's quest. The narrative follows Kerry's youthful idealism into the crucible of war, his disenchantment, and his effort to redeem both himself and his country. The film also takes on such specifics as the stories behind his medals, the purpose and scope of the VVAW, the drama of the march on Washington, the details of Kerry's Senate testimony, and the reasons for the tossing of the medals. The film cannot be taken as a direct response to *Stolen Honor* insofar as it in no way addresses the major charge that Kerry's actions were detrimental to POWs still in captivity. This is not to say that the film does not contain powerful arguments, however, such as the central notion that Kerry's motives were pure and his actions patriotic.

Aesthetically, *Going Upriver* is more cinematic than *Stolen Honor*. Though not strictly observational, *Going Upriver* does not mediate the story through a narrator. Rather, the story is carried by the interviewees, whose words tie together photos, archival Vietnam footage, and footage of Kerry himself at various events. With some action-packed exceptions, the first third of the film portraying Kerry's time in Vietnam is dreamlike and surreal. There is an abundance of negative audio space in which no one is speaking. There are many quiet shots of the Vietnam countryside and wide sunsets. The camera hovers over photographs with a slow zoom in the style of Ken Burns's *The Civil War* (1990) series. At one point, one of Kerry's letters home regarding the death of his friend Richard Pershing is read in the stoic manner that has become Burns's signature. The archival footage of U.S. napalming runs over villages is a muffled, slow-motion ride over a bed of sparse Vietnamese bells or other minimalist music. The aesthetic captures a Vietnam War that is an unholy mixture of fire and water, at once "beautiful and terrifying," as one of the interviewees, Georgia senator Max Cleland, describes. The cumulative effect of these choices is a contemplative distance and reverence.

In contrast to *Stolen Honor*, *Going Upriver* gives a certain place to the Vietnamese people, at the very least making them characters in the drama. The film offers postcard shots not only of the countryside but also of the houses, fishing boats, and daily life of Vietnamese civilians. GIs grieving over American bodies are pictured alongside Vietnamese weeping over their dead. In this way, *Going Upriver* draws the battle lines at a much different place than in *Stolen Honor*. American soldiers and the Vietnamese people find themselves both victims of a larger force, perhaps "playing a deadly game for blind gods," as veteran and poet Yusef Komunyakaa later put it.[51] The blind gods in the drama are those such as General William Westmoreland, Lyndon Johnson, and Richard Nixon, safely making decisions out of harm's way. These leaders are painted as less evil than self-absorbed and ignorant to the reality of the war. This idea is exemplified by a creatively contrived scene where Vietnamese barroom patrons watch Nixon give a televised speech. Though it is clear that the footage was intercut to achieve this effect, the point-of-view melds our gaze as viewers with that of the Vietnamese, positioning them as worthy subjects (rather than objects) of history. Through the eyes of the Vietnamese, Nixon's remarks about winning the mind of the American public seem particularly distant. The scene creates a sense of an absurd gulf between American leaders and those who are affected most by their decisions. Later in the film, the main purpose of Kerry's stateside actions will be the closing of this gulf by demanding accountability for disastrous policies. He will be the protagonist in a story of redemption.

The film provides a complex explanation of the purpose (or purposelessness) of the war. *Going Upriver* stops quite short of the claim that the Vietnam War was a calculated act of American imperialism. Indeed, the Kennedy administration's initial decision to commit American troops, the narrative goes, appealed to a young idealistic and patriotic John Kerry at Yale. The film turns against the war precisely when the American public did, after the 1968 Tet Offensive debacle, when Vietnam officially became, in Walter Cronkite's famous words, "mired in stalemate." Neil Sheehan, the *New York Times* reporter who first printed sections of the *Pentagon Papers*, tells this story in the film. Sheehan argues that most Americans believed President Johnson when he put forward the (in)famous domino theory. We thought we were defending a small nation against a monstrous Communist aggressor. Later, we were to find that we would never win, that the Vietnamese would continue fighting whatever the cost, because they were fighting a war for national independence. Thus, the film takes the soft critical stance that we were victims of "Cold War myths" and that Vietnam was a tragedy of mistaken identity. Beyond this, the film implies a staple assumption of American imperial political rhetoric from Vietnam forward: only unwinnable wars are illegitimate.[52] Because the main purpose of the film is the telling of Kerry's heroic story, however, the filmmakers are wise not to squander sympathy on interpretations of the war that aim too wide of center.

Going Upriver is most direct in its rejoinder to ~~Stolen Honor~~ in exploring Kerry's motivations. The film portrays Kerry as coming from a strong family to become an all-American athlete and civic leader at Yale. A story of Kerry collecting recycling bottles at the Stop 'N' Shop for money eases his patrician image. Kerry associates himself closely with John Kennedy, who does not appear in the rogues' gallery of Vietnam presidents with Johnson and Nixon. We hear that Kerry admired Kennedy and that Kennedy's admonitions of service deeply affected Kerry and his decision to enlist. We also hear of Kerry's heartbreak at the news of Kennedy's assassination. Later in the film, after Kerry had delivered his Senate testimony, clips from an audiotaped conversation between Nixon and his chief of staff, Bob Haldeman, are played in which Haldeman declares Kerry to be a "Kennedy-type guy; he looks just like a Kennedy, and he talks exactly like a Kennedy." The film derives much of Kerry's ethos from this association.

Kerry's time on the Swift Boat provides a test of his character. The film relates that at first he was naively eager to captain a Swift Boat. Kerry was a strong and democratic leader, as one of his shipmates remembers. Soon, however, the navy began sending the crew on suicide missions up the Mekong River to draw enemy fire. Here the film claims that Swift Boats sustained 75–90 percent casualty rates. Additionally, they were sent into free fire zones, where they were ordered to shoot anything that moved, count the dead as Viet Cong, and burn down huts as an intimidation tactic. Kerry recounts in a recorded 1970 interview:

> I remember this one body, just lying in this open field, with blue shorts and a light blue shirt, and this was the guy's uniform. I couldn't help but remark that with all of us running around in our flak jackets and our M-16 and fifty-caliber guns—it seemed rather amazing that he was this enemy that was causing such an amazing conflagration. And as we left with this hut that had been set on fire by one of the men, burning, and with this body lying all alone in the field—it was a very poignant scene that has always remained with me. After all of the shooting and killing and the supposed carrying out of orders that were for the benefit of these people, there was this dead Vietnamese on his own ground lying there alone with no honors, no ceremony, nothing in a sense to justify his death except what he died with and died for.

Kerry's recollection is played over actual footage of the incident, which included shots of the man in the blue shirt and the burning of his hut. This account represents the beginning of Kerry's disillusionment and his questioning of the wisdom of the leadership.

Proceeding from this anecdote, we encounter a dual argument. First is the atrocity argument, which focuses on the "free fire zone" policy implemented by General Westmoreland. Senators Max Cleland and Bob Kerrey, Neil Sheehan, and other former soldiers testify to the horrors of this policy. Former marine Danny Barbeiro describes the free fire zones: "We literally had places we could go where if you saw a human being, you could kill them. You didn't have to find out who they were. Anybody, civilian, old man. We took this for granted in the Marine Corps." Cleland implies that these policies intentionally targeted civilians: "Peasants, civilians could move around a free fire zone. They don't know. Nobody drew out on a map what a free fire zone is. A free fire zone is a zone declared by the United States military." These accounts are related over gory footage of Vietnamese bodies. It is important to note that these accounts direct their outrage not at the soldiers who participated in these activities but at the leadership that required them to participate. We are told that Westmoreland was driven to provide high body count statistics. Sheehan argues that Westmoreland "knew what he was doing," quoting the general as justifying the free fire zones on the grounds that they "deprive the enemy of its population."

The second argument regards Kerry himself and his motivations. Kerry questioned the leadership in Vietnam. He told his officers, "It was wrong to go up the river just randomly shooting at villagers, and this wasn't the way to . . . 'win the hearts and minds of the people.'" Even so, the film continues with stories of heroism on the Swift Boat that earned Kerry his medals, acts of valor performed even in the face of his disillusionment. In doing so, the film makes an argument regarding Kerry's loyalty to the military, a loyalty tested and seemingly unshakable. In contrast to the narrative of *Stolen Honor*, Vietnam is presented as a drama in which American soldiers and Vietnamese alike were victimized by a misguided leadership. In this story, Kerry emerges from the impossible situation twice a patriot. At once, he has the courage to do his duty *and* exercise his conscience.

The story continues with Kerry's return to the United States and his joining with the antiwar movement. The tale of the VVAW is one of humble beginnings. The Winter Soldier Hearings, it is emphasized, are held in a hotel in the poor section of Detroit. Senator Bob Kerrey, noted Vietnam veteran, comments, "If there is a desire to go into politics, and you were talking to me in 1970 or '71, and saying I would like to run for Congress someday, and I'm also thinking about leading an effort to end the war, I would say pick one of the two, because you can't do both." As such, the film disputes the notion that Kerry participated in antiwar activities for political gain. Additionally, the medal-throwing ceremony is presented as an enormous psychological sacrifice where veterans renounced the very symbols for which they risked their lives. Thus, the film counters at every turn the idea that the antiwar movement for Kerry was an easy, opportunistic route to political power. Indeed, the film's title, *Going Upriver*, metaphorically captures this central argument.

Kerry is also portrayed at several points in contrast to the average antiwar protester. He is clean-cut and demure, sometimes drawing the ire of the counterculture because of his establishment looks. He circulates among the agitated VVAW crowd at the Capitol Building, calming nerves. As one VVAW member recounts, Kerry was last in line to toss his medals over the fence, saying only, "'I don't do this to oppose anyone. I'm only doing this to help my country wake up.' And then, like so many of his brothers, he didn't wind up and throw. He kind of lobbed, and then left." Whereas *Stolen Honor* likens Kerry to a spotlight-hoarding agitator—an Abbie Hoffman—*Going Upriver* portrays him as a statesman who did not let power or resentment derail his love of country. As a kind of Christ character, he is tempted, and each test yields evidence of his true motivations.

At several points, the film disputes the notion that antiwar efforts in general were anti-soldier or anti-American. If anything, the film implies, the soldiers and nation were victims of the higher leadership. We are shown footage, for example, of Kerry condemning the Nixon White House for disallowing a grieving mother entrance to the Arlington National Cemetery. In another scene, the film explains that the protest symbol of the upside-down flag was not anti-American but was a military symbol of distress. Some VVAW protesters are shown with the letters "P.O.W." scrawled on their foreheads, drawing attention to the White House policy of surrounding the veterans with armed guards and overhead helicopters. (*Stolen Honor* deploys this same image, incidentally, as evidence of long-haired VVAW protesters mocking actual POWs.) Here the Capitol police, some having served in Vietnam, are presented as sympathetic to the VVAW cause. We see footage of Kerry defusing the notion that protesters might become violent: "It's ridiculous to assume that veterans, who saw the violence in Vietnam, are going to go to Washington, D.C., to perpetrate violence. That's what we're here to stop." We hear a story where a member of the Daughters of the American Revolution tells a VVAW marcher that the protest "will not go over well with our troops." The response from a veteran is, "Lady, we are the troops." Finally, the film mends the rift between the protesters and the more democratic reaches of the government, featuring the Capital Hill office workers, senators, and congresspersons who poured out of the Capitol Building to join the VVAW effort.

The film's climax, and the narrative's most confrontational moment, is Kerry's testimony in front of the Senate Foreign Relations Committee. Here the dramatic conflict between the top policy-makers and the troops is most acute. The film plays a long section of Kerry's statement that impugns the leadership using the standards of its own military. The following is a short excerpt:

> We are here to ask, and we are here to ask vehemently, where are the leaders of our country? Where is the leadership? We're here to ask where are McNamara, Rostow, Bundy, Gilpatrick, and so many others? Where are they now that we, the men they sent off to war, have returned? These are the commanders who have deserted their troops. And there is no more serious crime in the laws of war. The army says they never leave their wounded. The marines say they never even leave their dead. These men have left all the casualties and retreated behind a pious shield of public rectitude. They've left the real stuff of their reputations bleaching behind them in the sun in this country. . . .

The testimony continues with a rhetoric that joins the Vietnam soldier and the antiwar protester into the single figure of the soldier-for-peace, who "undertakes one last mission" to wipe out the barbarity, fear, and hatred that have driven America. As such, the film seals its central narrative of an America whose leadership has violated the trust of its people, the honor of its soldiers, and its basic values.

Flashbacks

In a sense, a narrative of the past must have the friction of contradiction in order to be burned into the collective psyche. Between *Stolen Honor* and *Going Upriver*, we find two dueling ironic narratives, both of self-sabotage. *Stolen Honor* features the absurdity of one soldier torturing his comrades on behalf of the enemy. *Going Upriver*'s core narrative is of an ignorant civilian commanding the war-worn soldier to take on a suicide mission with the purpose of "destroying the village in order to save it."[53] The narratives fan out into the larger world, describing structures of power that go well beyond the military. They are stories about media, government, and the wild card of American public opinion. They are stories about what it means to exercise moral integrity in a world of ignorance, powerful interests, and monsters.

Memories, however, are not the sole province of the past. They are, as sociologist Maurice Halbwachs suggests, retrofitted for the collective needs of the present.[54] We know that the needs of the 2004 presidential election produced a flurry of discourse about the meaning of Kerry's war service and his activism afterward. The debates, however, go beyond Kerry-the-candidate and whether he had the "stuff" to be president in a "time of terror." The nation was wrestling with the meaning of Vietnam at a moment when public opinion was split regarding an ongoing occupation of another distant land, Iraq. The ghosts of Vietnam had been summoned again of necessity, emerging in a cluster of meanings by which America could understand its turmoil and find its conscience. Once again, a nation struggled to define the basic terms of the debate, the narratives by which war itself is understood as a conflict.

Notes

1. Jessica Clark, "Political Realities: Documentaries Rush in to Fill Journalism Void," *In These Times* (2004), http://www.inthesetimes.com/site/main/article/1003.

2. See Mark Memmott, "Bush Leads in Negative Ads, but Kerry Has Help," *USA Today*, May 18, 2004. Not only had the Bush campaign produced more negative ads than the Kerry campaign, but the Bush campaign spent nearly two-thirds of its advertising budget early on airing seven negative ads. For an

extended discussion of Republican co-opting populist rhetoric, see Thomas Frank, *What's the Matter with Kansas? How Conservatives Won the Heart of America* (New York: Metropolitan Books, 2004).

3. For an excellent treatment of the politics of masculinity, see Stephen Ducat, *The Wimp Factor: Gender Gaps, Holy Wars, and the Politics of Anxious Masculinity* (Boston: Beacon Press, 2004).

4. "Windsurfing," Bush-Cheney '04, Inc., television advertisement, September 23, 2004. All 2004 official candidate ads can be viewed at *The Living Room Candidate*, http://livingroomcandidate.movingimage.us/.

5. Damien Cave, "Flip Flopper," *New York Times*, December 26, 2004, 5.

6. Evidence for Kerry's "flip-floppiness" most often came in the form of a quotation that was repeated ad infinitum in presidential speeches and the press: "I actually did vote for the $87 billion before I voted against it." White House chief advisor Karl Rove called the quotation "the gift that kept giving." See "Defending the American Way," *Irish Times*, December 30, 2004. The comment, made in front of an audience of veterans, was later clarified by Kerry as referring to two versions of the same bill—a first version that would have garnered the money from taxes on those making more than $200,000 (a version Bush threatened to veto), and a second version that did not include this provision. See David E. Rosenbaum, "Fact Check," *New York Times*, October 26, 2004.

7. Walter J. Robinson, "1-Year Gap in Bush's Guard Duty; No Record of Airman at Drills 1972–73," *Boston Globe*, May 23, 2000. See also George Gardner and Lois Romano, "At Height of Vietnam, Bush Picks Guard," *Washington Post*, July 28, 1999.

8. Lois Romano, "Bush's Guard Duty in Question; Democrats Say President Shirked His Duty in 1972," *Washington Post*, February 3, 2004. As of September 2004, neither Bush nor Kerry had released his entire service file. See Michael Dobbs, "Assembling Full War Records a Challenge," *Washington Post*, September 30, 2004.

9. See Jacques Steinberg and Bill Carter, "CBS Dismisses 4 over Broadcast on Bush Service," *New York Times*, January 11, 2005.

10. "Three Minutes," Kerry-Edwards '04, Inc., television advertisement, July 10, 2004.

11. "Text of John Kerry's Acceptance Speech at the Democratic National Convention," *Washington Post* (2004), http://www.washingtonpost.com/wp-dyn/articles/A25678-2004Jul29.html.

12. Karl Rove once told reporters, "Look, I don't attack people on their weaknesses. That usually doesn't get the job done. Voters already perceive weaknesses. You've got to go after the other guy's strengths. That's how you win." Quoted in James Moore, "Smear Artist," *Salon.com*, August 28, 2004.

13. Indeed, the Bush administration chose the "high road" when it came to the Swift Boat ads with the president publicly issuing the statement, "I think the senator served admirably and ought to be proud of his record." See Sheldon Alberts, "Bush Denounces Anti-Kerry Ads; Unimpressed Rivals Say President Has Yet to Set the Record Straight," *Ottawa Citizen*, August 24, 2004, A8.

14. See a history of O'Neil's involvement with the Nixon White House in Michael Dobbs, "After Decades, Renewed War on Old Conflict," *Washington Post*, August 28, 2004. For a complete outline of the networks linking the Bush White House and the Swift Boat Veterans for Truth, see Kate Zernike and Jim Rutenberg, "Friendly Fire: The Birth of an Attack on Kerry," *New York Times*, August 20, 2004.

15. Paul Farhi, "Veterans Group Criticizes Kerry's War Record," *Washington Post*, May 5, 2004.

16. Gardner later claimed to have received a threatening phone call from the Kerry campaign for his outspokenness. Of the twelve who served on Kerry's Swift Boat, only two refused to stand with him at the Democratic National Convention. One was Gardner; the other chose to remain silent. See Mary Laney, "How Kerry Whistleblower Suffered for Truth," *Chicago Sun-Times*, November 29, 2004.

17. This charge, which O'Neil makes in his book *Unfit for Command*, circulated widely. At the Republican National Convention, one delegate handed out Band-Aids for the participants that read, "It was just a self-inflicted scratch, but you see I got a Purple Heart for it." The appearance of the Band-Aids caused a minor controversy with a veterans' group called The Military Order of the Purple Heart. The Bush administration finally issued a statement that it "did not approve." See Jim Rutenberg, "Delegates Mock Kerry's Wounds, Angering Veterans," *New York Times*, September 1, 2004.

18. "Any Questions?" Swift Boat Veterans for Truth, television advertisement, August 4, 2004. All SBVT ads can be viewed at http://www.swiftvets.com/.

19. "Gunner," Swift Boat Veterans for Truth, television advertisement, August 26, 2004.

20. The dispute quickly formed a tautology. Kerry made the claim to imply that the government was lying to the American people about its operations in Vietnam. The response by Kerry's critics was often that there is no way this could be true, because it was official government policy to stay out of Cambodia—that "he would have been court-martialed for doing so." See Michael Kranish, "Kerry Disputes Allegations on Cambodia," *Boston Globe*, August 18, 2004.

21. "Medals," Swift Boat Veterans for Truth, television advertisement, August 31, 2004.

22. "Friends," Swift Boat Veterans for Truth, television advertisement, September 21, 2004. Kerry had openly attended the Paris Peace Talks of 1971 with North Vietnamese diplomats before returning home and volunteering the fact in front of the Senate committee four months later. Paul Farhi, "Ad Says Kerry 'Secretly' Met with Enemy; but He Told Congress of It," *Washington Post*, September 22, 2004.

23. "Never Forget," Swift Boat Veterans for Truth, television advertisement, September 30, 2004. See also "Why?" Swift Boat Veterans for Truth, television advertisement, October 13, 2004.

24. Retired Air Force colonel Kenneth Cordier, for example, appeared in both the Swift Boat ads and the film. Cordier had worked on the Bush campaign but resigned his post when the Bush administration attempted to distance itself from the Swift Boat campaign. See Jim Vandehei and Paul Farhi, "POW's Shown in Film Join Swift Boat Group's Anti-Kerry Efforts," *Washington Post*, October 14, 2004.

25. Ibid.

26. Paul Farhi, "Sinclair Stations to Air Anti-Kerry Documentary," *Washington Post*, October 11, 2004, A7. The decision to cancel *Nightline* even drew fire from Republicans. Arizona senator John McCain called the decision not to air the *Nightline* episode "unpatriotic" and "a gross disservice to the public." Bill Carter, "Debate over 'Nightline' Tribute to War Dead Grows, as McCain Weighs In," *New York Times*, May 1, 2004. The policy of minimizing exposure of dead U.S. soldiers is part of a broader "clean war" media strategy by the Bush administration. See Dana Milbank, "Curtains Ordered for Media Coverage of Returning Coffins," *Washington Post*, October 21, 2003.

27. *News Central* was taped at Sinclair headquarters in Baltimore and drew criticism for its apparent attempt to disguise itself as a local editorial program. Sinclair's chairman, David Smith, is open about his wish to emulate Fox News on a local affiliate level. See Aaron Barnhart, "TV Trend Blends Views with News," *Milwaukee Journal Sentinel*, November 24, 2004. In 2004, Sinclair got into legal trouble with the General Accounting Office when it aired a preproduced "video news release" on some of its local news programs promoting the Bush administration's Medicare package. See Dennis Roddy, "She's Not a Reporter—She Just Plays One on TV," *Pittsburgh Post-Gazette*, March 20, 2004.

28. Bill Carter, "Broadcaster's Stock Picks Up after Change on Kerry Film," *New York Times*, October 21, 2004. See also Bill Carter et al., "Risks Seen for TV Chain Showing Film about Kerry," *New York Times*, October 18, 2004.

29. John Griffin, "Why Kerry Will Be U.S. President: Director Predicts. Movie of Kerry's War Service Makes Liars of His Critics," *Montreal Gazette*, October 2, 2004.

30. Ibid.

31. Mark Mohan, "Movie Review Past Tense: Kerry's Vietnam," *Portland Oregonian*, October 1, 2004, 32.

32. Bill Nichols, *Representing Reality: Issues and Concepts in Documentary* (Bloomington: Indiana University Press, 1991).

33. Sherwood, while working with a Gannett News Service group in 1980, was a co-winner of the Pulitzer Prize for exposing a Vatican group, the Pauline Fathers, in a fund-raising scandal. He has worked for several new agencies since then, but his most notable work was the pro–Unification Church book *Inquisition: The Persecution and Prosecution of Reverend Sun Myung Moon*. Having worked for the *Washington Times*, a conservative paper owned by the Unification Church, Sherwood has been accused of compromising his journalism with public relations. Rory O'Connor, writer and producer of the PBS *Frontline* documentary "The Resurrection of Reverend Moon," which aired in 1992, contended that Sherwood wrote the book in collaboration with Reverend Moon. See Rory O'Connor, "Sinclair Plays Fast and Loose with the News," *MediaChannel.org* (2004), http://www.mediachannel.org/views/dissector/affalert277.shtml. Sherwood also served as special media advisor to the secretary of the navy during the Reagan administration. He is currently executive vice president and director of communications for the WVC3 Group, an anti-terrorism security firm based in Reston, Virginia.

34. This statement should be tempered with the acknowledgment that the political documentary leads a double life within a history of extremes—both as a voice for the voiceless and as tool of the state. This is why so many progressive documentaries of the 2004 election cycle could be labeled "propaganda," though they were critical of powerful interests. For a history of the early institutional uses of documentary in the Soviet Union, Great Britain, and the United States, see Jack C. Ellis, *The Documentary Idea: A Critical History of English-Language Documentary Film and Video* (Englewood Cliffs, N.J.: Prentice Hall, 1989).

35. Most other major Vietnam documentaries were television series. These come in the form of journalistic retrospectives, such as the immensely successful seven-part *Vietnam: A Television History*, produced by and aired on PBS in 1983. The 1988 HBO documentary *Dear America—Letters Home from Vietnam* was a human history of the war. Apart from these, the field of the Vietnam documentary is littered with other journalistic histories and military interest films, mainly for television and video.

36. For a theoretical discussion of the symbolics of pain and their relationship to truth-telling, see Elaine Scarry, *The Body in Pain* (New York: Oxford University Press, 1985).

37. George W. Bush, "Address to the Joint Session of Congress and the American People," (2001), http://whitehouse.gov/news/releases/2001/09/20010920-8.html.

38. Fonda traveled to Vietnam to protest the U.S. bombing of dikes on the Red River Delta, which the *Pentagon Papers* revealed would mean the deaths of 200,000 civilians. In 1988, Fonda met with Barbara Walters on *20/20* and apologized for causing pain to Vietnam veterans. She released her memoirs, *My Life So Far*, in April 2005. Fonda maintains that her actions were manipulated by the North Vietnamese for propaganda purposes. See Dylan Foley, "Fonda, 'Lighting Rod,' Icon Actress Recounts Her Troubles with the Men and Myths of Vietnam," *Denver Post*, April 17, 2005.

39. Fonda did make a statement in April 1972 on Hanoi radio regarding her visit, and it is often cited by her critics as a further indictment of her patriotism. The probable offending segment is this:

> One thing that I have learned beyond a shadow of a doubt since I've been in this country is that Nixon will never be able to break the spirit of these people; he'll never be able to turn Vietnam, north and south, into a neo-colony of the United States by bombing, by invading, by attacking in any way. One has only to go into the countryside and listen to the peasants describe the lives they led before the revolution to understand why every bomb that is dropped only strengthens their determination to resist. But now, despite the bombs, despite the crimes being created—being committed against them by Richard Nixon, these people own their own land, build their own schools—the children learning, literacy—illiteracy is being wiped out, there is no more prostitution as there was during the time when this was a French colony. In other words, the people have taken power into their own hands, and they are controlling their own lives. (qtd. in *US Congress House Committee on Internal Security, Travel to Hostile Areas,* H.R. 16742, 92nd Cong., 2nd sess., 1972).

40. The photo comes from a 1970 antiwar protest at Valley Forge, Pennsylvania. This was during Kerry's very early involvement with the VVAW and two years before Fonda's infamous visit to Vietnam. Both Kerry and Fonda claim they were only passing acquaintances at the time. The photo first surfaced on conservative Web site NewsMax.com when questions of Bush's military service were in the news. See "Kerry Takes New Fire over Vietnam," *CNN Online*, (2004), http://cnn.com/2004/ALLPOLITICS/02/11/eleco4.prez.kerry.fonda/.

41. The Winter Soldier Hearings and their portrayal have been the source of much controversy and attention. Recently, one who testified at the Winter Soldier Hearings, Steven Pitkin, claimed that he had been coached by Kerry to testify to having witnessed atrocities that he now says he did not witness. See "Vietnam Vet: I Lied about Atrocities," *Fox News Online* (2004), http://www.foxnews.com/story/0,2933,132405,00.html. Another former marine, Kenneth Campbell, initiated a lawsuit against the producers of *Stolen Honor* for suggesting he fabricated his testimony. See Kate Zerneke, "Ex-Marine Sues over Portrayal in Kerry Film," *New York Times*, October 19, 2004. Interestingly, the ninety-five-minute raw footage of the Winter Soldier Hearings, which has circulated underground for years, was set for limited theatrical release in August 2005. The incidents of torture at Abu Ghraib prison in Iraq in 2003, critics argue, have given the film a kind of general interest. David M. Halbfinger, "Film Echoes Present in Atrocities of the Past," *New York Times*, August 9, 2005.

42. Between September 1970 and September 1971, troop levels in Southeast Asia declined from 450,000 to 254,000. Kerry spoke in front of the Senate in April 1971. "Military Personnel Historical Reports: Active Duty Military Personnel by Regional Area and by Country," Department of Defense, http://siadapp.dmdc.osd.mil/personnel/MILITARY/history/309hist.htm.

43. Quoted in Andrew Miga, "Kerry Tempers 1971 'Atrocity' Remarks," *Boston Herald*, April 19, 2004.

44. The casualty numbers, of course, argue that southeast Asia was the true loser of the war. The number of civilians killed ranges from 1.5 million to 4 million. In the 2003 film *The Fog of War, a somewhat apologetic* Robert McNamara, secretary of defense during much of the war, cites the number of civilian dead at 3.2 million. The casualties continue to mount from unexploded ordnance, particularly cluster bomblets and land mines, and Agent Orange poisoning. Regarding individual atrocities, the Pentagon officially claims to have convicted 278 persons of war crimes over the course of the war. See Michael Kranish and Bryan Bender, "Kerry's Stand on Abuses Gets Backlash; Former Commanders Criticize 1971 Talk of Vietnam Atrocities," *Boston Globe*, May 13, 2004. In 2003, the *Toledo Blade* won a Pulitzer Prize for a series of articles investigating an elite army platoon called "Tiger Force" and its record of atrocities. See "Elite Unit Savaged Civilians in Vietnam," *Toledo Blade*, October 22, 2003.

45. For a discussion of the Vietnam Syndrome and efforts to control wartime journalism, see Susan Carruthers, *Media at War: Communication and Conflict in the Twentieth Century* (New York: St. Martin's Press, 2000). Various experi-

ments with press control throughout the 1980s and 1990s resulted in development of tightly controlled press pools and finally the embedded reporter system used in the 2003 invasion of Iraq. We should note that significant opposition in the United States to the involvement in Vietnam came very late in the war, and it took a significant antiwar movement before the press took notice. For compelling arguments against the conventional wisdom that the press hindered the U.S. effort in Vietnam, see William M. Hammond, *Reporting Vietnam: Media and Military at War* (Lawrence: University Press of Kansas, 1998). See also Daniel C. Hallin, *The "Uncensored War": The Media and Vietnam* (New York: Oxford University Press, 1986).

46. See James S. Olson and Randy Roberts, *My Lai: A Brief History with Documents* (New York: Bedford Books, 1998).

47. Lieutenant Calley was the only one convicted for My Lai. His initial life sentence of hard labor was commuted to three and one half years under house arrest under the recommendation of President Nixon.

48. The rhetoric of "bad apples" was echoed more recently in the 2004 Abu Ghraib torture scandal. While human rights groups had been denouncing the routine torture of prisoners at the hands of the U.S. military since 2003, the story broke much later, again with the help of Seymour Hersh. Here again, the blame was primarily laid at the feet of two of the prison guards, Lynndie England and her fiancé at the time, Charles Graner. Seymour Hersh, "Torture at Abu Ghraib: American Soldiers Brutalize Iraqis; How Far up Does the Responsibility Go?," *New Yorker*, May 10, 2004. Also see "Torture; Leadership Failure, at the Top," *Minneapolis Star Tribune*, May 12, 2004.

49. One substantiated spitting incident occurred in Kansas City on April 19, 2005. A Vietnam veteran waited ninety minutes at a book signing to spit tobacco juice in Jane Fonda's face. David Goldiner, "Annoy Jane: Vet Spits in Her Face!," *New York Daily News*, April 21, 2005.

50. Jerry Lembcke, *The Spitting Image: Myth, Memory, and the Legacy of Vietnam* (New York: New York University Press, 1998).

51. See the poem "Thank You" in Yusef Komunyakaa, *Dien Cai Dau* (Hanover, N.H.: Wesleyan University Press, 1998).

52. That nastiest of all American political words, "quagmire," is a testament to this. See a discussion of this term as it relates to legitimate and illegitimate violence in Michael Hardt and Antonio Negri, *Multitude* (New York: Penguin Press, 2004), 30.

53. The memorable phrase "We had to destroy the village in order to save it" is attributed to a U.S. soldier in a report filed by Peter Arnett regarding the destruction of the town of Ben Tre in the Mekong Delta region. The authenticity

of this defining phrase from the Vietnam era is disputed by some. See Mona Charen, *Useful Idiots: How Liberals Got It Wrong in the Cold War and Still Blame America First* (Washington, D.C.: Regnery Publishing, 2003), 33.

54. Maurice Halbwachs, *On Collective Memory*, trans. Lewis A. Coser (Chicago: University of Chicago Press, 1992), 51.

5

Martin J. Medhurst

Theology, Politics, and the Evangelical Base

George W. Bush: Faith in the White House

Faith in the White House strives to anoint Bush as some kind of divine warrior-king.

George W. Bush: Faith in the White House is a work of supreme arrogance and misinformation; a film of such simplistic moralizing and propagandistic fury that it stopped just short of offering up Bush *himself* as Christ the Redeemer.

If any video can be called preaching to the converted, this is it. The message is that George Bush is doing God's work and we should all re-elect him to continue God's work.

To say that *George W. Bush: Faith in the White House* is controversial would be an understatement. It has been attacked in the pages of the *New York Times*, lambasted by the *New Republic*, and excoriated by on-line pundits and has provided fodder for bloggers of all stripes.[1] Indeed, the responses to the film could themselves be an instructive object of analysis, since they reveal interesting motives and attitudes not just about George W. Bush but about religion in general, Christian faith in particular, and the ways in which religion, politics, and culture interact in these ever-so-tenuously-united states. But that is another essay. This essay examines the rhetorical dimensions of the film itself; that is, it treats the film as a message designed to communicate a set of meanings to a particular audience and for a specific purpose. One may disagree with the makers, oppose the message, reject the evidence, and lament that any audience might find such a film persuasive, but that is not the task of a rhetorical critic.[2] The task of the critic is to account for why certain rhetorical potentialities, when organized, stylized, and delivered in a particular manner, succeed (or fail) in finding or creating an audience that resonates with the message and thus is more predisposed to believe or act in accordance with the purposes of the makers than it was before being exposed to the message. Cicero said that the purposes of rhetoric are three—to teach, to delight, and to move. In the case of *George W. Bush: Faith in the White House*, the purpose seems to be to achieve all three of these ends simultaneously. The film teaches viewers about Bush's conversion and his subsequent testimony of faith in God. It delights viewers by showing Bush as a man who will not compromise his faith, even in the face of repeated criticism and attack. And it moves the audience both to belief and to action—to belief in the proposition that Bush really is a sincere man of faith (one who "walks the talk") and to the action of supporting him for reelection.

George W. Bush: Faith in the White House is a film made by evangelicals, addressed primarily to evangelicals, and designed in large measure to meet the ego-needs of evangelicals at the beginning of the twenty-first century. That is my contention. Before trying to prove it, however, we must establish at the outset a common understanding of a slippery term—"evangelical Christian." So configured, "evangelical" becomes an adjective modifying "Christian." An evangelical is a particular kind of Christian. Americans are used to Christians being divided into two large classes, Protestants and Catholics, and in delineating the branches of Protestantism by denominational categories—Presbyterians, Methodists, Episcopalians, Baptists, and the like. As neat and seemingly clean as this category system is, it is basically useless as a roadmap for understanding contemporary Christianity, for the major fault lines of Christianity no longer lie along denominational grounds or even in the divide between Protestants and Catholics. Instead, the major division is between those whom James Davison Hunter designates as "orthodox" and those whom he designates as "progressives."[3] Evangelical Christians fall into the orthodox category.

Without being too reductionistic, we can say that orthodox Christians accept the Bible as God's written word and the propositional teachings of the Bible as universally true for all people in all times and places. The central teaching is that the God of the Bible—the God of Abraham, Isaac, and Jacob, the God who called the world into being by the power of his Word and who created humankind from the dust of the earth—became incarnate in the man Jesus of Nazareth. Jesus lived a sinless life and willingly sacrificed himself on the cross at Golgotha so that all people in all times and places might believe in him and be saved. God confirmed that Jesus was his unique Son by raising him from the dead on the third day, thus forever breaking the power of sin and death. Orthodox Christians believe that all humans are eternal spirits; the physical body dies, but the spirit lives forever, either in the presence of God (heaven) or separated from God (hell). It therefore behooves such Christians to witness to this saving power of God in Christ Jesus in an effort to persuade as many people as possible to avail themselves of God's saving grace. Such persuasion might take place through preaching, teaching, or personal testimony or through more organized efforts such as revivals, crusades, or televangelism. Whatever the medium, that which is preached is the "good news"—the evangel—of Jesus Christ. Evangelicals are those Christians who accept the teachings of Jesus, believe the Bible to be God's authoritative word, and seek to convince others to accept Jesus as their Lord and Savior.

Evangelicals are found in every Protestant denomination; even some Roman Catholics now refer to themselves as evangelicals. It is variously estimated that anywhere from 30 to 50 million Americans can be properly classified as evangelical Christians, even if the term "evangelical" is not one with which they personally identify. George W. Bush is one such Christian. Though he does not apply the terms "evangelical" or "born again" to himself, he nonetheless is considered to be an evangelical because he (1) has a conversion story, (2) publicly identifies Jesus Christ as his Lord and Savior, (3) regularly prays and reads the Bible, (4) speaks publicly and unashamedly about his "faith," and (5) tries to use his faith as a guide to everyday decision-making. For evangelicals, each of these five dimensions is important, which is why all five of them are illustrated in *George W. Bush: Faith in the White House*.

Reading the Film

The film begins with a graphic, using white letters on a black background: "This documentary was produced independently and without any input from the White House, the Bush Administration, or the Bush/Cheney Election Campaign. It is based on independent research." This disclaimer is, strictly speaking, true; it is also disingenuous. Are we really to believe that a documentary produced in an election year, released in August 2004, targeted to the base of the Republican Party, and featuring the incumbent president has nothing to do with the White House, the administration, or the election campaign? Yes, it was "independently produced." But the significance of that claim depends on what one means by "independently." It is true, insofar as I can determine, that the film was not directly inspired by the White House, produced under the watchful eye of Karl Rove, or funded by the Republican

National Committee or one of its subsets. Even so, it was produced by a professional film company with a long history of ties to the evangelical right,[4] it was based largely on three books whose authors *did* have direct access to the White House,[5] and it features interviews with several people who were close political allies of the president.[6] It may have been "independently produced," but in no way was it an "independent" or disinterested production. To the contrary, it was a production funded, written, produced, and directed by individuals with deep ties to the evangelical base. Yet such criticism, while warranted, probably misses the point for the intended audience—evangelical Christians. This is not a documentary produced by a political party to convince undecided voters. This is a documentary produced by evangelicals for evangelicals, and for it to be effective, the filmmakers must first convince the viewers that what they are about to see is not political propaganda, not "pandering to the religious right," as the film itself asserts, but firsthand testimony from their fellow evangelical believers. In other words, the viewer is invited to believe that this is not a film about politics but rather a film about faith. This is a vitally important move strategically because most evangelicals are neither acolytes of the religious right nor particularly interested in politics.[7] Talk about partisan politics will turn many of them off; talk about faith will invite them to attend more closely to the claims advanced.

How do we know that this film was intended primarily for the evangelical audience? Both external and internal evidence point to that conclusion. The film premiered at an evangelical trade show, was distributed by direct mail to churches throughout the nation, was marketed publicly through Christian bookstores, and was broadcast only on Christian television stations and networks.[8] It was never shown in general theatrical release. This external evidence all points to evangelicals as the target audience. So, too, does the internal evidence. Not only does the film feature testimonials from such well-known evangelicals as James Robison, Doug Wead, and Ted Haggard (then president of the National Association of Evangelicals), but it makes repeated references to such high-profile evangelical ministers as Billy Graham and Arthur Blessitt. Conspicuously absent from the film are any prominent leaders of the religious right. There are no references to or visuals of Pat Robertson, James Dobson, Jerry Falwell, Richard Land, Charles Colson, D. James Kennedy, Donald Wildmon, Lou Shelton, Ralph Reed, or any other well-known figure with an explicit political agenda. The closest the film comes to showing any link to the hardcore religious right is one testimonial from Don Hodel, who is identified in a graphic as "Former Secretary of the Interior Reagan Administration." What is not indicated in any way is Hodel's current position as CEO of Focus on the Family or his previous position as president of the Christian Coalition, facts that most evangelicals would not know and might not appreciate. This is a carefully crafted, almost choreographed effort to keep the focus on the issue of faith. The film accomplishes this through the use of five devices: (1) a dialectical narrative structure, (2) testimonial, (3) historical analogy, (4) representative anecdote, and (5) historical reconstruction.

The host and narrator of the film is Janet Parshall, the nationally syndicated radio talk-show host of *Janet Parshall's America*. Parshall is one of a handful of conservative women talk-show hosts. Her radio program "reaches 3.5 million listeners five days a week."[9] A former aide to Beverly LaHaye, the president of Concerned Women for America, Parshall is well-known in evangelical circles and was elected in 1998 to the board of directors of the National Religious Broadcasters. She has served on its executive board since 2001. Parshall as host/narrator provides the narrative structure for the film through a series of dialectical questions that are clearly designed to focus the narrative on one issue only—the faith of George W. Bush. They are also designed in an agonistic fashion to suggest that there is a contest—or a war—between Bush's faith and his critics of various persuasions. This is an interesting and, I believe, effective device because it rhetorically places Bush in the very position in which evangelicals have historically found themselves—as people of faith who are misunderstood, ostracized, and made fun of and whose faith is constantly under attack from the larger culture.[10] One purpose of the narrative structure is to help audience members identify Bush as one of themselves. How do we know that he is an evangelical? Because he has been made to suffer just as evangelicals have suffered. It begins with Parshall's opening set of questions: "Historians may quibble, but the fact is George Washington, Abraham Lincoln, and George W. Bush are the only presidents who have had to contend with the ravages of war on our own soil. The reliance placed on God by both Washington and Lincoln is well documented. But what do we know about George W. Bush? Is he a man of faith?" Parshall sets the stage by rhetorically aligning Bush with the two greatest—and in some senses most mythic—presidents of the Republic. This serves several purposes. First, it sets up a historical analogy that will be carried throughout the film and thus establishes a dominant motif that will reappear at crucial moments in the narration. Second, it identifies Bush with the two heroes of the Republic in such a way that any criticism of Bush is implicitly also a criticism of Washington and Lincoln. It thus serves as a rhetorical buffer for the president. And third, it misstates—intentionally I believe—the historical facts. As numerous critics have pointed out, Parshall's statement leaves out the War of 1812, which, among other outrages, resulted in the burning of the nation's Capitol.[11] Surely that qualifies as "war on our own soil." Anticipating such criticism, Parshall starts with a qualifier—"Historians may quibble." That's an odd way to phrase an opening statement unless one already knows that what one is about to say is not wholly factual. But the choice, if that is what it was, serves two purposes for the filmmakers. First, it effaces the man who was president in 1812—James Madison—and second, it reduces that cinematic choice to a mere "quibble." By so doing, the film constructs potential critics, be they historians or others, as people who can be expected to carp. The term "quibble" thus serves as a sort of rhetorical insurance policy for the filmmakers. It was important to eliminate Madison both because the filmmakers wanted to establish Bush as the rightful heir to the American Founding, represented by Washington and Lincoln, and because Madison, along with Jefferson, was a great champion of strict separation of church and state, a position anathema to the filmmakers and to most evangelicals.

Parshall's question "Is he a man of faith?" is immediately answered by showing a clip from the December 13, 1999, Iowa debate where Bush, in answer to a question about which philosopher most influenced his thinking, replied: "Christ, because he changed my heart." Here is the first of multiple testimonies, some by Bush and many by others on Bush's behalf, that signal to the evangelical base that Bush is one of them. In this brief statement, Bush fulfills two evangelical imperatives: He claims Christ as Lord and he does so publicly. This then sets up Parshall for her next set of narrative interrogatives: "Could it be that a candidate for president of the United States would actually fly in the face of political correctness and espouse not just religious convictions but a firm belief in Jesus Christ? Critics and pundits were quick to suggest Bush had committed political suicide and asked, 'Is this candidate totally out of touch with the American mainstream, or is he just a politician cynically pandering to the voters of the religious right?'" Again, the term "Jesus Christ" is used to distinguish Bush's expression of faith from more general religious sentiments. But more important, Parshall constructs two categories that are crucial to understanding the rhetorical strategy of the film—"the American mainstream" and "voters of the religious right." For non-evangelicals who view this film, the immediate reaction is that it is directed to the religious right. But the strategy of the filmmakers is to construct their viewers as "the American mainstream"—those who follow in the footsteps of Washington and Lincoln, those who understand the historical relationship of God to America, and those who will not be pandered to by politicians who want their votes but do not truly live out their Christian faith. If the film is meant to prove anything, it is that Bush is not a panderer but a true man of faith and that this faith is a true expression of Americanism—indeed, *is* mainstream Americanism—because it conforms to the faith of the Founding Fathers.

As if in answer to Parshall's question about pandering, the film cuts to a graphic of a statement Bush made in the *Maranatha Christian Journal* in October 2000: "My faith is an integral part of my whole being, that's what faith is. I don't think you can separate faith from who you are." Again, the statement does double duty, both reassuring evangelicals that Bush's faith informs his life and introducing the term "separate." Just as Bush the person does not separate his faith from his life, so, the film will argue, should one not separate God from government. There is thus a synecdochal relationship established whereby Bush becomes the part (a man of faith) who stands for the whole (a nation built on faith). The president is but the latest in what we will learn is a long line of faith-guided chief executives.

Parshall then reappears with still more questions: "Had the nation elected a man of faith and strong Christian principles or simply a clever political opportunist? The answer to those questions would turn out to be more critical than anyone could have possibly imagined. Only seven months into his presidency, the tragic events of September 11th . . . forced us to deal with the complexities of a world in which America was no longer safe from catastrophic attack." As Parshall speaks about the "tragic events of September 11th," the viewer sees shots of the Twin Towers burning, plumes of black smoke rising heavenward, debris and destruction on the ground, and one tower collapsing. Then Parshall asks: "Is George Bush a man with the spiritual strength to meet this awful challenge, or is he just another pandering politician paying lip service to God?"

The answer comes immediately as the film cuts back to the Iowa debate, where the moderator asks Bush to explain his earlier answer. Bush replies: "Well, if they don't know, it's going to be hard to explain. When you turn your heart and your life over to Christ, when you accept Christ as Savior, it changes your heart and changes your life. And that's what happened to me." Not only has Bush given his own personal testimony of faith in Christ, but his faith has been rhetorically and visually linked to the "spiritual strength" needed to deal with terrorism. The three terms "spiritual," "strength," and "terrorism" soon become combined in the viewer's mind as Bush's ability to stand up to his critics—those concerned about his breach of traditional church-state etiquette—comes to stand metonymically for his ability to confront the terrorists. One who has the "moral clarity" to see and appreciate the role of faith in governing is also one who has the "moral clarity" to see what must be done in the war on terror.

Parshall puts the question directly: "Could it be that religious moral clarity is precisely what the public is looking for in a leader?" She continues: "But do most Americans necessarily connect a man of faith with a person they can trust?

Indeed, the president's critics are quick to claim that precisely the opposite is true." The film then cuts to a graphic of screen actor Richard Gere as an unseen narrator reads the voice-over of Gere's words: "One thing I've learned in my life is never to trust anyone who thinks that he exclusively has God on his side. Especially when he's the President of the United States." The theme here is trust, and the choice is clear: Do you trust the values of Hollywood (Gere) or the values of Christian faith (Bush)? Much of the rest of the film is an effort to build trust through a systematic construction of Bush's character. We will learn that Bush is trustworthy, loyal, disciplined, kind, sincere, truthful, ethical, and, like Christ, a "servant leader."

If Bush's critics are used as foils to suggest his ability to stand tough when confronted with opposition, then the culture war in general is presented as the domestic equivalent of international terrorism. As the camera zooms in on Bush at prayer, it is clear that he is standing in front of American soldiers, as he is framed against a khaki background—a not-so-subtle reminder of the war on terror. Rabbi Daniel Lapin then appears on camera to charge: "From the outside you've got attacks on America and on the rest of the Western world from radical Islamic fundamentalism. At the same time, there's a struggle going on inside America, and it's a struggle between those who regard Judeo-Christian values as vital for our nation's survival and those who view those values as horrible obstructions to progress. The future of our nation depends upon the outcome of this struggle." As Lapin's phrase "those who regard Judeo-Christian values" is spoken, the viewer sees a protester with a sign that says "Stop Abortion Now." As the rabbi completes his statement by referring to those "who view those values as horrible obstructions to progress," the viewer sees pro-choice demonstrators holding signs that say "Proud To Be Pro-Choice," "Defend Abortion Rights" and "Keep Abortion Legal." The death and terror of 9/11 have now found their domestic equivalent. Against both of these "evils" Bush will do battle, for the very "survival" of our nation depends on winning the war without and the war within, for both attack our values and seek the destruction of both body and soul.

Parshall secures the point as the viewer watches George Washington praying at Valley Forge: "Is George Bush a man of sufficient spiritual strength and dedication to lead the nation through the difficult times we are facing both inside the nation and from without?" The answer, we learn, is yes, as sequential testimonies are offered by evangelist James Robison, Catholic publisher Deal Hudson, writer Thomas Freiling, and political activist Robert Woodson. While the first three make short statements focusing on Bush's character, Woodson tells a story about how Bush comforted his family in the face of the tragic death of their son. This is the first of three extended testimonies that I am calling

"representative anecdotes." They are vignettes used to illustrate personal characteristics of George Bush—not Bush the policy-maker but Bush the Christian,
one who acts in his personal life the way that evangelicals would expect any
Christian to act when faced with similar circumstances. In this first vignette
with Woodson, we hear about how Bush called Woodson from Air Force One
upon learning of the death of his son, how he called the widow, and how days
later the president still had tears in his eyes as he recalled Rob Woodson's
life. So emotionally touched was Bush that Woodson felt as though he would
have to comfort the president, just as the president had comforted him. As he
relates this story, Woodson's eyes fill with tears and his voice is halting as he
says, "I will never forget this man as long as I live for what he did to comfort
us." The role of these vignettes is to illustrate how Bush fulfills the mandates
of the scriptures. For evangelicals, all of life is to be lived in accordance with
the teachings of the Bible. Some of those teachings are that a Christian is to
take care of the widows (1 Tim. 5:3) and to comfort those who mourn (2 Cor.
1:4). Bush is shown enacting the biblical directives.

"How did the president come to be such a man of faith, of prayer, and of
love?" Parshall asks. The answer, presented in the second segment of the film,
is that he grew up in a loving Christian family and later in life experienced
what evangelicals would call being "born again" as he committed his life to
Christ. This section of the film deals with Bush's youth in Midland, Texas,
and introduces more testimony—from west Texas friend E. Donald Poage,
authors Stephen Mansfield and David Aikman (whose books were primary
sources for the film), Robert Woodson, Uncle William "Bucky" Bush, and
evangelist James Robison. The segment begins with one of several reenactments
of events that happened in the past. In this case, it begins with the baptism of
Bush, proceeds through his efforts to comfort his mother as she grieved over
the death of his sister Robin, and ends with his emergence as a family man
who, in the words of Poage, believed in "faith, family, and friends."

But Bush is also shown pursuing "the good life." This is an especially
important part of this segment, because one cannot be "saved" unless one
first has been "lost." Bush's battle with alcohol was well known, and it was
widely believed by some analysts that the report of Bush's 1976 DWI on the
brink of the 2000 election had cost him much-needed evangelical votes. So,
from both a religious perspective (the need for sin) and a political perspective
(the need for more votes), it behooved the filmmakers to talk at length about
Bush's conversion. It starts with a report from Woodson who quotes Bush as
having told him that "only through the grace of God was I delivered from
my problems." After testimonies from Aikman ("It was a stunning change"),
Bucky Bush ("He was suddenly stone-cold sober"), and Robison ("He began

to live for others"), Bush appears to testify for himself: "Faith can help change our culture. Faith gives us purpose to right wrongs. And faith can change lives. I know. I know firsthand."

"What was it," Parshall asks, "that brought about such a profound change in a young man who, to that point, had expressed no interest in politics?" This is the setup to transition into a detailed account of Bush's conversion story. For an evangelical audience, it is particularly important that a specific time and place be identified where one experienced Christian conversion or being "born again." Bush, however, had never used the term "born again" in reference to himself, nor did he include a specific instance in his campaign biography, *A Charge to Keep*. But the film, drawing on Mansfield's book, recounts Bush's 1984 meeting with evangelist Arthur Blessitt in Midland. This brings on another historical reenactment as Donald Poage recalls his discussions with Bush about Blessitt and that Bush indicated that he had prayed with the evangelist, whom he considered to be the "real deal."[12]

As the reenactment comes to an end, Parshall appears on-screen to secure the point: "According to many of his close associates, the meeting with Blessitt in 1984 marked the beginning of a born-again Christian experience that would culminate several years later in Kennebunkport, Maine, during a meeting with another famous evangelist." We then see another historical reenactment as the Bush family gathers around Billy Graham for what is described as "an informal Bible camp." After one such meeting, Bush and Graham took a walk along the beach. Graham is reported to have asked Bush, "Are you right with God?," to which Bush is said to have replied, "No, but I want to be." This story, which was reported in Bush's campaign biography ("Graham planted a mustard seed in my soul"), is the clincher for evangelicals, for whom Billy Graham is the chief model.[13] To have been converted by Graham is to be placed among the tens of thousands who have responded to Graham's invitation to come "Just as I Am." It is to be given an evangelical imprimatur—approval by the closest thing that evangelical Protestants have to a pope.

Like all true conversions, this one was soon put to the test. This change in Bush's life calls forth the second representative anecdote, this time in the form of a historical reenactment narrated by Doug Wead, former White House aide to the first President Bush. In the vignette, Bush is tempted by a young female campaign staffer who just wants to help him "relax." Bush is shown loudly rebuffing her advances and proclaiming "not interested. I'm a married man. Glad she got the message." In the second half of this two-part morality tale, Wead recounts how a congressman tried to sweeten a proposition for Bush by telling him "there's something in it for you," at which point Bush curtly cuts off the meeting and shows (almost shoves) the congressman out of his office.

It was because of this rock-solid character, we are led to believe, that Bush prevailed over incumbent governor Ann Richards in the 1994 Texas gubernatorial race. During that race, according to Bush friend Michael Minor, "people saw evidence of the truth in him. They saw his goodness, his kindness, his truthfulness, his self-control. All of these things are evidence of his walk with God." For many listeners, such praise would be nothing but puffery. But to evangelicals, it was the very word of God, for the fruit of the Spirit is "love, joy, peace, patience, kindness, goodness, faithfulness, gentleness and self-control" (Gal. 5:22, NIV). This double-barreled vignette thus serves as proof to the evangelical audience that Bush's actions square with his profession of faith.

But when Bush reached Washington, D.C., Parshall tells us, he encountered opposition to the "faith-based initiatives" that he had employed in Texas. Using a graphic with a quote from Susan Jacoby of the *Los Angeles Times*, an offscreen voice intones: "There is no precedent in American history for the Bush administration's determination to infuse government with a highly specific set of religious values." The filmmakers then cut to author William Federer, who says:

> I find that a curious view of history, as George Washington in his 1789 inaugural address said: "The propitious smiles of heaven can never be expected on a nation that disregards the eternal rules of order and right which heaven itself has ordained." Our thirtieth president, Calvin Coolidge, wrote: "The foundations of our society and our government rest so much on the teachings of the Bible that it would be difficult to support them if faith in those teachings would cease to be practically universal in our country."

By this point in the film, viewers have heard quotations supporting religious influence in government from Washington, Adams, Lincoln, and Coolidge. Before the film is over, the viewer will see quotes from Madison, John Quincy Adams, and Dwight D. Eisenhower and will hear references to Kennedy and Truman. So organized, it appears that the whole of American history is testifying to the role of religion in the nation's governance. The strategy is the same throughout—to reassure evangelicals that they represent the true beliefs of the founders and that the attacks on Bush are the same kinds of attacks that have historically been made upon them. To recount attacks on Bush is to evoke recall in the mind of the evangelical audience and to foster a deep identification-through-suffering between that audience and Bush. The more Bush is "beat up" by his critics, the more evangelicals identify with him. Secular critics will complain that the voice of the critic in the film is nothing more than a straw man—set up only for the purpose of being knocked down. While that is true, it misses the rhetorical function served by these erstwhile critical voices. It is not George Bush that is being attacked; it is the whole structure of evangelical belief and practice that Bush has now come to represent.

Parshall reappears: "Is it possible that George Bush, by his faith-based example, is leading the nation in a reawakening of those principles upon which it was founded?" The use of the term "reawakening" does double duty, as it gestures back to the First and Second Great Awakenings, which many evangelicals consider their spiritual heritage, as well as to the present, as the sleeping giant of American evangelicalism reawakens to its rightful place in the life of the nation. If there is any doubt that such a reawakening is necessary, the sequence that follows lays that doubt to rest, as three examples underscore the attempts of public school students to live out their faith, only to be rebuffed by school authorities who threaten that "any student uttering the word Jesus at the school's graduation" will be "arrested and locked up." The examples set up the testimonies by U.S. senator Zell Miller and Chief Justice William Rehnquist that the First Amendment does not require strict separation of church and state. But we soon learn that it is none other than George W. Bush who is leading this reawakening, as Parshall assures the viewer that "there have been a great many changes at the White House. The president encourages Bible study, opens meetings with prayer, and unabashedly references God in his public pronouncements." In other words, the president of the United States does exactly those same actions that the schoolchildren of America are being punished for doing.

After several more graphics testifying to the religious character of the Bush White House, the third representative anecdote is offered. This is the story of Sam Haynam, a thirteen-year-old cystic fibrosis patient whose request to the Starlight Foundation was that he be able to meet the president of the United States. Sam wanted to meet the president, he testifies, to tell him "how much I appreciated the president being a Christian and a man of faith." The vignette relates how Sam and his family went to the White House and gave President Bush a Bible that included a FROG bookmark. When the president inquired about the bookmark, Sam informed him that the letters stood for "Fully Rely on God," to which Bush responded, "Well, then, Sam, I guess that means that I'm a frog, too." As the vignette draws to a close, Sam's father appears on-screen to testify that as he thanked the president for meeting with his son, "there were almost like tears in his eyes." This is the second reference to the president's tears, and they are both in the context of providing comfort to those in need. But to an evangelical audience, especially those segments of evangelicalism that come out of the Pentecostal or charismatic movements, tears function as a sign of total commitment to God, a sign of having surrendered one's emotions, as well as one's intellect, to the leading of the Holy Spirit. It is a sign of authenticity.

But even authentic faith is under attack, as the screen fills with a picture of Barry Lynn, president of Americans United for Separation of Church and State. An offscreen voice reads Lynn's words: "We continue to careen dangerously down the path of government-supported religion. . . . Madison would have been horrified at the notion that Congress or the president would embark on the reckless journey of taxpayer funding of religion." The pattern now well-established, Parshall reappears to challenge the assertion: "But is that true? Did the founders in fact intend to keep religion in general and Christianity in particular out of government and public life? Is George W. Bush at cross-purposes with the men who drafted the First Amendment?" Not surprisingly, the answer is no, as the viewers hear from both Madison and John Quincy Adams:

> MADISON: We have staked the whole of our political institutions upon the capacity of mankind for self-government, upon the capacity of each and all of us to govern ourselves according to the Ten Commandments of God.
>
> ADAMS: The highest glory of the American Revolution was this. It connected in one indissoluble bond the principles of civil government with the principles of Christianity.

Parshall then reappears to inform the viewer that "in point of fact, in 1782, the United States Congress voted a resolution stating: 'The Congress of the United States recommends and approves the Holy Bible for use in all schools.'"

Much could be said about this exchange. A critic looking for weaknesses in the argument would doubtless point out that Lynn was referring to "taxpayer funding" and that none of the quotes speak to that issue. Such a critic would also note that the Constitution was not approved until 1789. All of this, while true, misses the rhetorical significance of the exchange for the audience to whom it is directed. First, for evangelicals, there is no greater devil figure in the battle over church-state issues than Barry Lynn, who, predictably and accurately, invokes Madison. Earlier in the film, Madison has been effaced in order to keep the focus on Washington and Lincoln. But this opportunity is just too good to pass up, because it allows the filmmakers to "refute" their archenemy Lynn using Madison's own words and to introduce the topic of the Ten Commandments at the same time.[14] Since the battle over displays of the Ten Commandments was front-page news at the time of the film's release, it was a perfect quote for advancing one side of the culture war under the pretext of responding to Lynn. Likewise, the quote from Adams reinforces the view that the evangelicals are, in fact, the true representatives of the American mainstream, for they are the ones who see an "indissoluble bond" between government and Christian principles. After Lincoln and Eisenhower are brought forth to testify, Bush appears on-screen to offer his own testimony: "My relationship with God through Christ has given me meaning and direction. My faith has made a big difference in my personal life and in my public life as well." Parshall then reappears to secure the point: "George W. Bush, it seems, is right in line with the Founding Fathers."

But Parshall is not finished. Again, she turns to the interrogative mode: "But will the president pay a political price for commitment to those principles?" Though other presidents have made references to God and some have specifically recommended the principles of Christianity, only George W. Bush has been repeatedly attacked for his faith. Parshall wonders, "Could it be that in what is perhaps America's greatest crisis since the Civil War, faith from the White House is needed more than ever? Is it possible that the calamity that now faces the nation calls for a greater, not a lesser, devotion to faith? Will we discover that the test now facing the world is more than a test of physical strength?" The viewer has already learned that Bush felt a "calling" to run for president, that he had a "premonition" that his services would be needed, and that, in his own words, "there is something incredibly reassuring in the belief that there is a divine plan that exceeds all human plans." Without directly saying so, the film strongly implies that Bush is part of God's divine plan for America at this hour. And the defining "test" of the hour is terrorism.

It is important to note that the viewer has not seen or heard a direct reference to terrorism since the opening sequence of the film. Everything since the opening has focused on issues of the culture war—the Ten Commandments, prayer in school, abortion, same-sex marriage, Bible reading, faith-based programs—and that is clearly by design. By focusing the majority of the film on what Rabbi Lapin called "the war within," the filmmakers, through the psychological processes of association and transfer, can make one kind of "test of faith" into another kind. The war within tests our devotion to Christian principles in the public square; the war without tests our "faith" in American leadership. But we have already learned that that leadership, in the person of George W. Bush, relies on God. It is not a stretch, therefore, to conclude that if Bush puts his faith in God and seeks his will, the actions he undertakes as leader of the nation must be those that God approves.

Now images of 9/11 reappear—the Twin Towers burning, one tower collapsing, smoke and debris filling the air, an aerial shot of the black patch of ground where once the towers stood. With the nation, which we now clearly understand was built on Christian principles, under attack, Parshall asks, "How would his sense of destiny serve him and the nation? How would he stand up to the monstrous evil that now faced America? Would we see him rise up in righteous wrath or sink to his knees in prayer? Or would he do both?" The visuals reveal the answer. Despite still more criticism from those who charge that America seeks "domination of the entire world," we are told by Stephen Mansfield that "like Lincoln" during the Civil War, Bush "wanted to be on God's side of the issue." We then see shots of the Bush family in the National Cathedral, and Parshall asks: "Does the expressed and apparently deeply held faith of the man who occupies the White House bring us closer together as a nation, or does it drive us apart?" In the context of 9/11 and the memorial service at the National Cathedral—a unifying event if ever there was one in American history—the question answers itself. The (personal) faith of the man has become the (public) faith of the nation. And, as the old Christian hymn puts it, that faith locates the viewer as a "Christian soldier . . . marching as to war, / With the cross of Jesus going on before."[15]

Amid the rubble of Ground Zero, we now see Bush with his bullhorn. But instead of the oft-heard line about knocking down buildings, we hear Bush say: "America today is on bended knee in prayer for the people whose lives were lost here, for the workers who work here, for the families who mourn." Even in the midst of tragedy, Bush is still seen as comforting the afflicted, just as he comforted Robert Woodson and Sam Haynam earlier in the film. He is still practicing his Christian principles, so when the filmmakers edit the Ground Zero sequence to join Bush's statement about prayer with his promise about retribution—"and before long the people who knocked down these buildings are going to hear from all of us"—it is experienced only as the "righteous wrath" that Parshall had foreshadowed. It's no longer either prayer or retribution but prayer and retribution, the retribution being, perhaps, the answer to the prayer.

Surely Bush has been guided by prayer, for the viewer sees and hears about the schools, hospitals, clinics, vaccinations, courts of law, power generation, and commerce that have now sprung up in Iraq and Afghanistan. Parshall assures the viewer that "things are changing in the Middle East and changing for the better." But lest the viewer think that Bush's God is only a God of war, the filmmakers show Bush addressing the United Nations on the subject of "modern-day slavery" and the sex trade. We hear Bush intone: "We must show new energy in fighting back an old evil." Evils, we are led to understand, come in many forms, and all must be fought. "But will George W. Bush be allowed to finish the battle against the forces of evil that threaten our very existence?" asks Parshall. The battle against the evils of sin and terrorism has now morphed into the battle for reelection, for only if he is reelected can

Bush "finish the battle." But here, as before, there are agents who would seek to prevent Bush from fulfilling his God-given mandate.

Chief among those who would prevent Bush from finishing the battle is Michael Moore, director of the anti-Bush documentary *Fahrenheit 9/11*. Though Moore's name is never invoked, the viewer sees his face on the cover of magazines such as *Film Comment, Entertainment,* and *Time.* But Moore and his documentary are quickly dispatched by means of a quote from Christopher Hitchens that identifies *Fahrenheit 9/11* as a work of "moral frivolity." For a film repeatedly hyped as an "alternative" to Moore's film, *George W. Bush: Faith in the White House* devotes less than twenty-four seconds to its presumed nemesis and addresses none of the issues raised by *Fahrenheit 9/11.*

As if to contrast with the presumed "moral frivolity" of Moore's film, Bush is shown fulfilling his moral duty to the troops injured in Iraq and Afghanistan. Through a historical reconstruction, Bush is pictured visiting the bedside of a fallen solider. Aikman narrates the scene as he informs viewers that Bush "knelt down by the bedside, took the stump in his hands, said a small prayer, then kissed the bandage." As a man of his word (and of the Word), Bush then is shown running with amputee Private Mike McNaughton, fulfilling a promise he had made to McNaughton while he was still in the hospital. The message is not subtle—here is a man of his word, a man one can count on to do what he says he will do.

Parshall delivers the final challenge, this time starting with assertions rather than questions: "President George W. Bush has set the example for maintaining faith in the face of unrelenting criticism. It is vitally important for Christians to be fully engaged in the religious and cultural conflicts of the twentieth century. Will the faith of George Bush be sufficient to keep us in God's hands today? Perhaps, if we all join our faith to his." The film then closes with shots of Bush quoting Romans 8:38: "As we've been assured, 'neither death, nor life, nor angels, nor principalities, nor powers, nor things present, nor things to come, nor height, nor depth, can separate us from God's love.' May he bless the souls of the departed. May he comfort our own. And may he always guide our country. God bless America." As Bush is finishing this statement, the viewer sees him embracing a child and then a mother and finally standing at Ground Zero with that lone firefighter, hand draped around his shoulder.

The message is clear: If we will "join our faith to his," then Bush will be able to finish the battle that others have started, both internally and externally. Indeed, the film spends far more footage on the internal battle, because it is that fight that most concerns the target audience. By establishing Bush's credentials in the culture war, the filmmakers can use the elasticity of "faith" to link the internal battle to the external war effort. If evangelicals link their faith to Bush's in one sphere, should they not also do the same in the war on terror? If he is to finish the battle, so the logic of the film suggests, we must support him with our votes.

Implications

This film raises far more issues than it answers. Considered solely from the perspective of a political documentary targeted to a specific audience for the purpose of solidifying and motivating the evangelical base, it must be considered a rousing success. Karl Rove said in 2001 that his primary goal for the 2004 election was to turn out the approximately four million evangelicals who, by his own calculations, should have voted in the 2000 election but did not.[16] Post-election analysis shows that the percentage of white evangelical voters did, in fact, increase in 2004, though not by the amount Rove desired.[17] It is, of course, impossible to make a direct cause-effect connection between any single piece of discourse and something as complex as group voting patterns. Even so, it seems clear that *George W. Bush: Faith in the White House* was one of numerous efforts to turn out the evangelical base, even if one not directly under the control of the Republican Party. Indeed, its very success as an artistically structured appeal can be traced directly to the fact that it was made by fellow evangelicals, not by a political campaign firm. I have tried in this critique to take notice of those aspects of the film that would be particularly appealing to the evangelical mind: the focus on Jesus; the numerous shots of Bush at prayer; the high esteem in which the Bible is held; the constant public witness to Bush's faith, both by himself and by others who know him well; and the overarching sense that Bush's values and principles—and by extension those of his fellow evangelicals—are constantly under attack and in danger of being vanquished. The "logical" conclusion of such an experience seems clear: we must all stick together.

I use the term "we" because like Bush and the filmmakers, I too am an evangelical Christian—a Catholic evangelical, to be precise. I grew up in a fundamentalist, Pentecostal church, attended the nation's most well known institution of evangelical higher education, wrote my first scholarly article more than thirty years ago on the relationship between fundamentalism and right-wing politics, and converted to Catholicism at age thirty-eight.[18] I am also, as many people know, a philosophical and political conservative—and yes, I twice voted for George W. Bush. There is much to criticize about this film from a purely secular point of view: the reduction of everything to a simple matter of "faith"; a caricature of issues, such as separation of church and state, over which the best minds in America continue to struggle; the quotations from the founders, often taken out of context and never interrogated; the use of extreme examples from the culture war as though they are in some way representative of the norm; a not-so-subtle appeal to a flag-waving kind of (unthinking?) patriotism; outright misstatements of fact; and what many will view as an inappropriate reduction of the political to the personal. These and other weaknesses clearly mar the film from an objective point of view. But the filmmakers never set out to be objective in the first place. This is a film that proceeds from a particular theological point of view and one that is directed to an audience that shares that brand of theology. It would seem most appropriate, therefore, to end with some theological reflections on the film.

There are six aspects of the film that I as a Catholic evangelical find theologically troubling. All of them have to do with the way language is deployed. First, when Parshall claims that we are battling "the forces of evil that threaten our very existence," I have to wonder how this squares with Ephesians 6:12. That verse starts with the claim that "we wrestle not against flesh and blood, but against principalities, against powers, against the rulers of the darkness of this world" (KJV). To equate an earthly enemy with the "forces of evil" is either to reduce evil to a purely natural category or to imbue the terrorists with supernatural power. Either way, such language seems to fly in the face of evangelical theology. Evangelicals also believe in eternal life. Therefore, no one could "threaten our very existence," for to be "absent from the body . . . [is] to be present with the Lord" (2 Cor. 5:8, KJV). Evangelicals consider themselves to be merely sojourners on this earth, people whose true home is with God in heaven. Killing the body does not extinguish the person.

Second, the film's location of Bush's conversion in his decision to quit "smoking, drinking, cursing, and carousing with his friends" seems both to reduce the idea of sin to nothing more than personal vices and to divert the viewer's focus from what the Bible calls the "weightier matters" of justice, mercy, and faithfulness (Matt. 23:23, KJV). While this problem is somewhat offset by James Robison's later comment that it was "not what [Bush] stopped doing, but what he began to do—he began to live for others," it is still a mixed message with respect to how Christian conversion is to be reckoned.

Third, when Bucky Bush is discussing his nephew's sense of discipline and decorum, he says that George W. Bush holds the presidency as a "sacred trust" and views the Oval Office as a "sacred place." While all would agree that the institution of the presidency and the seat of executive power are worthy of respect and perhaps even a certain sense of awe, it is wholly inappropriate, from an evangelical point of view, to ascribe the term "sacred" to them. Sacred means set apart for God. As devout a believer as Bush may be and as revered a locale as the Oval Office may seem, neither are sacred. They are matters of human choice, not divine mandate.

Fourth, the reenactment where Bush provides comfort to his mother after the death of his sister Robin uses language that to an evangelical ear ought to raise some questions. The scene is narrated by David Aikman, who says: "When his father was away from home, George W. assumed a protective presence over his mother. And even though he was only a boy, he felt the most important thing in life was to comfort her." In evangelical theology, when one hears the terms "protective presence" and "comfort" in the same sequence, the immediate association is to the Holy Spirit. In the Bible, the Spirit of God is described as a "protection over them . . . as with a shield" (Ps. 5:11–12, NIV). The Spirit is also called the "Comforter" in John chapters 14–16. I am not arguing that the film identifies Bush with God—which some secular critics have charged—but rather that in this instance, the film seems to suggest that Bush is performing functions that in an evangelical worldview are reserved for the Holy Spirit. The fact that the term "comfort" is repeatedly linked to Bush throughout the film lends some force to this concern. Of course, Christians are supposed to comfort those in need, but it seems a little beyond the pale to wrench terms from one context and apply them wholesale to another. This was the same problem Bush encountered during his 2003 State of the Union speech when he used the term "wonder-working power" not in reference to the blood of the Lamb but in reference to the power of the American people. That's bad theology.

The fifth problem is similar to the fourth inasmuch as it revolves around a specific term. This time, it is Deal Hudson who testifies to Bush's appeal to various religious groups. Hudson says, "He's really a kind of perfect mediator between the mainstream, Catholics, and evangelicals." Of course, in evangelical theology there is only one "perfect mediator," and that is Jesus Christ. In 1 Timothy 2:5, it states: "For there is one God and one mediator between God and men, the man Christ Jesus." I do not believe that either Aikman or Deal is trying to say that Bush is God. What they are trying to do is associate Bush with godly attributes. They know that an evangelical audience will hear these claims within a biblical worldview and interpret them accordingly. But for non-evangelicals, the claims and associated images come perilously close to making Bush and God one and the same.

The final problem arises in Parshall's last narrative sequence when she asks, "Will the faith of George Bush be sufficient to keep us in God's hands today?" In some ways, this may be the most egregious statement from a theological perspective. It seems to say that our standing with God is somehow dependent on the faith of George Bush. This is problematic at several levels. First, the "faith of George Bush" cannot be either sufficient or insufficient with respect to securing one's relationship with God. That relationship, for

Protestant evangelicals, is secured only by the individual, not by some third-party mediator. Second, the statement seems to imply that if Bush's faith is not sufficient, we will not be kept in God's hands—as though God is somehow limited by Bush's faith or lack thereof. Third, the use of "today" at the end of the statement seems to imply that it might be different tomorrow—that we might be in God's hands today, but if Bush's faith waivers, we might not be all right tomorrow. This is utter nonsense from a theological point of view, but rhetorically it allows the filmmakers to effect the transition to the next sentence: "Perhaps, if we all join our faith to his." The notion of "sufficiency" now takes on a quantitative dimension. We have to "add our faith" to his—presumably in the form of votes—in order to secure God's protection. Such rhetoric may be good politics, but it is terrible theology.

The existence of these six problems should give everyone, especially evangelicals, pause. For as every evangelical knows, not everyone who cries "Lord, Lord" is going to enter into the kingdom of heaven (Matt. 7:21). In everyday life, but especially during election season, one needs to be not only innocent but also discerning (Matt. 10:16). As evangelicals continue to enter the American mainstream, they must become better at discerning truth from error, more willing to consider the positions of others, better able to distinguish faith (eternal) from politics (contingent), and more critical of the rhetoric of those who presume to speak in their name. The future of our country as "one nation under God, indivisible, with liberty and justice for all" may depend on it.

Notes

1. The opening quotations, in order of appearance, come from "Ammo for the Enemy," *The Revealer*, September 30, 2004, http://www.therevealer.org/archives/timely_000932.php; Matt Cale, "Ruthless: George W. Bush: Faith in the White House," *Ruthless Reviews*, March 7, 2006, http://www.ruthlessreviews.com/movies/g/georgewbush.html; and Rusty Pipes, "DVD: George W. Bush: Faith in the White House," *Cosmik*, 2004, http://www.cosmik.com/aa-november04/ev/ev-faith_in_white_house.html. See also Frank Rich, "Now on DVD: The Passion of the Bush," *New York Times*, October 3, 2004, sec. 2, p. 1; and Amy Sullivan, "Empty Pew: Why W. Doesn't Go to Church," *New Republic Online*, October 5, 2004, https://ssl.tnr.com/p/docsub.mhtml?I=20041011&s=sullivan101104. For some of the more vicious reviews of the film and the Bush presidency, see Ayelish McGarvey, "As God Is His Witness," *American Prospect Online*, October 19, 2004, http://www.prospect.org/web/printfriendly-view.ww?id=8790; Amy Goodman et al., "God and the Presidency: An In-Depth Examination of Faith in the Bush White House,"

Democracy Now!, October 20, 2004, http://www.democracynow.org/print.
pl?sid=04/10/20/1423216; and Chris Rice, "There He Goes Again: Director David Balsiger Creates Another Metanarrative," *Cornerstone Magazine*,
http://www.cornerstonemag.com/pages/show_page.asp?670.

2. This position on the role and function of the rhetorical critic is not,
of course, universally shared. For another perspective, see James F. Klumpp
and Thomas A. Hollihan, "Rhetorical Criticism as Moral Action," *Quarterly
Journal of Speech* 75 (1989): 84–96.

3. James Davison Hunter, *Culture Wars: The Struggle to Define America*
(New York: Basic Books, 1991), 67–132. For an application of Hunter's "cul-
ture wars" thesis to the rhetoric of Bush, see my chapter "George W. Bush,
Public Faith, and the Culture War over Same-Sex Marriage," in *The Prospect
of Presidential Rhetoric*, ed. James Arnt Aune and Martin J. Medhurst (College
Station: Texas A&M University Press, 2008).

4. The film was produced by Grizzly Adams Productions, Inc., whose CEO
is Charles E. Sellier. Sellier is listed as the supervising producer on *George
W. Bush: Faith in the White House*. He wrote the original novel *The Life and
Times of Grizzly Adams* and produced the 1974 movie of the same title. The
next year, Sellier became president of Sunn Classic Pictures. Following the
success of the Grizzly Adams television series that ran from 1977–78, Sellier
used the proceeds to set up his own production company. Sellier already knew
how to make lucrative films. Two of his Sunn Classic productions—*The Life
and Times of Grizzly Adams* and *In Search of Noah's Ark*—are still among the
top ten in all-time rental revenues for independent film productions. Working closely with Sellier since the mid-1970s has been David W. Balsiger, who
is listed as the director of *George W. Bush: Faith in the White House*. Balsiger
is the author of three books that have sold more than a million copies—*In
Search of Noah's Ark*, *The Lincoln Conspiracy*, and *The Satan Seller* (coauthored
with Mike Warnke). Balsiger has produced and/or directed multiple films for
Grizzly Adams Productions, where he and Sellier form a production/direction
team. Sellier has multiple ties to the evangelical world, including the position
of executive consultant to the Total Living Network, a network of Christian
television stations. Reading through the Grizzly Adams Web site, two things
become immediately clear: making money is the number one goal, and fam-
ily-friendly television and film is the way to make money; see http://www.
grizzlyadams.tv/corporate.tpl?cart=1125684153684669. This judgment parallels
that of *Slate* staff writer Bryan Curtis, who attended the conservative American Renaissance Film Festival on September 12, 2004, where David Balsiger
spoke between showings of the Bush documentary. According to Curtis's

report: "Whereas most directors saw conservative filmmaking as a part of the larger Republican jihad, Balsiger saw it as a way to make a fortune." See *Slate*, September 13, 2004, http://slate.msn.com/id/2106624/.

5. The books are David Aikman, *A Man of Faith: The Spiritual Journey of George W. Bush* (Nashville: W Publishing Group, 2004); Thomas M. Freiling, *George W. Bush on God and Country: The President Speaks Out about Faith, Principle, and Patriotism* (Fairfax, Va.: Allegiance Press, 2004); and Stephen Mansfield, *The Faith of George W. Bush* (New York: Tarcher, 2003). All three authors were given access to Bush friends, White House operatives, and Bush relatives. Indeed, Aikman claims that the only person he was not given access to was Reverend Kirbyjon Caldwell, the black minister from Houston, Texas, who is a spiritual confidante of the president's. It is also interesting to note that Freiling coauthored another book in 2004 titled *We Pray for Election Day: A Prayer and Action Guide to Reclaim America on November 2, 2004*. The Xulon Press Web site notes that he "previously worked as a political consultant and for the U.S. House of Representatives." See http://www.xulonpress.com/founder.htm.

6. People such as Doug Wead, Robert Woodson, and Deal Hudson have been political advisors to Bush. Wead was a special assistant to the president in the George H. W. Bush White House. Woodson is a longtime black conservative activist. Hudson, the only self-identified Catholic among those who offer testimony, participates in the weekly conference call between the White House and the evangelical and Catholic communities. For more background on these ties, see Amy Tilton Jones, "George Bush and the Religious Right," in *The Rhetorical Presidency of George H. W. Bush*, ed. Martin J. Medhurst (College Station: Texas A&M University Press, 2006), 149–70; and Joe Feuerherd, "The Real Deal: How a Philosophy Professor with a Checkered Past Became the Most Influential Catholic Layman in George W. Bush's Washington," *National Catholic Reporter*, August 19, 2004, http://www.nationalcatholicreporter.org/update/bn081904.htm.

7. There is a common misperception that all fundamentalists and evangelicals are right-wing activists. As a former activist myself, I could only hope that such was true. It was not and is not. Most conservative Christians care little or nothing about politics. Why should they? Their home is in heaven and their dominant focus is on family and church. This fact is subtly recognized at several places in the film, as, for example, when Bush friend Donald Poage notes: "Politics was certainly something people talked about, but most of the men in Midland frankly weren't interested in things outside of Texas too much." Janet Parshall opines that Bush was a "young man who, to that point, had expressed no interest in politics"—a statement that is demonstrably false

but that serves the purpose of the film. And James Robison says: "He said, 'You know, God really did change my life.' He said, 'You know, I never wanted anything to do with politics. . . . I wanted to be remembered as the man who walked in Wal-Mart to buy fishing lures, and used to be governor, my dad was president—that's the only way I want people to think about me.'" All of these statements reflect not George W. Bush but the predominant mode of thinking among most evangelicals. By nature and inclination, most evangelicals have "no interest in politics." That's why Karl Rove and the Republican Party have to work so hard to motivate them to vote.

8. The film premiered at the Christian Booksellers Association annual convention on June 28, 2004. It was then shown in a hospitality suite at the New Yorker Hotel during the Republican National Convention on August 31, 2004, under the sponsorship of William J. Murray's organization, the Religious Freedom Coalition. Murray is the Christian son of the late atheist activist Madelyn Murray O'Hair. The video and DVD versions were released to Christian bookstores on August 30, 2004, and to all other outlets on October 5, 2004. Distribution to the Christian market was handled through FaithWorks and to the secular market through GoodTimes Entertainment. According to David Balsiger, one million copies of the film were produced. Approximately 300,000 of these were distributed by direct mail to churches and religious organizations. Between September and November of 2004, the film aired on Christian television stations around the country. According to a press release from Grizzly Adams Productions, the film was scheduled to air on "nine Christian television networks which includes seven domestic/international satellites, 62 broadcast stations, 510 broadcast affiliates, and over 3,000 cable outlets." These outlets, according to the release, "plan multiple showings of GAP's 52-minute news documentary, *Faith in the White House*—with over half of the broadcasts scheduled in prime time during September and October. The combined broadcast schedule will reach the largest possible audience of faith-based viewers—an estimated 60 million households." The same release identifies those networks as "FamilyNet TV (satellite/320 affiliates), INSP-Inspiration Network (2,500 cable outlets), Daystar Television Network (five satellites/39 stations), WAZT-TV Network (six stations), Total Living Network (satellite/four satellite stations/500 cables/65 affiliates), Cornerstone TV Network (5 stations/125 affiliates), Faith TV-Florida, WLMB-TV Network (three stations—Ohio/Michigan), and KSCE-TV El Paso (four Spanish stations—New Mexico)." The press release as well as the entire press kit for the film is available on the Grizzly Adams Web site noted above. While my analysis is based on the VHS version of the film, the DVD version does include some extra material, including "Responses to *Fahrenheit 9/11*." Yet these "responses"

are text-only documents that are, according to media critic Mark Moring, "accessible only when the DVD is plugged into a computer's DVD-ROM player. These responses include an essay and an *F 9/11* review from the Christian website MOVIEGUIDE, plus an excerpt from *Unfairenheit 9/11: The Lies of Michael Moore*, by Christopher Hitchens." See Moring, "George W. Bush: Faith in the White House," *ChristianityToday.com*, August 24, 2004, http://www. christianitytoday.com/movies/reviews/georgewbush.html.

9. See "Radio's Parshall Wrong on Social Security," *Media Matters for America*, February 25, 2005, http://mediamatters.org/items/printable/200502250003. See also "Janet Parshall," *Center for Media and Democracy's Source Watch*, March 1, 2005, http://www.sourcewatch.org/index.php?title=Janet_Parshall.

10. Steven Waldman, proprietor of beliefnet.com, has written an insightful analysis of why Bush appeals to evangelicals. One of the reasons identified by Waldman is "persecution." See Steven Waldman, "The Real Reason Evangelicals Love Bush," *beliefnet.com*, September 2, 2004, http://www.beliefnet. com/story/152/story_15216.html. For other informed views on Bush and religion, see Alan Cooperman, "Openly Religious, to a Point," *Washington Post*, September 16, 2004, http://www.washingtonpost.com/ac2/wp-dyn/A24634–2004Sep15?language=printer; Howard Fineman, "Bush and God," *Newsweek*, March 10, 2003, http://people.cas.sc.edu/rosati/fineman.god.newsweek.303. htm; Joseph M. Knippenberg, "A President, Not a Preacher," *The Claremont Institute*, September 2, 2004, http://www.Claremont.org/writings/crb/fall 2004/knippenberg.html?FRMAT=print; David Gergen, "Leadership in the Bush White House," *Harvard Business School Working Knowledge*, October 27, 2003, http://hbswk.hbs.edu/tools/print_item.jhtml?id=3745&t+innovation; and "Frontline: The Jesus Factor," transcript, *PBS*, http://www.pbs.org/wgbh/ pages/frontline/shows/jesus/.

11. For critiques that focus on some of the historical inaccuracies in the film, see Rice, "There He Goes Again"; David Wilkerson, "Indoctrinating or Educating? Political DVD's in Youth Ministry," *Youthworker Journal*, http://www. youthspecialties.com/articles/topics/culture/political.php; and "George W. Bush: Faith in the White House," *The Mayor Speaks*, http://www.joelcomm. com/george_w_bush_faith_in_the_white_house.html. For in-depth ethical critiques of other Balsiger films, see Brendan McKay, "Secrets of the Bible Code Invented," 1998–99, http://cs.anu.edu.au/~bdm/dilugim/secrets.html; and Gary Posner, M.D., "An All-Too-Unpleasant *Encounter with the Unexplained*," *Tampa Bay Skeptics Report Online*, vol. 13, no. 3 (Winter 2000–01), http://www.tampabayskeptics.org/v13n3rpt.html. By my own count, there are at least seven inaccuracies in the film. These include the claims that (1) only Washington and Lincoln had "to contend with the ravages of war" on American

soil prior to the administration of George W. Bush, (2) Bush was a successful businessman in the oil industry, (3) it was a near-miracle that Bush beat Ann Richards in the 1994 Texas gubernatorial race, (4) some 22 million children had been inoculated in Iraq (a country with a total population of only 25 million), (5) Bush had expressed no interest in politics prior to his father's presidential campaign, (6) Bush is "right in line" with the founders on matters of religion and government, and (7) George H. W. Bush "set aside" wealth to make it on his own. There are other statements made that are certainly debatable, but these seven are demonstrably false. These do not include such other inaccuracies as the misspelling of "Rehnquist" and "Afghanistan."

12. And Blessitt thought Bush to be the "real deal," too. After the 1984 meeting, Blessitt recorded what had happened in his diary. See "The Day I Prayed with George W. Bush to Receive Jesus" on Blessitt's official Web site, http://www.blessitt.com/bush.html.

13. George W. Bush, *A Charge to Keep* (New York: William Morrow, 1999), 136.

14. Ironically, the quotation from Madison is nowhere to be found in his official papers. This spurious quote has been traced to a book published in 1939, which was the source from which it was taken by David Barton for his 1989 book *The Myth of Separation*. Barton's book became a key resource for conservatives waging battles about separation of church and state. For the full story about the erroneous Madison quote and Barton's role in reviving it, see Nate Blakeslee, "King of the Christocrats," *Texas Monthly* (September 2006): 172–75, 252–54, 265–76. As Blakeslee notes, "Barton published his retraction ten years ago, yet the fraudulent Madison quote still pops up like a bad penny all over the Internet" (268). Whether the scriptwriters found the quote in Barton's book or on the Internet is not clear. What is clear is that a minimal amount of research would have revealed the quotation to be falsely attributed to Madison.

15. "Onward Christian Soldiers," words by Sabine Baring-Gould; music by Arthur S. Sullivan, *Cyberhymnal.org*, http://www.cyberhymnal.org/htm/o/n/onwardcs.htm.

16. Speaking at the American Enterprise Institute in December 2001, Rove said: "If you look at the model of the electorate, and you look at the model of who voted, the big discrepancy is among self-identified, white, evangelical Protestants, Pentecostals, and fundamentalists. . . . [T]here should have been 19 million of them, and instead there were 15 million of them. Just over four million of them failed to turn out and vote . . . that you would have anticipated voting in a normal presidential election." See "Those 4 Million 'Missing' Evangelicals," *The Carpetbagger Report*, September 14, 2004, http://www. the carpetbaggerreport.com/archives/2529.html.

17. On the role of the evangelical vote in the 2004 presidential election, see Bill Schneider, "Bush's Secret Weapon," *CNN.com*, November 8, 2004, http://cnn.allpolitics.printthis.clickability.com/pt/cpt?action=cpt&title=CNN.com++Bush . . . ; "Religion and the Presidential Vote: Bush's Gains Broad-Based," *Pew Research Center*, December 6, 2004, http://people-press.org/commentary/display.php3?AnalysisID=103; and "2004 Election Exit Poll Results," *beliefnet.com*, http://beliefnet.com/story/155/story_15546.html.

18. For more on my relationship to evangelicalism and my early scholarship on religion and politics, see Martin J. Medhurst, "Rhetorical Invention and the Pentecostal Tradition," *Rhetoric and Public Affairs* 7 (2004): 555–72; "Fundamentalism—Step to the Right?" *Journal of the Illinois Speech and Theatre Association* 29 (1975): 54–61; "McGovern at Wheaton: A Quest for Redemption," *Communication Quarterly* 25 (1977): 32–39; and "American Cosmology and the Rhetoric of Inaugural Prayer," *Central States Speech Journal* 28 (1977): 272–82. For more recent work on the use of religious language by George W. Bush, see Martin J. Medhurst, "Religious Rhetoric and the *Ethos* of Democracy: A Case Study of the 2000 Presidential Campaign," in *The Ethos of Rhetoric*, ed. Michael J. Hyde (Columbia: University of South Carolina Press, 2004), 114–35.

For a different kind of theological critique of Bush's religious discourse, see Jim Wallis, "Dangerous Religion: George W. Bush's Theology of Empire," *Sojourners Magazine*, vol. 132, no. 5 (September–October 2003): 20–26, http://www.sojo.net/indx.cfm?action+magazine.article&mode=printer_friendly&issue=soj . . . In the film *George W. Bush: Faith in the White House*, Wallis's words are the first of the "critics'" voices to be heard.

6

Robert E. Terrill

Mimesis and Miscarriage in *Unprecedented*

The project that resulted in *Unprecedented: The 2000 Presidential Election* began when documentary filmmakers Joan Sekler and Richard Ray Perez watched George W. Bush take the oath of office to become the forty-third president of the United States in January 2001. They "saw more people protesting the legitimacy of what had happened than supporting him" but noted that this "was never reported by the media."[1] Sekler cashed out her retirement funds to begin working on the film, then approached producer Earl Katz with "some very, very rough footage that Richard Perez had shot."[2] Katz found the footage compelling and agreed to become co-executive producer with Robert Greenwald. Sekler and Perez eventually interviewed over one hundred people and combed through hours of broadcast news footage, which they edited into an hour-long film. They rushed to have *Unprecedented* released just before the 2002 midterm elections, and then in 2004 a "campaign edition" was released on DVD with approximately thirty minutes of additional material, including an introduction and conclusion by actor Danny Glover. The film has won numerous awards, including the Grand Festival Award at the Berkeley Film and Video Festival and the Grand Jury Prize for Best Documentary and the Director's Award at the New York International Film Festival, and has become a part of a series of films produced by Greenwald, including *Uncovered: The War on Iraq, Outfoxed: Rupert Murdoch's War on Journalism*, and *Unconstitutional: The War on Our Civil Liberties* (all 2004).

Perez has described the film not only as "a wake-up call to say, the way we conduct our elections isn't necessarily democratic,"[3] but also as an effort "to inspire people to come together to do something to fix these problems."[4] Perez intends, in other words, not only to shed light on a significant issue but also to call an audience to action. Lisa Selin Davis explains that "times have changed since *Titicut Follies* (1967) begot massive reform in mental health care or *The Thin Blue Line* (1988) helped clear Randall Adams of murder charges. These days, social issue filmmakers are doing more than trying to get their movies up on the big screen. They're . . . motivating audiences to stop eating their dinners and do something."[5] This understanding of the potential for documentary film to mobilize its audience is consonant with what Thomas Waugh has termed a "committed documentary," which he defines as a "specific ideological undertaking, a declaration of solidarity with the goal of radical socio-political transformation," and "a specific political positioning: activism, or intervention in the process of change itself."[6] *Unprecedented* exhibits this purpose throughout, but it expends its energy in the presentation of evidence rather than in a call to action.

Unprecedented makes three arguments. The first is that the state of Florida targeted African Americans and other likely Democratic voters through the misuse of a "felon purge list" to remove "anywhere from 57,000 to 91,000 voters from the rolls—more than half of them Democrats, and most of them non-felons."[7] This argument draws upon the work of Greg Palast, who in a series of essays published primarily in Britain's *Guardian* and *Observer* and then collected in *The Best Democracy Money Can Buy* (2000) detailed the way that Republican political functionaries in Florida manipulated the purge list to skew the election.[8] The second argument portrays the recount process and subsequent Supreme Court decision as sites of fraud, excess, and error, and the third argument is that if the manual recount of the Florida ballots had been handled in accordance with state law and good sense, then Al Gore probably would have won the election. For the purposes of this essay, the analysis concentrates on the 2004 DVD release of the film and treats the added introduction and conclusion as parts of the first and third arguments, respectively.

Arguments are presented to arouse the audience, but *Unprecedented* offers no viable modes of action for the members of the audience to take once they are aroused. In other words, *Unprecedented* does not fully deploy the *mimetic* potential of documentary. While the film does attempt to portray what many believe was a miscarriage of the political process, and while the form of the film—including its pacing and editing—may invite its audience to experience some sense of the disruption caused by the 2000 election in Florida, it does not portray for its audience any individuals or groups who act in a way worthy of emulation.

Film scholars seem largely in agreement concerning the rhetorical function of documentary film but theorize this function from a relatively anemic understanding of rhetoric. A more robust sense of rhetoric might contribute to a more nuanced conceptualization of the rhetorical relationship between a committed documentary and its audience. In particular, "mimesis" might be understood as a rhetorical strategy through which modes of ethical political judgment and action might be made available to the audience of a committed documentary.

Rhetorical Mimesis

In *Representing Reality*, his landmark book on documentary film, Bill Nichols argues that documentary has a "kinship" with what he calls "discourses of sobriety," which include "science, economics, politics, foreign policy, education, religion, welfare."[9] These are discourses of sobriety because they are "seldom receptive to 'make-believe' characters, events, or entire worlds" and because "they regard their relation to the real as direct, immediate, transparent."[10] Documentary film, however, "has never been accepted as a full equal" with other such discourses because of "the imagistic company it keeps."[11] In other words, documentary film can never become a full-fledged discourse of sobriety because it consists of images—and images, as Plato taught us long ago, are deceiving. This situation is something of a paradox, because photographic images generally are apprehended as having a special relationship to reality that Nichols calls *indexical*, referring "to signs that bear a physical trace of what they refer to, such as the fingerprint, X ray, or photograph."[12] Photographs, in other words, seem to capture reality mechanically, objectively, without human interference. As Nichols explains, "The primary importance of this indexical quality to the photographic image . . . is less in the unassailable authenticity of the bond between image and referent than in the *impression of authenticity* it conveys to a viewer."[13] It would seem that documentary film, if understood as a sort of moving indexical photograph, should share this same presumption. But, Nichols argues, documentary never can be entirely "sober" because it "fails to identify any structure or purpose of its own entirely absent from fiction or narrative."[14]

For Nichols, documentary is a hybrid genre, providing both visual pleasure and logical argument; it requires its audience to attend to rational assertions while at the same time it offers aesthetic resources designed to provoke emotional response. Documentary film, therefore, is not distinct from fictional film in any absolute sense but does display the evidentiary reasoning of the sober discourses. Understanding a form of discourse like documentary film,

Nichols argues, requires avoiding the extremes of a Platonic quest for indexical transparency and a Baudrillardian resignation to a universe of simulacra.[15] Like any medium, documentary cannot provide direct, immediate, or transparent access to reality, but because of its impression of authenticity, it directs the attention of its audience to reality in ways unavailable to fiction film.

Nichols turns to rhetoric as he develops a lens through which to view documentary film as a simultaneously aesthetic and argumentative form of discourse, but he defines "rhetoric" as "the means by which the author attempts to convey his or her outlook persuasively to the viewer" and the "means by which effects are achieved."[16] This is a narrowly rational and instrumental understanding of rhetoric that seems inadequate to the task of analyzing so complex a mode of public discourse as documentary film, and its shortcomings might be traced to Nichols's reliance upon Aristotle. As Eugene Garver notes, the "Aristotelian rhetorician succeeds when he has found the available means of persuasion, and that is a rational end."[17] Ekaterina V. Haskins has argued that Aristotle explicitly severed aesthetics from rhetoric, dividing the two concerns between his *Poetics* and his *Rhetoric* and relegating rhetoric to "the bottom of the hierarchy of legitimate disciplines."[18] Stripped of its aesthetic and emotive register and limited to rational argument, this conception of rhetoric cannot account for the ways that discourse might move its audience to take action. As Haskins puts it, Aristotelian rhetoric encourages "a distinctly transparent literate conception of the logos as reflection of the cosmos, not a creative force that shapes thought, action, and identity of human agents."[19]

The audience in such a conception is not constituted through discourse but instead consists of a preexisting reservoir of attitudes and beliefs that might be exploited by a savvy filmmaker. Nichols's discussion of ethos, pathos, and logos is indicative. Ethical proof, Nichols explains, often involves the use of "on-screen commentators and television anchorpeople" because audiences ascribe to these figures an ethical or "fair" stance. Ethical standards evidently are innate within an audience rather than invented in and through rhetorical discourse. Similarly, emotional proofs "in general depend on our preexisting emotional attachments to representations" rather than on the potential for discourse to suggest or encourage such emotional attachments. Demonstrative proof is disconnected from these other modes because it is concerned only with "making evidence persuasive, not [with] ensuring that it is fair, accurate, or even authentic," as though the presentation of unfair, inaccurate, or inauthentic evidence would have no bearing on the perceived quality of a rhetor's ethical or emotional proof.[20] This view leaves little room for understanding the potential of rhetoric to shape its audience by structuring the ethical and emotional standards through which demonstrative proofs might be assessed and thus cannot account for the potential of rhetoric to call an audience to judgment and action.

Paula Rabinowitz and Jane M. Gaines provide provocative emendations to Nichols's ideas, especially as they suggest a more active role for the audience. Rabinowitz, for example, argues that "by insisting on the dynamic relationship of viewer to view, documentary forms [can be understood to] invoke performance within their audiences as much as within their objects."[21] This is an active audience that cannot be accounted for within Nichols's instrumental rhetoric; rather than an audience merely acted upon, this is an audience that is invited to act. Rabinowitz continues: "If performance and action are at the center of documentary rhetoric, then it seems that what is being produced is less a psychoanalytical and more an ethnographic scene; an encounter in which observation slides into participation which somehow exceeds transference and identification."[22] That is, a documentary film does not invite the members of its audience merely to imagine themselves as participants within a projected narrative, but it instructs its audience in modes of participation and performance within the "real" world that is indexed by the projection. "If classical narrative constructs a subject of desire through mechanisms akin to the psychoanalytical processes of identification and refusal in the spectator," Rabinowitz explains, then "the historical documentary—the documentary that seeks to intervene in history—mobilizes a subject of agency. This subject desires too, but the desire is directed toward the social and political arenas of everyday experiences as well as world-historical events shaping those lives and away from the purely psychosexual manifestations of lack and plenitude, differentiation and identification, which characterize the fetishistic forms of narrative desire."[23] Ideally, for Rabinowitz, a political documentary "calls its audience to action."[24]

Rabinowitz draws from Terry Eagleton a more performative and constitutive understanding of rhetoric than that which Nichols extracts from Aristotle.[25] But she does not address the specific strategies through which documentary film might encourage an audience to act. Gaines suggests such a strategy, proposing "political mimesis" as a theory to account for the "relationship between bodies in two locations—on the screen and in the audience."[26] Specifically, political mimesis is intended to "account for . . . the fact that radical filmmakers have historically used mimesis not only in the interests of consciousness change but also in the service of making activists more active—of making them more *like* the moving bodies on the screen."[27] She is concerned, Gaines explains, "with the question of what it might be that *moves* viewers to want to act, that moves them to do something instead of nothing in relation to the political situation illustrated on the screen."[28] While Rabinowitz suggests that committed documentaries call their audiences to act, Gaines suggests that, through political mimesis, committed documentaries might call upon their audiences to act like the figures being screened. She describes political mimesis as "the starting point for the consideration of what the one body makes the other do."[29]

While Nichols's description of film's indexical quality directs our attention to one locus of mimesis—the relationship between the film and its object—Gaines directs our attention to another. This locus, residing in the relationship between the film and its audience, also is the locus of rhetoric, but we have seen that an Aristotelian conception of rhetoric cannot adequately account for political documentary as a hybrid genre integrating both aesthetic and persuasive appeals with the purpose of rousing its audience to civic action.

Isocrates, Aristotle's Athenian contemporary and pedagogical rival, offers a conception of rhetoric better suited to understanding the rhetorical dimensions of political documentary. Rabinowitz argues that "documentary . . . is meant to instruct through evidence,"[30] and viewing political documentary in an Isocratean frame helps to emphasize its educative potential. "While Isocrates's discourses about rhetoric are designed to contribute to civic education and civic virtue," Garver points out, "Aristotle's are not."[31] Haskins argues that "Isocrates and Aristotle constitute two distinct, even antagonistic, paradigms of reflection about discourse and human agency" and notes that a key difference between these models of rhetoric is that "Isocrates views rhetorical performance as constitutive of one's political agency, [while] Aristotle relegates performance to an external stylistic function."[32] In other words, an Aristotelian rhetoric marginalizes the performative interrelationship between rhetor and audience as merely aesthetic, while an Isocratean rhetoric emphasizes this performative moment as a significant locus of civic education.

The medium of this civic education is mimesis. As Robert Hariman notes, Isocratean rhetoric is not focused "on the question of how literary art is capable of imitating reality"[33] but instead on the potentially mimetic relationship between discourse and audience. In a learning process governed by mimesis, students analyze exemplars that embody instantiated values, strategies, and judgments as they are performed through public discourse and then invent new discourses that are informed by this analysis. "In contrast with Plato's harsh judgment of democratic imitation as a numbing repetition," Haskins argues that Isocrates "presents a different kind of *mimesis*—not a satirical representation but a creative reenactment."[34] This creative reenactment—what Hariman calls "flexible" or "inventive" imitation—is intended not to discipline through duplication but instead as a "means of self-fashioning."[35] Just as Gaines wishes to disassociate political mimesis from understandings of mimesis as "naïve realism, mindless imitation, mechanical copying, and even animality,"[36] Michael Leff explains that the goal of this mimetic pedagogy, often referred to as *imitatio*, is "not the mere repetition or mechanistic reproduction of something found in an existing text" but rather a hermeneutical practice that requires and fosters active judgment.[37] The task is not to do as the text does but to invent as the rhetor invents—not to produce a text that seems like the exemplar but to critique the exemplar as a performance of ways of thinking and acting that might be applicable in some present or future circumstance. The intended product is not a slavish copy but is instead the internalized patterns of judgment and action that might encourage the invention of discourses radically different from the originals.

An Isocratean conception of rhetoric addresses both the aesthetic and the argumentative components of discourse, understanding that an audience can be both persuaded to agree and moved to act. As such, this view begins to answer Gaines's call for "putting the sensuous back into the theory of political aesthetics."[38] The rhetorical potential of documentary film, in this view, relies not on an audience who merely provides the rhetor with resources that might be exploited in persuasion but instead on an audience who is actively engaged in judgment and action. The audience is encouraged not to ape the bodies on the screen but to assess possibilities of action and judgment that can be revealed only through interpretive work. Following from this amended understanding of political mimesis, a committed documentary should not ask the members of its audience to mimic the actions on the screen but instead to engage in inventive acts of their own.

But *Unprecedented* does not present a viable resource for political mimesis. It instead presents a Kafka-esque world in which effective moral action appears impossible. The people it portrays are uniformly either frustrated and impotent or self-interested and corrupt. As portrayed in this film, the 2000 election is merely another episode in the continuing post-Reconstruction effort to deny African Americans the right to vote, the Florida recount is confused and inconclusive, the Supreme Court is a rogue band of politicized power brokers, and improved voting technology is only another tool through which the ruling elite retain their positions. The audience is left without ethical guidance: no one challenges power and prevails, no one emerges as a principled political actor, and no one models a viable way to behave. In other words, and as the following textual analysis suggests, *Unprecedented* mimetically represents the truncated political miscarriage of the 2000 presidential election in Florida but fails to provide mimetic resources through which that miscarriage might be effectively addressed.

Repeated Impediments

The first third of the film exhibits a curious recursive quality. The narrative begins with the 2000 election, then twice jumps to a specific moment in the past before moving forward in time toward the election. This repeated pattern of presenting political back-story and then deferring forward movement helps to establish the 2000 election as an especially troublesome episode within a larger historical narrative, suggesting perhaps that getting past it requires building up some sort of kinetic momentum through repeated narrative trajectories.

The documentary opens with a close-up of Danny Glover looking at us, one of only three moments of direct address in the film: "I'm Danny Glover. The 2000 presidential election was a flashpoint event in American political history that tested the integrity of our democratic system."[39] Glover's introduction establishes the election in Florida as a synecdoche for the 2000 election in general—it is a flashpoint in American history, not just Floridian history—so that the corruptions that marred the election in Florida stand in for the corruptions that mar American democracy. A full-screen graphic fades in, reminding us that Al Gore won the popular vote in 2000 with 48,809,906 votes to 48,549,563 for George W. Bush. The graphic changes to a map of the United States, with states colored red and blue, and we zoom in on Florida, which glows yellow. Glover reminds us that "Florida became the battleground for the presidency of the United States," and his exordium concludes: "The documentary you are about to see is a chronicle of what happened in Florida and the chilling story of the undermining of democracy in America."

The remainder of this first section of the film establishes themes of chaos, confusion, and menace that will run throughout. Following the fade that closes Glover's introduction, the producer's name and the names of the filmmakers appear in stark white lettering against a black background. A single low piano note plays, and then we hear the sound of a protest crowd. Another low piano note, reminiscent of the notes that signal the appearance of the shark in *Jaws*, and then a crane shot presents us with George W. Bush's inaugural parade so that the motorcade seems to be heading directly toward us. Representing the moment that inspired the filmmakers to make the documentary, Bush emerges from his limousine to boos and cheers and takes the oath of office. This film would call us to action in response to this image, just as the filmmakers were called to action.

Following a second fade to black, we hear the first words of the first interview of the film, which would have been the first words of the 2002 version of the documentary: "It was mass confusion," declares Cathy Dubin, identified as a member of the Democratic Party in Palm Beach County. A series of rapid-fire images follows: a well-kempt, gray-haired white man holding a placard tells us that he is a veteran, a marine with a Purple Heart, and that he is "entitled to my vote" but that "they have just taken it away from me"; Thomasina Williams, voting rights attorney with the National Association for the Advancement of Colored People, explains that the organization had received reports of people being harassed by police while waiting in line to vote; local radio host Andy Johnson tells us that he received "calls from a lot of people who complained that they had gone to vote and that the local precinct didn't have their name on the list"; an African American man wonders why his name was not on the list; Yvonne Montalvo, poll volunteer, Orlando, explains that "there were no bilingual pollers, there were no bilingual translators, there was no one there." The speakers each talk to an off-camera interviewer, and there is no background music to smooth the transitions. In his introduction, Glover said that the "frenzied media created a cloud of confusion as they scrambled to make sense of this event," and this paratactic series of images invites the viewer to share in the disconnection and bewilderment being described. Pam Iorio, supervisor of elections, Hillsborough County, seems to sum it up, saying that "the story of the 2000 presidential election is a multifaceted story that has to do with decision-making at a lot of different levels and inconsistencies in policies and voting systems and technologies."

The first historical narrative begins when the narrator, actor Peter Coyote, tells us that "the story of the 2000 presidential election started long before election day"; the film then focuses on Jeb Bush's relationship with African American voters in Florida. That the relationship is an uneasy one is suggested by images of an African American man holding a placard that reads "NAACP Says Keep Affirmative Action" and of a sign held high above a crowd of protesters that reads "Jeb Crow." John Lantingua, Pulitzer Prize–winning investigative journalist, establishes the historical starting point for this particular narrative, noting that during Jeb Bush's unsuccessful campaign for Florida in 1994, he was asked what he would do, if elected, for Florida's African American community. "He gave a two-word answer," Lantingua tells us, "which was proved to be both accurate and prophetic. His answer was 'probably nothing.'"

When elected in 1998 with, as the narrator tells us, only 10 percent of the African American vote, Jeb Bush was asked, according to Lantingua, what he was going to do to "reassure black voters. And he said that 'I guess I'm going to have to reach out to that community.'" While we are shown photo-op pictures of Jeb shaking hands with African Americans, Lantingua continues: "And what he did was 'reach out' and take away almost all of the affirmative action programs in the state." In response, the African American leaders organized an "Arrive with Five" campaign, aggressively registering new black voters and encouraging them to bring five other voters to the polls with them. Sharon

Lettman-Pacheco, of the People for the American Way Foundation, describes the campaign; the narrator then informs us that in the 2000 election, "65 percent more black voters went to the polls than in the previous election." A middle-aged African American woman leaving the polls tells us proudly that she "voted Democrat all the way."

These images provide multiple mimetic opportunities as people protest, organize, march, speak at rallies, and vote—all possible and appropriate modes of civic participation that follow upon a prudent assessment of the political situation. The forward movement comes to an abrupt halt, however, when the narrator returns us to the chaos of November 7, noting that "when Election Day came, there were unexpected obstacles." Andrew Gillum of Florida A&M University tells of reports of voters finding that their names were no longer on the voting rolls. "Many more voting irregularities were confirmed," the narrator tells us, "when the NAACP held hearings a few days after the election." In C-SPAN footage of that hearing, Kweisi Mfume, NAACP president and CEO, explains that "this effort is to establish a record, a public record, which will further assist the Justice Department—which doesn't seem to be actively trying to establish its own record—with respect to whether or not there have been violations of civil rights and civil rights law." His voice is faded down as the narrator introduces the next argumentative section of the film, but the implication seems clear: the protesting, organizing, marching, speaking, and voting all have come to naught. The enthusiastic community-building modeled by the African Americans has given way to a procedural effort to establish a record of violations—a record that, Mfume strongly suggests, probably will be ignored anyway.

The second of the two recursive historical narratives in this first section of the documentary begins while Mfume's image is still on-screen and the volume fades. The narrator tells us, in what seems a continuation of Mfume's thought, that "the most serious voting rights violation was the misuse of something called the felon purge list." The narrative links the infamous "felon purge list" to the post-Reconstruction disenfranchisement of African American voters; thus, it begins in the present, jumps to the past, and progresses back toward the present.

The editing is particularly frenzied, and perhaps some sense of the pacing of the montage can be related through a brief synopsis of approximately five minutes of film: Greg Palast, author of *The Best Democracy Money Can Buy*, explains that the voter purge list consisted of names of voters removed from the rolls by Florida's secretary of state, Katherine Harris; as he mentions her name, she floats across the screen as a low-resolution specter. The narrator explains that it was Harris's job to implement this list, and this time we see her at a press conference being introduced by Jeb Bush. Reverend Willie Whiting, a pastor in Tallahassee, recalls being denied the right to vote because he was listed as an ex-felon, even though he had served as a federal juror. John Lantingua tells us that Database Technologies (DBT) was chosen to create the lists. While the narrator explains that "Florida officials told DBT to use 'loose parameters' in setting up the database," database headers such as "voter birth date" and "felon birth date" float around the screen, and Palast explains several examples that are illustrated with graphics, showing how the state's call for loose parameters resulted in many "false positive" matches. Ion Sanchez, supervisor of elections in Leon County, reviewed the purge list he received from Harris's office name by name and was able to confirm that only 33 of the 690 people listed actually were felons; an image of an e-mail printout shows that Jeb Bush's administration encouraged these false positives.

Without breaking the editing rhythm, the camera begins to pan slowly, Ken Burns–style, across several racist newspaper cartoons from the nineteenth century. John Nichols, author of *Jews for Buchanan* (2001), explains that "the law to deny ex-felons the ability to vote was written into the state constitution in 1868 by ex-Confederate soldiers who did it because they were being forced to allow blacks to vote by the federal government, and so they wrote this law in, specifically to deny as many blacks as possible their franchise." We are told further that "blacks represented more than half the names on this purge list" and that "since blacks vote over 90 percent Democratic, the state's instructions eliminated thousands of Democratic voters from the rolls." The purge also denied the right to vote in Florida to ex-felons who had had their voting rights restored in other states, so these ex-felons had to petition to have their voting rights *re*-restored. As we see George W. Bush sitting next to his brother Jeb on an airplane, Palast explains that "90 to 93 percent of the people who come out of prison vote Democratic, so they knew exactly who they were removing from the voter rolls."

Unlike the first historical narrative, this one offers no promising mimetic potential that suddenly is cut off. The effect of this brief narrative instead is to crush the viewer beneath a unified wall of impenetrable corruption. Jeb Bush's office, relying upon nineteenth-century race laws, ordered the purges; the political operative implementing the purge was co-chair of Bush's campaign in Florida; DBT was instructed to cast as wide a net as possible so that many nonfelons were included on the list; all of these people knew that most of the purged voters were African American and would have been expected to vote Democratic. We are presented with a seamless narrative spanning over a century of corruption that rolls relentlessly forward into the present, providing little opportunity for intervention. Palast sums up the effacement of human agency, saying that "now we're back to the basic issue: do black people have the right to vote? Except this time it's not George Wallace standing in the doorway of a schoolhouse saying 'segregation now and forever.' Now it's done quietly, and with computers." The utter futility of trying to engage the individuals involved is illustrated with white lettering against a black screen, informing us that "Jeb Bush denied our request for an interview" and that "Katherine Harris did not respond to repeated requests."

The documentary begins, then, by establishing the 2000 election in Florida as a synecdoche for American elections in general and presents the audience with two historical narratives that establish that the corruption of the 2000 election was not an aberration but instead an episode within a larger and continuing narrative. Human bodies in action—marching, speaking, voting—are first shown to be ineffective and then are effaced altogether as agency is reframed as behind-the-scenes maneuvering and computerized manipulation.

Cloistered Politics

The second major argument, occupying approximately the center third of the film, focuses on the legal and political wrangling over the manual recount and the decision of the Supreme Court that followed in the wake of the 2000 election. The screen goes dark as an unnamed MSNBC reporter states that "I don't think that anyone who went to bed last night could imagine waking up this morning and not knowing who the president of the United States is." When he appears on-screen, as though with the dawn, he is disheveled and harried, showing several newspapers with conflicting reports of the election outcome. A graphic fills the screen, showing that Al Gore unambiguously won the popular vote but that the election remains undecided. Another unnamed MSNBC reporter holds up a copy of the *Daily Mail* with the headline "President Who?"

In this section, the logic of the opening sequence is speeded up and repeated so that a series of potentially promising developments is presented, but each is immediately foiled. Because the election results were so close, we are told, Florida law mandates a recount, but then Jack Tapper, author of *Down and Dirty: The Plot to Steal the Presidency* (2001), tells us that "to this day there has not been a true statewide recount as mandated by state law." We see Jeb Bush recusing himself from the Florida election board to "ensure that there is not the slightest appearance of a conflict of interest," but then we are told that many members of his staff immediately began to work for the Bush campaign. Tapper tells us that George W. Bush, while governor of Texas, had signed into law "one of the most liberal hand recount laws that exists," but then the narrator states that "the Republicans began to advance the idea that there was something wrong with manual recounts," and we see news footage of James Baker saying that "the nation has left manual counting in favor of machine counting because it is less subject to human error and potential mischief." The narrator tells us that the manual recount from Broward County resulted in a net gain of 563 votes for Gore and that in Volusia County the gain was 96 votes for Gore, but then the Republicans attempted to have overseas absentee military ballots counted, even though they did not meet standards set by Florida law and therefore were, as Mark Herron, attorney for the Florida Democratic Party, puts it, "illegal as hell." The film shows the manual recount proceeding in an orderly manner, with teams of people studying each ballot closely, but then we see what Mark Seibel, news editor for the *Miami Herald*, calls a "Republican mini-riot" outside the rooms where the recount is taking place, incited by Republican staffers flown in from Washington, D.C.[40] The Florida Supreme Court moves the deadline for the manual recount to November 26, but then the Republicans take the issue to the more conservative U.S. Supreme Court.

The Supreme Court decision, of course, is the climax of this story. But by this point, the rhythmic and repeated denial of human agency has rendered the audience inert. Without offering any figure who has acted in both a moral and effective way, the film has minimized its potential to move its audience. Vincent Bugliosi reminds us that "we look up to the United States Supreme Court as a revered institution like no other" and that we "rely on them to be above the fray," but the statement seems ironic. This segment of the documentary aims to show that the Supreme Court is *not* above the fray of political maneuver and influence but that it *is* beyond the reach of ordinary citizens. After the Court reaches its decision, we can only, like the "lawyers, students, and history buffs" who are shown lined up in the night, "grab a copy of the ruling that ended it all." We're shown a printed copy of the ruling, but we cannot read it. We're shown the judges, but at some unnamed photo opportunity not connected with the 2000 election. The Supreme Court is not only "above the fray" but entirely inscrutable—the judges and their rulings are unavailable for any dialogue, unruffled by any crisis, and unapproachable by average citizens.

Though insulated and remote, the Supreme Court—unlike the audience— is not rendered politically inert. Jamin Raskin, professor of law at American University, reminds us that "the Supreme Court's a political institution, and we should be clear about that. Politics is inextricably bound up with the interpretation of the law. There's no use in pretending as if most of the time the Supreme Court acts like judges and in this one case they acted like politicians. No . . . politics is always part of what they do." Bugliosi suggests that this was a direct intervention in a specific political event, noting that "this is probably the first time in the 210-year history of the United States Supreme Court that the court limited its ruling to the case in front of it. They knew that if that ruling were applied elsewhere, it would invalidate elections throughout the entire country." Ed Baker, professor of law at University of Pennsylvania, agrees. Alan Dershowitz and John Nichols both review the reasons that conservative justices Scalia, Thomas, and O'Connor should have recused themselves because of conflicts of interest.

Throughout this section, various pundits and professors stand in for ordinary citizens, modeling the only action available—analysis. This is not judgment, for it cannot culminate in action; there simply is nothing to be done. The only succor seems to be in the opinions of the four dissenting judges, whose head shots float across the screen. We are told that all agreed that the solution was to establish uniform recount procedures and then to continue the recount. Of the dissenting opinions, the narrator tells us that the most forceful was from Justice John Paul Stevens; as the camera slowly zooms in on an image of his face, the following quotation scrolls upward beside him and the narrator reads it aloud: "Although we may never know with complete certainty the winner of this year's presidential election, the identity of the loser is perfectly clear. It is the Nation's confidence in the judge as an impartial guardian of the rule of law." Indeed, the Supreme Court that *Unprecedented* presents to its audience is isolated, capricious, and politically biased, incapable of either protecting or reflecting the interests of the American public.

Diminished Returns

The final third of the documentary includes the original ending of the film together with the new ending added for the 2004 DVD release. It continues the pattern familiar from the first two-thirds of the film in that potentially productive modes of judgment and action are presented but then are shown to be inconclusive or ineffective.

For example, we see boxes of ballots being loaded on trucks and transported with a police escort as the narrator informs us that a media consortium, including the *Washington Post, Orlando Sentinel, New York Times*, and *Los Angeles Times*, conducted a thorough analysis of the 175,000 ballots that were never read in Florida. This would seem to suggest that some relatively clear answers should be forthcoming about who actually won the election, and Dan Keating, the *Washington Post* database editor, declares simply that "based on what is marked on the ballots, if you look at every ballot, it would indicate that more people voted for Gore." But then Sean Holton, projects editor for the *Orlando Sentinel*, says that they found that "anywhere from 2,000 to 25,000 ballots, out of these 175,000 ballots, were, in fact, legal votes," which narrows considerably the potential impact of the unread ballots while at the same time opening a fairly wide range of votes as potentially readable. Keating explains that an "over-vote" occurs when a voter punches the ballot for the candidate and then also writes in the name of the candidate, but then, as the camera zooms in on a headline from the *Washington Post* that states "Florida Recounts Would Have Favored Bush," the narrator tells us that "it is only when the state's *under-votes* are counted that George Bush would have retained his lead" (emphasis added). The viewer has been given no unambiguous statement about the outcome of the recount and thus no unambiguous endorsement of the idea that counting all of the votes would have resulted in a different—or even more just—election outcome.

The next segment opens with the blatant doublespeak of Florida election officials, who have played the role of villain throughout the documentary, but then the villain role is enlarged in an unexpected way. Clayton Roberts, Florida director of elections, and Katherine Harris are shown in C-SPAN footage listening to a question at an unnamed hearing: "How can some counties be counted, and others not have, without discrimination?" With Harris look-ing on approvingly, Roberts—after a long pause—answers that "I . . . I don't think that they can. But there are some counties where the supervisors have interpreted the statutes to not require a machine recount in that automatic machine recount." While the images of Harris and Roberts linger on the screen, Francis Fox Piven, co-author of *Why Americans Don't Vote* (1989), tells us that "the people who commit a kind of voter fraud regularly in American elections are the people who run those elections." The implication is clear: Harris and Roberts are the sort of election officials who regularly commit voter fraud.

Over images of Warren Christopher and James Baker, Piven notes that "American elections are run by the parties." Then the Gore campaign is cri-tiqued for seeking a recount only in heavily Democratic counties instead of seeking a recount of all 175,000 unread ballots. The irony is brought home by John Nichols: "After the election, their job was to make sure that the votes were counted. *All* the votes, not just their own. They got so concerned about finding the five hundred votes that they needed that they forgot their broader responsibility. . . . The Gore camp would have won . . . had they been good citizens." The election waters have been fouled not only by Jeb Bush, Katherine Harris, Clayton Roberts, and the other Republican functionaries but also by Al Gore, who to this point has been cast as an innocent victim. No one at all, it seems, has acted with the greater good in mind.

The segment that originally closed the documentary begins with Juanita Cohen, a resident of Lake Park, explaining that it is "a hard task for an African American person to really go out and vote, because we're not sure if this person is really for us or against us." *Unprecedented* models no procedure through which it might become easier for African Americans—or anyone else—to make informed voting decisions. As Gwendolyn Johnson, a Wellington resident, explains: "They [the candidates, or the parties] have the money, and they have the plans." Barbara Devane, a white grassroots organizer with We All Count, reminds us to "always remember that one person can make a difference in this world," but *Unprecedented* has shown us no one who has made a difference, either by voting or through any other means. Of course, it has shown us people successfully stealing an election.

The shot that ended the original version of the documentary is Kweisi Mfume delivering the following speech at the NAACP hearing: "We recognize that this strange and sometimes twisted democracy that we have is our democracy nonetheless. It is what we make it. And so as stewards of that democracy, I think we have a very special responsibility to make sure that we improve upon it, and that we leave a democracy and a democratic form of government and quite frankly a republic to the next generation that they can be proud of and recognize that it is one that has survived the test of time and it will survive this and it will get better because of this." The message of this documentary, in contrast, is that those in power seek to deprive others of their rights, that seemingly noble acts actually are political maneuvers, that the highest court of the land is both corrupt and aloof, and that the processes that are supposed to protect our democratic culture are hopelessly flawed. Despite Mfume's statement, the documentary gives its viewers little reason to believe that going to the polls is a politically effective mode of action.

Throughout the documentary, human agents have been shown to be unreliable or disenfranchised and thus have offered no models for productive mimesis, but the final section warns that the viewer should not hold out hope for a technological solution that might bypass human bias and error. Danny Glover returns and offers a brief update that closes the "chapter of American history" represented by the 2000 presidential election in Florida. He then warns us of "a new set of challenges to our democratic system," addressing the camera directly to say that "Congress passed federal legislation to replace outdated voting systems. Many states responded by purchasing fully computerized, touch-screen voting machines." Among the problems with such a proposal, as Stanford University professor David Dill tells us, is that "there is absolutely no way to check" for voter fraud when using an electronic touch-screen voting machine. Several experts tell us how easily such machines can be rigged. Glover, in a voice-over, tells us that "in Georgia, some unexpected election results undermined voter confidence in the new technology." After a vote that resulted in six upsets, including the election of a Republican governor for the first time since the Civil War, "there was no way to recount anything or to audit anything." In addition, according to Avi Ruben of the Information Security Institute at Johns Hopkins University, "when anybody asks . . . how does the machine work, can we see the design of the machine, can we see the code, the voting machine companies say, 'No, that's proprietary.'" Computerized voting represents a closed system, as impervious to citizen intervention or influence as the Supreme Court. And perhaps as biased. Glover's voice tells us, for example, that "the owners and board members of companies that manufacture touch-screen voting systems have unsettling conflicts of interest. Some actively raise money for political parties and candidates, and one elected official was a head of a voting machine company—a company whose machines later would count his votes." Ruben sums up the argument: "You shouldn't have to trust computer scientists; we don't want them running the world. And you shouldn't have to trust politicians. You should be able to verify for yourself that your vote counted and that there's some hope that in a recount your vote will continue to count."

As the documentary's theme music comes up, Dill tells us that "people have to act now. Basically, elections have been handed over to the election community, which consists of vendors, election officials, and the people who orbit around them. As a rule, they are gung-ho for this conversion to touch-screen machines. Stopping that is going to depend on the American people. It has to be a grassroots effort to persuade the people that represent us that this is not what we want. We want a system we can trust." But this documentary has shown us no grassroots organization that was not undermined through bureaucratic manipulation or maneuvering and no government entity, public personage, or private individual who was not misinformed, ineffective, or corrupt. In this context, Glover's peroration rings hollow: surrounded by the technological apparatus of a modern digital production studio, he faces the camera in a medium close shot and tells us that "the United States was founded on the principles of democracy, equality, and individual freedom. The survival of our republic is our responsibility. Elections provide us the opportunity to uphold these ideals by participating in our democracy by exercising and protecting our precious right to vote. . . . I encourage you to exercise your right to vote."

Missed Opportunity

Unprecedented may offer an accurate portrayal of the "real" world of the 2000 presidential election, and through its form it may invite its audiences to experience some of the chaos and frustration that characterized that historical moment. Shedding light on public issues is a vital contribution made by political documentaries. But while this film may mimetically reproduce the events in Florida, it offers its audience no mimetic models worthy of reproduction. Democratic culture depends upon a populace that is encouraged and enabled to intervene through direct participation, and *Unprecedented* offers no resources toward this end. It does not call its audience to action.

This curiously inert quality is especially ironic given the avowed purpose of political films such as *Unprecedented* to ignite or participate in a progressive revival. Because of their ability to represent reality, documentary films perhaps possess an unusual rhetorical potential, a concrete realization of the suasory force of Aristotle's "bringing-before-the-eyes."[41] Because of the pervasiveness of such mediated representations in contemporary culture, political documentaries might be able to collect a broader and more diverse audience than that ever available to orators. But as Jeffrey Isaac explains in *The Poverty of Progressivism* (2003), a progressive revival seems unlikely. He argues that the decline of liberal Protestantism and the rise of antihumanist fundamentalism have eviscerated progressive politics of the Christian theology that once motivated a good number of its adherents; that modern research universities are largely devoid of the public purposiveness that once undergirded the social contract; and that the politicized class conflict that drove much progressive reform has simply vanished from contemporary public discourse. Leftist politics in America has never recovered from the fragmentation of the 1960s, and the public sphere is perhaps irrecoverably anemic.[42]

Isaac's assessment is compelling, but there may be one further poverty of progressivism that documentary film is especially well suited to ameliorate—not through its reflective, indexical quality but instead through its productive mimetic potential. This potential is clarified by extending Gaines's ideas with an Isocratean notion of rhetoric and by attending particularly to the ways in which public discourse, such as political documentary, might model for its audience modes of judgment and action. As Hariman notes, "Isocrates teaches us that inventive imitation is an important element of democratic discourse."[43] Democratic citizenship is neither a pledged oath nor an accident of birth but a sustained performance of cultural production, and citizens in a democratic culture must be provided viable models of civic conduct and critique. The doubled mimesis of documentary film—its imitation of reality and its invitation to its audiences—presents a potent means of providing these models. Documentary possesses an unusual capacity to school its audiences in strategies of interpretation and intervention. If progressive politics is to regain traction in American public life, there should exist within public discourse a supply of exemplary individuals and collectivities engaged in successful intervention in the public sphere, for it is through such exemplars that a public might be mobilized.

It may be true, as Gaines suggests, that the connection between political documentary and social change is merely a myth that filmmakers tell among themselves.[44] Certainly, there can be no magic bullet that would enable any single documentary, no matter how eloquent, to inspire mass movement on a national scale. No single film could either elect a president or prevent one from being elected. But if documentary film is to translate its remarkable power to bring social issues before the eyes of its audiences into a faculty to motivate them toward addressing those social issues, it cannot ignore the potentials of political mimesis as thoroughly as does *Unprecedented*.

Notes

1. "Nüz: Jim Crow Laws Rising," *Metro Santa Cruz*, May 21–28, 2003, http://www.metroactive.com/papers/cruz/05.21.03/nuz-0321.html (accessed June 9, 2005).

2. "Earl Katz, Co-Executive Producer of the Documentary 'Unprecedented: The 2000 Presidential Election': A BuzzFlash Interview," *BuzzFlash*, January 29, 2003, http://www.buzzflash.com/interviews/03/01/29_Unprecedented. html (accessed June 6, 2005).

3. Rod Harman, "An 'Unprecedented' Examination of Florida's Flawed 2000 Election," *Bradenton Herald*, September 22, 2002, http://www.bradenton.com/ mld/bradenton/news/local/4125711.htm (accessed June 7, 2005).

4. Coralie Carlson, "Critical Documentary on Florida 2000 Election Screened in Miami," *Florida Times-Union*, September 20, 2002, http://www. jacksonville.com/tu-online/apnews/stories/092002/D7M5N0001.html (accessed June 9, 2005).

5. Lisa Selin Davis, "Do-Something Documentaries: Effecting Change beyond Affecting Attitudes," *The Independent: A Magazine for Video and Filmmakers* 28, no. 3 (2005): 40–43. Davis describes the emerging interrelationship between political documentaries and "outreach" through related Web sites and political organizations. Pat Aufderheide provides a more thorough analysis of these interrelationships and quotes Robert Greenwald as saying, with respect to "house parties" and the Internet as modes of distribution for documentaries such as *Unprecedented*, that "frankly, I think what we've learned about distribution may be more important in the long run than the films themselves." Pat Aufderheide, "The Changing Documentary Marketplace," *Cineaste* (Summer 2005): 24–28. While this topic is an important part of the story of the political role that *Unprecedented* and other documentaries have played in recent American elections, it lies beyond the scope of this essay. I thank my colleague Josh Malitsy for bringing Aufderheide's essay to my attention.

6. Thomas Waugh, *"Show Us Life": Toward a History and Aesthetics of the Committed Documentary* (Metuchen, N.J.: Scarecrow Press, 1984), xiv.

7. Harman, "An 'Unprecedented' Examination."

8. Greg Palast, *The Best Democracy Money Can Buy* (London: Pluto Press, 2002).

9. Bill Nichols, *Representing Reality: Issues and Concepts in Documentary* (Bloomington: Indiana University Press, 1991), 3.

10. Ibid., 4. Nichols is not implying that these discourses do have a direct, immediate, and transparent relationship with the real but that they portray themselves as having such a relationship.

11. Ibid.

12. Bill Nichols, *Blurred Boundaries: Questions of Meaning in Contemporary Culture* (Bloomington: Indiana University Press, 1994), ix. David Bordwell develops this sense of mimesis in *Narration in the Fiction Film* (Madison: University of Wisconsin Press, 1985), 3–15.

13. Nichols, *Representing Reality*, 150. Nichols seems to follow closely André Bazin's conception of the "ontology of the photographic image." André Bazin, *What Is Cinema?*, trans. H. Gray, vol. 1 (Berkeley: University of California Press, 1967), 9–16.

14. Nichols, *Representing Reality*, 6.

15. Ibid.

16. Ibid., 134.

17. Eugene Garver, "Philosophy, Rhetoric, and Civic Education in Aristotle and Isocrates," in *Isocrates and Civic Education*, ed. Takis Poulakos and David Depew (Austin: University of Texas Press, 2004), 194.

18. Ekaterina V. Haskins, *Logos and Power in Isocrates and Aristotle* (Columbia: University of South Carolina Press, 2004), 50.

19. Ibid., 29–30. A similarly narrow and instrumental view of rhetoric is articulated by David Bordwell in *Making Meaning: Inference and Rhetoric in the Interpretation of Cinema* (Cambridge, Mass.: Harvard University Press, 1989). Nichols understands the limitations of his conception of rhetoric and supplements it with discussions of "style" and "excess" in documentary film (*Representing Reality*, 134–36).

20. Nichols, *Representing Reality*, 135–36.

21. Paula Rabinowitz, *They Must Be Represented: The Politics of Documentary* (New York: Verso, 1994), 9.

22. Ibid., 9.

23. Ibid., 23–24.

24. Ibid., 26. Bluem concurs: "Documentary communication seeks to initiate a process which culminates in public action by presenting information, and to complete the process by making this presentation persuasive. Documentary seeks to inform but, above all, it seeks to influence." William

A. Bluem, "The Documentary Idea: A Frame of Reference (1965)," in *Nonfiction Film Theory and Criticism*, ed. Richard Meran Barsam (New York: E. P. Dutton, 1976), 77–78.

25. "Recent theorists of documentary, such as Thomas Guynn and Bill Nichols, have argued that the documentary film is primarily discursive; it seeks overtly to persuade its viewers by taking a side and arguing it. Rhetoric, according to Eagleton, does just that. It is fundamentally performative, interested in examining the ways discourses are constructed in order to achieve their desired effects. Interested and activist, rhetoric stakes a position from which to make its case" (Rabinowitz, *They Must Be Represented*, 11).

26. Jane M. Gaines, "Political Mimesis," in *Collecting Visible Evidence*, ed. Jane M. Gaines and Michael Renov (Minneapolis: University of Minnesota Press, 1999), 90. Gaines suggests that political documentary bears some kinship with Linda Williams's "body genres." See Linda Williams, "Film Bodies: Gender, Genre, and Excess," *Film Quarterly* 44 (1991).

27. Gaines, "Political Mimesis," 93. Documentary filmmaker Jill Godmilow similarly states that she desires her own films "to produce an audience of individuals who can learn some conceptual tools with which to articulate a critique—a critique applicable to all kinds of social and historical situations, not just to the materials at hand." Quoted in Ann-Louise Shapiro, "How Real Is the Reality in Documentary Film?" *History and Theory* 36 (1997): 83.

28. Gaines, "Political Mimesis," 89.

29. Ibid., 90. Gaines acknowledges that an "argument for mimesis as a form of knowledge will meet with resistance in the First World, especially because the concept has long been associated with not-knowing, or 'only imitating,' reproducing without adding anything, and learning by means of the body without the engagement of the mind" (93–94). Postcolonial critiques of mimesis have to do with its potential as a discourse of power through which the colonized can be made to be more like the colonizer. See, for example, Homi B. Bhabha, "Of Mimicry and Man: The Ambivalence of Colonial Discourse," in *The Location of Culture* (New York: Routledge, 1994), 85–92. I thank my colleague Jane Goodman for alerting me to this particular critique of mimesis.

30. Rabinowitz, *They Must Be Represented*, 18. Robert Greenwald suggests the pedagogical potential of this film specifically: "I remember thinking, this is important to do. I figured, if you're ignorant of history, it will be repeated. . . . So I envisioned that maybe in three or four years, a student would be doing a paper on the Florida election and would to go the library and dig this out and use it." Quoted in Stewart Oksenhorn, "What's Up? Docs," *Aspen Times*, September 30, 2004, http://www.aspentimes.com/apps/pbcs.dll/article?AID=/20040930 (accessed June 6, 2005).

31. Garver, "Philosophy, Rhetoric, and Civic Education," 204.

32. Haskins, *Logos and Power*, 30.

33. Robert Hariman, "Civic Education, Classical Imitation, and Democratic Polity," in *Isocrates and Civic Education*, ed. Takis Poulakos and David Depew (Austin: University of Texas, 2004), 218.

34. Haskins, *Logos and Power*, 76.

35. Hariman, "Civic Education," 226, 229, 224.

36. Gaines, "Political Mimesis," 93. Gaines breaks off her theoretical argument to discuss the mimetic potential of the infamous Rodney King video, which she describes as "an example par excellence of the powers of mimesis": "It seems that the footage of police brutally beating a black man *made* disaffected African Americans and Asians in South-Central Los Angeles riot and loot, when it was actually the *world* of the footage—the world within which police conduct humiliating strip searches on young black men—that *made* people riot" (96).

37. Michael Leff, "The Idea of Rhetoric as Interpretive Practice: A Humanist's Response to Gaonkar," in *Rhetorical Hermeneutics: Invention and Interpretation in the Age of Science*, ed. Alan G. Gross and William M. Keith (Albany: State University of New York Press, 1997), 97. George A. Kennedy provides a useful brief overview of mimesis in the rhetorical tradition in "Imitation," in *Encyclopedia of Rhetoric*, ed. T. O. Sloane (Oxford: Oxford University Press, 2001), 381–84. See also James Jasinski, "Invention," in *Sourcebook on Rhetoric: Key Concepts in Contemporary Rhetorical Studies* (Thousand Oaks, Calif.: Sage, 2001), 327–30.

38. Gaines, "Political Mimesis," 88.

39. The other two moments occur in the final section of the film, also added for the 2004 DVD release.

40. The film freezes one such demonstration and identifies each of the participants as a Republican congressional aid or an employee of the national Republican Party. See also Tim Padgett, "Mob Scene in Miami," *Time Europe*, December 4, 2000, http://www.time.com/time/europe/magazine/2000/1204/cover_riot.html (accessed June 22, 2005).

41. Sara Newman, "Aristotle's Notion of 'Bringing-Before-the-Eyes': Its Contributions to Aristotelian and Contemporary Conceptualizations of Metaphor, Style, and Audience," *Rhetorica* 20 (2002): 1–23.

42. Jeffrey C. Isaac, *The Poverty of Progressivism: The Future of American Democracy in a Time of Liberal Decline* (Lanham, Md.: Rowman and Littlefield, 2003), 77–116.

43. Hariman, "Civic Education," 229.

44. Gaines, "Political Mimesis," 85.

7

Susan Mackey-Kallis

Talking Heads Rock the House

Robert Greenwald's *Uncovered: The War on Iraq*

Robert Greenwald's documentary *Uncovered: The War on Iraq*, released into
theaters in October 2004, is one of a number of recent films about the 2003
Iraq war that critically deconstructs the Bush administration's rationale for
fighting it. Greenwald's film is joined, most notably, by Michael Moore's film
Fahrenheit 9/11, which grossed over $119 million in domestic box office; *Why
We Fight,* a Grand Jury Prize winner at the 2004 Sundance Film Festival;
Hijacking Catastrophe: 9/11, Fear and the Selling of American Empire, released
by the Media Education Foundation; and *WMD: Weapons of Mass Deception,*
produced by Danny Schechter. These five documentaries about the Iraq war are
in good company with at least another dozen political documentaries released
during the 2004 presidential campaign season.

Uncovered: The War on Iraq is a longer version of Greenwald's *Uncovered:
The Whole Truth about the Iraq War,* a somewhat less detailed examination of
similar issues completed in 2003 and prompted in part by Greenwald's introduction to the Veteran Intelligence Professionals for Sanity (VIPS), a nonpar-
tisan group of former CIA employees whose articulate critiques of the claims
being made in favor of the 2003 Iraq war were being quoted in such alternative
U.S. political journals as *Counterpunch* and *The Nation.* In an interview with
BuzzFlash, one of the Internet sites responsible for the distribution of his 2004
version of the film, Greenwald acknowledges these individuals as an impetus
for his project: "There are a large number of people who have worked within
the corridors of power from the CIA to the Pentagon to weapons inspection to

foreign service—people with hundreds of years of service to our country who are upset, angry and distraught at the lies that we have been told about the war. And these people are willing to step forward and go public."[1] Starting with Ray McGovern, a CIA analyst from 1964 to 1990 who regularly reported to the vice president and senior policy-makers from 1981 to 1985, Greenwald went on to interview such high-ranking individuals as Joe Wilson, former deputy chief of mission at the U.S. embassy in Iraq; John Dean, Richard Nixon's White House chief legal counsel during the Watergate scandal and a respected legal and political analyst; U.N. weapons inspector David Kay, who led the 1,400-member Iraq survey group appointed by President Bush in June 2003 to search for weapons of mass destruction after the war's formal conclusion; and Scott Ritter, a former marine captain and the U.N.'s top weapons inspector in Iraq until 1998. Greenwald's on-camera interviews of CIA operatives, image analysts, politicians, and diplomats resulted in a fifty-six-minute DVD, distributed through grassroots organizations. It received such positive critical response that Greenwald was able to secure financial backing for a longer version and a theatrical distribution agreement with Cinema Libre Studios.

Uncovered is also the second in a trilogy of "Un" films directed and/or produced by Greenwald, who has over fifty credits for directing and producing television movies, miniseries, and feature films and is the recipient of numerous awards.[2] *Unprecedented: The 2000 Presidential Election* (2002) examines the incompetence surrounding and possible manipulation of the vote count and recount in Florida (directed by Richard Ray Perez and Joan Sekler); *Unconstitutional: The War on Our Civil Liberties* (2004) describes the erosion of American's civil liberties after September 11, 2001 (directed by Nonny de la Pena). Greenwald is also the director/producer of *Outfoxed: Rupert Murdoch's War on Journalism* (2004), which examines the right-wing bias of Fox News.

The style of *Uncovered: The War on Iraq* is not particularly innovative—talking heads and tight editing are used to deconstruct network news footage of Bush administration voices. Nor is Greenwald's argument a new one, that the administration manipulated and ignored intelligence information about WMDs and terrorism in Iraq in order to justify the invasion of Iraq and later to silence critics by shifting the terms of the debate. *Uncovered* is innovative in the way it was disseminated, in its ability to quickly find an audience, and because of Greenwald's access to an A-list of highly placed Washington insiders with a great deal of credibility and authority. This chapter examines the film's deconstruction of the Bush administration's arguments for war against Iraq and the film's counterargument regarding what should constitute patriotism in an era of preemptive war and global imperialism. It begins with a discussion of the growing impact of "new political documentaries" such as Greenwald's, which are successful due to the new methods of inexpensive production and new channels of distribution, the rise of political election attack ads and biographical candidate films to which these documentaries are often a response, the increasingly polarized political climate that has added fuel and finances to the fires of the partisan advocacy groups that often pay for and distribute these films, the increased public appetite for extended critical treatment of complicated foreign and domestic policy issues as a result of both 9/11 and the mainstream media's tendency toward either "sound-bite" coverage or "journalism-free" live coverage, and the public's increased acceptance of both the grainy, "low-budget" cinema verité "reality show" and "live new coverage" style and the partisan debate style of political talk radio and television. This chapter also explores the implications of such developments for the future of political documentaries and for an educated public.

The Political Documentarian's Dilemma: Getting the Word (and Images) Out

With the notable exception of *Fahrenheit 9/11*, which had a box office take well in excess of $100 million, most political documentaries released in 2004 made less than half a million dollars in limited theatrical release. These documentaries often had a difficult time getting aired on television. Although there is a greater chance of distribution through cable, cable stations are often wary of screening such partisan political films because they fear damage to their reputations for offering "balanced" coverage of issues.[3] Sinclair Broadcast Group, owner of sixty-two cable stations, for example, canceled its airing of the anti–John Kerry film *Stolen Honor* at the last minute, opting instead to show excerpts of the film in conjunction with a program on Vietnam POWs.[4]

Lacking access to theatrical distribution, many filmmakers have taken advantage of the ability to market and sell their films through their own Web sites or those of sympathetic political groups or through on-line distribution channels such as Amazon or Netflix. At the time of the writing of this chapter, *Uncovered* cost ten dollars to purchase on-line, and prior to the 2004 election, copies were often made available as a free download for interested political organizations. Speaking in 2004 with BuzzFlash, one of his distributors, about his plans for *Uncovered*, Greenwald notes that

> BuzzFlash, AlterNet, *The Nation* and MoveOn.org are leading the
> way in the Internet distribution. . . . This is a powerful, democratic
> and alternative way to get the film into people's hands. I am very
> excited about our alternative distribution. . . . We have different
> sponsors in different cities, and more to come. I encourage all
> BuzzFlash readers to get a copy and screen it, no permissions

necessary. . . . You can use it at your school, club, church, or family get-together, use it as a fundraiser, use it to generate discussion.[5]

Greenwald acknowledges the drawbacks to accepting funding from such partisan groups as MoveOn and the Center for American Progress to make his films. Asked about this in an interview, he explains:

> Sure, some groups will attack me for taking money. . . . But it's well worth it. They [the organizations] never tell me what to do. Even when I did *Uncovered*, at a very volatile time. They never looked at a frame until I was finished. Number two, they are part of the alternative distribution and that's how the word gets out there, through the Internet, through the screenings, through the house parties. That's my primary means. The fact that we are now in movie theatres and we have commercial DVD distribution is a gift that I never thought would happen.[6]

Inexpensive Digital Production Format

The explosion of the new political documentary—indeed, Greenwald's recent career as a political documentarian (since 2002)—has also been made possible by the technological changes in film production. The convergence of video and film technology into digital has made for relatively inexpensive shooting and editing costs. Lorie Conway, a Boston-based producer and documentary filmmaker, explains: "Armed with digital cameras and sound equipment, and using computer-based editing, these savvy filmmakers have become a source of alternative explanation. . . . In this era of digital images, nearly everything that's been said on the air or off can be captured on camera and become grist for documentary filmmakers to use."[7] All of Greenwald's documentaries exhibit these qualities—talking-head interviews shot with pickup crews, extensive use of local and national archival footage with built-in high production value, and cheap but effective post-production graphics and sound. In an interview with *Movie Maker* magazine, Greenwald elaborates: "We have technology that can drive cost radically down. I can do these [films] for $300,000 or $400,000. Sometimes I'm not even in the room when I interview people. With *Outfoxed* we had millions and millions of dollars in production value—it happened to come from Fox News."[8]

A Response to Audience Acceptance of Film Conventions of Live Coverage

Audiences' positive reception of these partisan documentaries may come from their acceptance of the filmic conventions of live breaking news coverage—the same conventions that are the hallmark of reality entertainment programming on mainstream media. Audiences have become more comfortable with handheld cameras, grainy film stock, low lighting, low budgets, short production time, and the "unscripted" quality that marks reality television and live breaking news coverage as well as the partisan political documentary. Morgan Spurlock, director of *Super Size Me*, a 2004 documentary about the serious impact of a McDonald's-only diet, notes, "People think, well, it's interesting to see a normal person on TV. So, why not go see a real person in film. It's not that big of a stretch."[9]

A Response to Other Election Films and to a Changing Electorate

The "new political documentary" as anti-candidate propaganda may also be a response to the rise of the biographical political candidate film. Ronald Reagan's 1984 Republican National Convention film, *It's Morning in America Again*, gave a face to this growing genre, set a precedent for the shape of modern visual political rhetoric, and became the template for all such films that would follow it.[10] Every serious presidential candidate since 1984, including George W. Bush, has produced such a film.

The candidate biography film was itself a response to a number of shifting factors in the political landscape. According to J. Cherie Strachan and Kathleen E. Kendall, with the declining influence of party affiliation on voter choice, the voting public has come to depend on direct access to candidate imagery. "At the same time, candidates have embraced image construction because it can now accomplish more with a far greater variety of persuasive visual symbols."[11] Such biographical candidate films and their increasing prominence in national elections cry out for counterpoint in the form of such anti-candidate films as *Bush's Brain*, *Stolen Honor*, and *Uncovered: The War on Iraq*.

Although there is a long tradition of the political campaign documentary, styled perhaps after Timothy Crouse's *The Boys on the Bus* and Hunter S. Thompson's *Fear and Loathing: On the Campaign Trail*, both written journalistic accounts of the 1972 presidential campaign, only recently has the "balanced" campaign documentary morphed into the more activist partisan documentary. The traditional political campaign film, for example, predominantly follows the candidate on the campaign trail and is usually released after the election. A recent example is the critically acclaimed *War Room*, produced by R. J. Cutler and released in 1993 after the 1992 presidential election. The film profiles James Carville, President Bill Clinton's national campaign manager, and documents Clinton's successful bid for the presidency in 1992. By contrast, the partisan "attack" documentary is released prior to an election with the explicit agenda of influencing the election's outcome.

The partisan film's more positive reception at the box office (Moore's *Fahrenheit 9/11* is again a case in point) may also be a result of the public's increased appetite for the "attack" political ad. Although audiences often express distaste for such ads, there is evidence that they work. With the increasing reach of cable television and the rise of dozens of politically partisan television talk shows such as Michael Savage's *Savage Nation* or Bill O'Reilly's *The O'Reilly Factor*, the public has also become more accustomed to occasionally vitriolic and usually partisan viewpoints about candidates and their political agendas. Once again, with the decline of party affiliation, the electorate now seeks out other forms of information about the candidates. Films such as Greenwald's *Uncovered: The War on Iraq* fit the bill.

A Response to America's Increasing Political Polarization

Another explanation for the prominence of these films is the relatively recent political polarization in America. Errol Morris, director of the Academy Award–winning feature-length documentary *The Fog of War* (2004), about former defense secretary Robert McNamara, believes that these films have "less to do with documentary filmmaking than how polarized the country is. We all feel it. This enormous anger."[12] According to Christian Christensen, the growth of these documentaries can be traced to the cultural wars in America. As he explains it, the political consensus and social conservatism of earlier decades in America gave way by the 1960s to the emergence of the civil and women's rights movements, the growing anti–Vietnam War sentiment, and the challenges to conservative lifestyle norms:

> While a certain segment of the US population saw this shift as victory, many conservatives saw it as an attack on their fundamental Judeo-Christian values. The "war" between these two groups—seen on a daily basis in the United States in battles over issues such as gay marriage, gun control, the role of Christianity in politics and abortion—continues to this day, with the media acting as the central battleground. Basically the "cultural war" is being fought, via institutions such as the media, over who had the right to define what is "acceptable" or "normal" behavior in US society.[13]

According to some scholars, the "cultural war" debate, although brewing for many decades, really took off during the 1992 presidential election season, which was defined by the Bush/Quayle Republican ticket as a battle over "family values."[14]

This increasingly polarized political climate has brought added financing to such partisan advocacy groups as MoveOn and United Citizen. Advocacy organizations of both the Left and the Right, not surprisingly, are ready, willing, and able to finance both the production and distribution of the work of independent documentarians such as Greenwald.

Writing in 1995, nine years before the 2004 watershed year in the partisan political documentary, James and Sara Combs predicted such a trend. In their book *Film Propaganda and American Politics,* they write, "We may expect in the future that many political issues, both chronic and immediate, will find expression in filmic propaganda. Ideological and issue groups are often well financed and willing to spend money on powerful visual and narrative films and tape that spread the word."[15] Michael Paradies Shoob, director of the 2004 film *Bush's Brain*, a documentary that might well fit what Combs and Combs were describing, characterizes this new political agenda of filmmakers: "The pose in the documentary world used to be, we're filmmakers and we're not out to change the political landscape. But Michael Moore unmasked us. We *are* out to change the political landscape."[16]

Indeed, partisanship *and* timeliness are key qualities of documentaries such as Greenwald's *Uncovered.* Michael Renov, associate dean of the School of Cinema and Television at the University of Southern California, explains that these films "want to have a direct impact on the elections. . . . It doesn't have to be a great film. It's all about the audience and its political impact first and foremost, with artistry and creativity playing a secondary role."[17] Greenwald, however, in an interview with Steve Appleford for the *Los Angeles Citybeat*, argues that his films have both long- and short-term influence: "I rushed *Uncovered* to get it out in the spring [of 2004], when the country was still debating the issue, and here we are in the fall, and the full-length version has even more resonance. Certainly the issues that *Outfoxed* raised about Fox News, as well as media consolidation, had an immediate impact on the coverage of the election, and a long-term impact."[18]

It may well be, however, that these films draw partisan audiences and simply reinforce existing political attitudes. Even if this is so, the role that they may play in motivating the faithful to get out and vote at election time should not be underestimated. And films such as Greenwald's *Uncovered* are clearly partisan and timely; as already noted, *Uncovered*, providing a scathing critique of the Bush administration's reasons for going to war against Iraq in 2003, was released in October 2004, just prior to the presidential election in November of that year.

A Response to Failures of the Mainstream Media

Are partisan political documentaries more than just a passing phase, assuming that American politics do not remain so bitterly polarized into "blue" and "red" states in the coming years? Other forces at work in American political culture might sustain these films. Morgan Spurlock views these films as a response to the failures of the mainstream media: "The news we get from the TV, magazines, and newspapers is all watered down. Especially TV. . . . They're pulling a curtain down in front of our eyes and we're starved for information."[19] Seeming to echo this view of the media while also offering a remedy, Greenwald asserts, "The primary media have become more and more the soundbite media. That's happening partly through media consolidation and profiteering at the very same time we, as a country, have never, ever in our history had a more complicated set of issues hitting us. . . . And you have a media that gives you information in 30 seconds. So where do you go? People go to the Internet, books, and documentary films."[20]

The new political documentary may be also a response to the ability of networks to provide extended live coverage of media events such as the Gulf War, 9/11, and the 2003 Iraq war. Such coverage, especially the coverage provided by "embedded" wartime journalists who are essentially guests of the U.S. government, may fall prey to an unintentional "framing" sympathetic to their host's point of view. Combs and Combs note: "The Gulf War and subsequent events augur a world in which media narrators and directors can 'frame' a breaking story in terms acceptable to the powers who control the wires. Thus a war, a summit, an oil spill, an uprising, or whatever could be interpreted by trained propaganda teams who broadcast the event." Such framing appears transparent to audiences who suppose that live coverage represents "reality" flowing through the lens of a camera. In this sense, "propagandists of the media could transform every event into a new kind of 'pseudo-event,' an event that appears on the 'world screen' in the framework of media interest, and we watch it unfold with the narration and imagery provided by media teams who give it official meaning." Such embedded journalists are offered exclusive access to areas often strictly controlled by the authorities, creating a "virtual monopoly on interpretation . . . from which is excluded competing opinions and perspectives that might challenge or undermine the official view."[21]

Combs and Combs, although predicting the rise of such films, are far from positive about such a development, believing that "such ideologically-based attacks undermine serious discussion of history and politics, since they invite suspicion as to the integrity of the discussants and suggest that all inquiry is, like their own approach, merely propaganda." Such films, they argue, create a dilemma whereby no one is able to transcend his or her own ideological orientation, suggesting that truth is unknowable except as it is bound up with "the local and personal bias of the discoverer." Although there are those who find value in such a model of visual debate and the unmasking of any possibility for objectivity on the filmmaker's part, there are downsides to such a development. In such an arena, as Combs and Combs note, film propaganda

> becomes an agency for refuting truth claims but not for "accuracy in media," since historical accuracy—demonstrable facts, plausible motivations, logical causality—is simply a tactic of the propagandist. Propaganda becomes the only possible communicative format or motive for the film documentary and this exists only to fool the credulous and to be "deconstructed" and exposed by its critics. But in the long run undermining efforts at historical or political reconstruction serves no "conserving" purpose, since audiences will have long since abandoned the ability or willingness to believe in any message.[22]

Washington Post writer William Booth seems to concur when he writes, "Despite all the hoopla, and with one big, fat notable exception, the political documentaries of 2004 have fizzled at the box office."[23] More people may have talked about the films of 2004 than actually saw them, but Spurlock believes that we will be seeing many more of them. "I promise you, if things go one way or another, you're going to see a lot more documentaries over the next four years."[24]

The Iraq war documentaries, in particular, according to Conway, "fill[ed] a press vacuum. . . . Filmmakers have become a source of alternative explanation for the war in Iraq and the news coverage of it, as well as critics of the administration's policies."[25] The second Iraq war demonstrated to millions around the world what the U.S. media was very good at—human interest stories, real-time coverage of events on the ground, and reporting the Bush administration's interpretations of what Americans were seeing on their TV sets. What the media was not so good at, not surprisingly, was presenting alternative views of the war, concerning both why it was fought and how it was being run. This was in part a result of the lack of overt criticism from Democratic leaders early on, many of whom seemed sensitive to the "anti-patriotic" label that was often quickly attached to those who disagreed with the Bush administration's war policy. "Deprived of such prominent dissenters, journalists' work revolved largely within this echo chamber, as the White House maintained firm control of the news agenda with its disciplined communication apparatus."[26] The task thus fell to the alternative media, both Web-based and otherwise, to examine and criticize the Iraq war. Conway points out that there is a long history of the publication of such alternative views, starting in the early twentieth century with the rise of "muckraker" journalism in response to the ideological excesses of mainstream newspapers pandering to corporate advertisers. This tradition continued during the Vietnam War in the coverage of antiwar protests and antiwar views provided by such media outlets as the *Village Voice* and *I. F. Stone's Weekly*.

Danny Schechter's documentary *WMD: Weapons of Mass Deception* (2004) addresses the issue of the media's failure to cover dissenting opinions of the war. According to Schechter, "Even as large numbers of Americans and people around the world dissented (to the war) their views were rarely seen and heard. . . . There was a patriotic correctness on the airwaves and a uniformity of viewpoint that did more selling than telling about the war."[27] Such "rally 'round the flag" patriotism on the part of journalists, however, faded after it became clear that the war's "official end" did not really mark the war's end. *Nightline* anchor Ted Koppel, who was embedded in Iraq for ABC, is shown in Schechter's film at a journalist seminar months after the war was declared over saying that "live coverage of war is not journalism." At another point in the film, three network news presidents are seen agreeing that their coverage should have more aggressively challenged the Bush administration's reasons for going to war. ABC's David Westin said, "We let the American people down in the weapons of mass destruction (WMD), and I sincerely regret that."[28] In sum, documentaries with a clearly articulated viewpoint may best be seen as a response to the failures of the "sound-bite" media and live embedded war coverage.

Critical Response to *Uncovered: The War on Iraq*

Critics for the most part gave Greenwald's *Uncovered* a positive reception, almost always comparing it to Moore's *Fahrenheit 9/11* while also proclaiming the film's future historical significance. A *New York Daily News* review of the film notes that Greenwald "doesn't resort to any of the editorial flim-flam and smug theater that undermines the credibility of Michael Moore's *Fahrenheit 9/11*. To a careful follower of post-9/11 political news, there is nothing in *Uncovered* that should come as a surprise. Excluding Fox News, it's all been covered. But recapping it in one tight, 83-minute film, and placing his sources in front of the camera, Greenwald has created a crisp historic document that is worth your time, even if the information in it was not worth the President's."[29] Making a similar comparison, another reviewer claims, "As a documentary, this one is far less humorous, satiric and dramatized than the Michael Moore approach. Instead, we have here a document that latter day historians are likely to refer to for a contemporary perspective of this administration's martial, economic and diplomatic legacy to the country. . . . To future historians, this testimonial condemnation will weigh heavily on the scales of presidential judgment."[30] According to another critic, "What makes *Uncovered* such a success is the diversity of the interviewees and the steady tone. . . . Contrast this quiet approach with the muckraking of Michael Moore and this pill is much easier to swallow. Greenwald's . . . mature handling of startling revelations is refreshing and most effective."[31] A reviewer for the BBC notes, "This is not a crowd-pleaser in the vein of Michael Moore's *Fahrenheit 9/11*—in some respects it is barely a movie at all. . . . As an argument, *Uncovered* is a triumph; as a historical document, it is of profound importance."[32]

Critics almost always commented on Greenwald's straightforward style in which archival footage of George W. Bush and such members of his administration as Condoleezza Rice, Colin Powell, Dick Cheney, and Donald Rumsfeld making arguments for war with Iraq and defending administration policy is intercut with critical commentary from highly placed weapons and security experts. Reviewers often remarked that it is the collective weight of so many voices—a total of twenty-six A-list experts repeatedly layered into the film as a running commentary—that ultimately "add[s] up to an effective denouncement of the phony premises for launching a war."[33] Another reviewer argues that "Greenwald has compiled a who's who of government insiders who all agree on one point: The reasons used to draw our country into Iraq were distorted."[34]

Greenwald's Vision of Why We Fought the Iraq War

In addition to acknowledging the VIPS as an impetus for his documentary, Greenwald says that he felt compelled to make his film when he saw the Bush administration's postwar justification for the Iraqi invasion shifting from finding WMDs to finding "evidence for weapons programs." This shift in the terms of the debate seemed to him to epitomize the slippery-slope arguments that had gained a foothold in Washington, due, in part, to the lack of strong public opposition prior to and during the war.[35] Greenwald's film examines the lack of opposition to the war by the public and the media, viewing it as an example of the increased acceptance of consensual thinking as the definition of patriotism in America.

Uncovered is organized in seven chapters. The first chapter begins with the brief introduction of the twenty-six experts who serve as the film's argumentative spine. This first chapter and the two that follow use these voices to argue that those in the Bush administration made up their minds to invade Iraq the day after the devastating terrorist attacks on New York City and Washington, D.C., on September 11, 2001. Collectively, these voices assert that key figures in the Bush cabinet manipulated or ignored intelligence information in order to convince the American people and the Congress that Saddam Hussein had links to al-Qaeda, the terrorist group responsible for the 9/11 attacks; that Hussein had weapons of mass destruction that he was prepared to use against America and our allies; that a preemptive strike was the only way to avoid this possibility; and that Iraqi oil reserves would pay for postwar reconstruction. All of these claims, the film reminds us, later proved to be false. We see numerous clips of President Bush, Secretary of Defense Donald Rumsfeld, and National Security Advisor Condoleezza Rice repeating slightly modified versions of the phrase "We don't want the smoking gun to be a mushroom cloud," thus implying that the administration could not wait for sufficiently strong evidence to invade (the "smoking gun") but would have to launch a preemptive strike to avoid a nuclear disaster. Some of Greenwald's experts assert that this was a powerfully persuasive and frightening image for the American people, but it was also a claim that was later proven false. The film's repetition of this claim also primes the viewer for the film's concluding argument regarding the spread of "American Empire" around the globe based on preemptive strikes.

The film's second chapter, "Terrorism," argues that the Bush administration, again possibly manipulating intelligence information, falsely claimed connections between al-Qaeda and Saddam Hussein's government. The film demonstrates that this claim was bolstered by the use of faulty information from Iraqi defectors who were in a position to gain from Hussein's removal and who were not in a position to have information about the activities of terrorist groups in Iraq or about the connection between Hussein's government and al-Qaeda and thus should not have been trusted.

The film's most powerful indictment of the Bush administration's rationale for war with Iraq comes in Greenwald's systematic deconstruction of the administration's claim, made both by President Bush in his January 28, 2003, State of the Union address to Congress and by Colin Powell in his 2003 address to the U.N. Security Council, that Saddam Hussein had weapons of mass destruction. Greenwald makes this argument in the film's third chapter, "Sixteen Words," a reference to the single statement, made by Bush in his State of the Union address, that the "British Government has recently learned that Saddam Hussein recently sought significant quantities of uranium from Africa." In this chapter, we see Ray McGovern, former CIA analyst, watching President Bush's speech on a monitor while providing a point-by-point analysis of the president's rationale for going to war with Iraq. McGovern discusses Bush's glaring inaccuracies and abuses of intelligence information, such as the infamous aluminum tubes described as usable for uranium production, a claim that later proved false, and, most notably, Bush's erroneous statement regarding evidence for the smuggling of "yellow cake," a somewhat enriched form of uranium, out of Niger to Iraq. Bush used both the aluminum tubes and the yellow cake in his speech as evidence for the existence of a nuclear weapons program in Iraq and thus as a strong reason for invading. In the film, Joe Wilson, former deputy chief of mission at the

U.S. embassy in Iraq, explains that Bush used the intelligence information about the yellow cake even after Wilson told the administration that it was false and probably even forged. Wilson had been sent to Africa by the CIA to investigate this intelligence information. He explains that his wife's identity was leaked to the press—an action that not only destroyed her career at the CIA and compromised agents with whom she had worked but also threatened her life—as revenge for Wilson's scathing criticism, in the *New York Times* and on *Meet the Press,* of the Bush administration's deliberate and knowing use of the faulty intelligence information. In the film, Wilson refers to highly placed individuals in the Bush administration as responsible for the leaks but does not identify any names. In October 2005, Lewis "Scooter" Libby, chief of staff for Vice President Cheney, and Karl Rove, Bush's campaign manger and deputy chief of staff, were both identified by the journalists who received the leaks as the individuals responsible for them. In the same month, "Scooter" Libby was indicted for perjury, lying under oath, and obstruction of justice for having lied to a grand jury about his role in leaking the CIA identity of Valerie Plame, Wilson's wife, to the press. Libby resigned his position. In March 2007, Libby was convicted of perjury and obstruction of justice. A few months later, President Bush commuted Libby's sentence. The alleged leak of Wilson's wife's identity as retribution for Wilson's public outrage over Bush's use of the "yellow cake" intelligence information in his speech is used in the film as evidence that the Bush administration may have intentionally used the bad information in the speech, despite Rice's statement, also in the film, that she did not know how the "sixteen words" had gotten back into Bush's speech after they had been removed at the request of former CIA director George Tenet. This segment of the film ends with John Dean, White House counsel to Richard Nixon during the last days of his administration, saying that "the most troubling things about the fact of the distortion and the misleading statements that Bush gave Congress is that it is a federal felony, it is a crime, to mislead and distort information."

The second half of Greenwald's film argues that the mainstream media failed to provide a forum for debate about the rationale for and goals of the war with Iraq. A chapter entitled "Cost of War" offers a brief but effective critique of the Bush administration's prewar argument that Iraq oil reserves would finance the country's postwar reconstruction. The film achieves this in less than five minutes by coupling prewar footage of President Bush and Secretary Rumsfeld making these claims with postwar newspaper headlines proclaiming the initial $87 billion appropriated for Iraq's reconstruction, the later appropriation of an additional $47 billion, and comments from Rice admitting that the administration had drastically underestimated the cost of rebuilding. This video montage so quickly and effectively undermines the Bush administration's prewar argument regarding Iraq reconstruction that the images speak for themselves. Greenwald needs no commentary by any of his twenty-six experts to bring the point home.

The film concludes with a chapter entitled "Neo-Cons," which offers a scathing indictment of what the film considers the imperialistic leanings of the Bush administration "neo-cons," individuals portrayed as dedicated to the notion that "might makes right," committed to a policy of "preemptive strikes" around the globe to protect American interests, and driven by the need to hasten the reach of "American Empire" and the growth of democracy around the globe despite the economic, political, and human costs of doing so.

Patriotism: Who Gets to Define the Term?

This last section of the film ends with a full-blown discussion of patriotism, including a consideration of what "passed" as patriotism before, during, and after the Iraq war and what should be defined as patriotism if we are to avoid another such war or the burden of global imperialism that it presumes. The conception of patriotism as active, often dissenting debate about the policies and goals of the government is threaded throughout Greenwald's film. One film reviewer writes, "Patriotism. Ever since the events of September 11th, 2001, the word seems to have been thrown around a lot, but as shown in Robert Greenwald's documentary . . . the true definition of patriotism may be harder to define than most people think."[36] According to another, "On the important question of what constitutes patriotism, the collective unity of these analysts' views [in Greenwald's film] will allow all good citizens to sleep well at night. It shouldn't be missed."[37]

Silent consent as patriotism emerged prior to the 1991 Gulf War when few elected leaders, Democratic or Republican, seemed willing to voice opposition to the war despite at least one national poll's indication that the country was evenly divided on whether or not to go to war.[38] Later polls showed much higher levels of support for the soldiers, for the war, and for the first Bush administration's policies in the Gulf War—a war fought by an international coalition responding to the perceived invasion of Kuwait by Iraq. Although the first Bush administration's interpretation of the intelligence information regarding the Kuwait invasion was also later called into question by a number of sources,[39] it is clear that by 1991, a climate of patriotism as not simply silent consent but active support for America's troops had replaced widespread debate about the goals and rationale for going to war.

The definition of patriotism as consent became increasingly operative in the 2003 Iraq war, which had less international support and no truly multilateral international coalition to speak of and did not have as a rationale for its invasion the invasion of one country by another. Mainstream media coverage before and during the war failed to present alternative views of the motives and conduct of the war. This was, in part, a result of the lack of overt criticism from Democratic Party leaders of the Bush administration's decision to invade Iraq. Concerned about being labeled "anti-patriotic" by the press, they were generally silent. A clip of Michael Savage from the MSNBC cable show *Savage Nation*, used by Greenwald in the film's fourth chapter, "War in Iraq," illustrates an extreme version of this idea of consensus patriotism: "These maniacs [referring to those who were protesting against the war in Iraq] are . . . reducing troop morale, confusing the American people, and emboldening our enemies; they are absolutely seditious or treasonous. As far as I am concerned, there is a huge difference . . . between a personal opinion and an opinion which degrades or debases our military in a time of war. It's a disgrace."

Greenwald demonstrates that such a reactionary view of patriotism was even evident in the mainstream media. He shows a clip in which CNN's Paula Zahn implies that Scott Ritter, head of weapons inspection in Iraq until 1998, must have been hallucinating for testifying to Congress that the aluminum tubes found in Iraq could not have been used to manufacture weapons-grade uranium. This clip is followed by one in which Ritter exclaims that he "was belittled. I was called a traitor. Paula Zahn of CNN accused me of drinking Saddam Hussein's Kool-Aid for making accurate statements in response to aluminum tubes." Ritter, according to one journalist, was victimized by "the press for what he did not find. Saying time and again on major news sources that as a weapons inspector he saw no reason Iraq should have been considered an imminent threat, Ritter was branded unpatriotic and even ridiculed."[40]

At one point in the film, Larry Johnson, former deputy director of Counter Terrorism, explains what happened to the mainstream media in its coverage of the Iraq war: "The media is supposed to be the Fourth Estate, but they totally climbed into bed with the administration on this." Johnson explains that "earlier on I felt that there was some real danger going into the war. I tried to get an op-ed into various major newspapers, and the word kept coming back, 'Nobody wants to hear this because we're going to war.'" The "rally 'round the flag" mentality that swept the country resulted in a virtual shutout of voices in opposition to the war, while those who did protest were labeled as unpatriotic.

Greenwald's argument regarding what constitutes consensual patriotism begins with the first frame of *Uncovered*. A graphic, in which a hand slowly pulls back an American flag like a curtain, reveals the White House, as the title *Uncovered* emerges on the screen. This may either imply that "patriotic nationalism" (as evidenced by the American flag) is covering or stifling debate regarding the White House's policies in Iraq or, conversely, a true patriot must pull back the curtain of patriotic lies covering the Bush administration in order to examine through healthy debate—Greenwald's film—what was done and why.

This deconstruction of what passes as patriotism in the current era continues in the film's treatment of the Bush administration's use of intelligence information. In the film, Robert Baer, a CIA analyst with twenty-one years of service, explains why the CIA was built in Langley, Virginia, and not inside the Beltway. "That's why they're not in Washington; they're in northern Virginia away from the White House, away from Congress—leave 'em alone, ask them what they think, but don't tell them to rethink their positions because then you come up with nonsense like we saw." A bit later in the film, we hear Dr. David MacMichael, another CIA analyst, explaining consensual thinking at the Department of Energy where the intelligence director of the department "simply ordered his experts who had raised questions about the evidence being used on the nuclear end of it to sit down and shut up so that the DOE would be on board." It is as if the film is comparing groupthink, in the first example, with self-censorship, in the second example, both of which contribute to assumed consensus. Milt Bearden, former CIA station chief in Pakistan with a thirty-year career, crystallizes the link between consensus thinking and patriotism by explaining the reason why, according to the film, consensual thinking has taken hold in Washington: "There is a sense in Washington now that you can't raise objections to this because you're not supporting the troops in the field."

The conclusion of *Uncovered* broadens the terms of the debate regarding what should constitute patriotism by using the various experts who commented throughout the film on the Bush administration's rationale for war. A clear sense of patriotism as healthy suspicion, as questioning one's government, and as fearlessness in the face of criticism emerges. MacMichael, for example, quotes Mark Twain's definition of patriotism in the film: "Patriotism is supporting your country all the time and your government when it deserves it." This is followed by a scene in which Chas Freeman, a thirty-year diplomat, asserts, "I don't think it's patriotic to stand by and remain silent while your country stumbles into disaster." Mel Goodman, a twenty-year CIA analyst, offers, "Patriotism is the last refuge of scoundrels, and I think these are scoundrels—they have no argument, they have no defense for what they did, so they are attacking the patriotism of others." Patrick Lang, former chief of Middle East intelligence at the Defense Intelligence Agency, opines that "it was Jefferson who said that our kind of government is not based on trust; it's based on, in fact, suspicion." Graham Fuller, former vice chairman of the National Council at the CIA, adds, "To suggest that if you have a different viewpoint than any given administration or that you're not supporting the president in policies that may be highly erroneous—I don't see that as unpatriotic at all; in fact, I would argue that any patriot with integrity is going to speak out if he or she believes that we are on the wrong course."

Clearly, *Uncovered: The War on Iraq* invites the audience to believe that America is headed in the wrong direction. Films such as this, *Uncovered* implies, are indeed patriotic in that they offer opposing viewpoints, challenge the mainstream media's interpretation of why we fought a war in Iraq, and examine the consequences, felt even now, of the decision to go to war in 2003. Greenwald's film, methodically and consistently constructed from talking heads and archival footage, provides an important historical record not only of what a number of officials both inside and outside the Bush administration were saying and thinking but of what twenty-six different experts, from the intelligence community service to the diplomatic corps, were saying and thinking about America's war against Iraq in 2003. Maybe it is possible for talking heads to "rock the house."

It is too soon to judge the effect of *Uncovered*. The war continues with no definite end in sight, and the Bush administration is still in office as this is written. Although the critics may not have all the answers, at least they get to raise the questions that may be on the minds of other scholars and of an educated public. This is not dissimilar to what the film itself has done. As one reviewer puts it, the power of *Uncovered* lies in the questions it asks: "Why push the Iraq/Africa connection after Wilson's report? Who manufactured the fake African documents? . . . Why was a connection between Hussein and Bin Laden created when it was well known they opposed one another? Did Colin Powell know his address to the U.N. was riddled with holes? Is there truly a connection between our involvement in Iraq and a long maligned program entitled 'Project for the New American Century'? Many people interviewed [in the film] were Republicans, and some of these issues . . . have been national news and to this day have not been addressed."[41]

Another question also remains: Can films like *Uncovered* continue to catch the attention of the American public? Michael Moore places in the front ranks of filmmakers in this genre and may have a monopoly on a formula that creates production and distribution contracts and profit margins about which other documentarians can only dream. Thanks to Moore's financial successes, however, studios are now taking a harder look at the documentary form. If nothing else, Moore's film demonstrated that political films with a clear message can find audiences, and where there are audiences, given low production costs like Greenwald's, there are profit margins as well. The picture is not completely rosy, however, since most theaters and distribution companies in the United States are controlled by a small number of large corporations. As such, it may remain tough for low-budget films like *Uncovered* to develop the necessary muscle to garner screening in larger venues. However, over the next few years, a continually polarized political climate, the uncertainty of upcoming political elections, an increasingly multimedia-attuned electorate already responsive to low-budget reality television and Web-based distribution of content, and the mainstream media's abdication of responsibility for quality journalism may add to the increased prominence, importance, and impact of political films such as Greenwald's *Uncovered: The War on Iraq*.

Notes

1. See Greenwald's interview at *BuzzFlash*, November 3, 2003, http://www. Buzzflash.com/interviews/03/11.

2. For a complete filmography, see *Internet Movie Database*, http://www. imdb.com/name/nm0339254.

3. Susan Mackey, *The 18-Minute Political Film Preceding Ronald Reagan's Acceptance Speech at the 1984 Republican National Convention* (Ph.D. diss., Pennsylvania State University, 1988).

4. William Booth, "Docu-Trauma: For Political Films, the Box Office Is More Bombo Than Boffo," *Washington Post*, November 2, 2004.

5. Greenwald interview, *BuzzFlash*.

6. Steve Appleford, "Robert Greenwald: 3rd Degree," *Los Angeles Citybeat*, September 30, 2004.

7. Lorie Conway, "Iraq War Documentaries Fill a Press Vacuum," *Nieman Report*, 59, no. 1 (2005): 107, http://www.nieman.harvard.edu/.

8. Rus Thompson, "Profile: Taking Aim at the Establishment," 56 (Fall 2004): 3, http://www.moviemaker.com/issues/56/greenwald.html.

9. Booth, "Docu-Trauma."

10. Joanne Morreale, *A New Beginning: A Textual Frame Analysis of the Political Campaign Film* (Albany: State University of New York Press, 1991); Joanne Morreale, *The Presidential Campaign Film: A Critical History* (Westport, Conn.: Praeger, 1993); J. Cherie Strachan and Kathleen E. Kendall, "Political Candidates' Convention Films: Finding the Perfect Image—An Overview of Political Image Making,'" in *Defining Visual Rhetorics,* ed. Charles Hill and Marguerite Helmers (Mahwah, N.J.: Lawrence Erlbaum, 2004).

home, it's Lefties 6, Righties 0."[3] The left wing of
tary movement was epitomized by works such as
hich assaults the Bush presidency from the 2000
asion and occupation of Iraq; *Bush's Brain* (2004),
ve's political career and his influence on the Bush
and *Unprecedented*, which investigates the vagaries of
ing on the disenfranchisement of African Americans.
hers, *Outfoxed* sought to engage in an impassioned
othing less than the future of a deeply divided nation
ty-first century.

y 2004 is being called the 'Year of the Documentary,'"
ues, "one need only look back at the record of distorted
overage by the corporate press in the run-up to the Iraq
of independent and revelatory documentaries filled a
liction of duty on the part of the corporate media."[4] At
ecifically credited "the influence of the Fox News Chan-
Murdoch's vast media empire," with providing inspira-
utfoxed but for a number of other works as well: "Several
makers, alarmed at the increasingly right wing slant of
coverage, have tried to counter that slant by telling 'the
in movies."[5]

s aim at the central role played by the media—specifically the
el (FNC)—in "manufacturing consent" for the state of affairs
ther films.[6] It also examines concentration of ownership in the
ommunications industry. The film was adopted as an anthem
ds who joined a growing movement to reshape national media
ew millennium. The media reform movement was marked by
nted display of public dissatisfaction with mainstream media
and an increasing concern over consolidation in an industry
eferred to simply as Big Media.[7] In 2003, for example, 750,000
rote to the Federal Communications Commission (FCC) urging
relax media ownership rules.[8]

s grassroots origins and guerilla tactics, it might seem strange that
ould begin and end with enthusiastic invocations of popular Hol-
ovies. In fact, however, the Hollywood bookends in the film are
propriate. The first, a reference to *The Godfather, Part 2* (1974), sets
for the problem to be examined in the film: a highly concentrated
ications industry in which a handful of major media companies func-
families in an organized crime syndicate while government regulators
like cops on the take. The second, a reference to *Network* (1976), sug-

11. Strachan and Kendall, "Political Candidates' Convention Films," 136.

12. Booth, "Docu-Trauma."

13. Christian Christensen, "The Politics of a Political Film," *Screen Education* 37 (2005): 20.

14. See, for example, Susan Mackey-Kallis, "Spectator Desire and Narrative Closure: The Reagan 18-Minute Political Film," *Southern Communication Journal* 56 (1991): 308–14; John Fiske, *Media Matters: Race and Gender in U.S. Politics* (Minneapolis: University of Minnesota Press, 1996); and Douglas Kellner, *Media Culture* (New York: Routledge, 1995).

15. James E. Combs and Sara T. Combs, *Film Propaganda and American Politics: An Analysis and Filmography* (New York: Garland, 1994), 154.

16. Booth, "Docu-Trauma."

17. Ibid.

18. Appleford, "Robert Greenwald."

19. Booth, "Docu-Trauma."

20. Appleford, "Robert Greenwald."

21. Combs and Combs, *Film Propaganda*, 160.

22. Ibid., 155.

23. Booth, "Docu-Trauma."

24. Ibid.

25. Conway, "Iraq War Documentaries."

26. Ibid.

27. Conway, "Iraq War Documentaries," 107–8.

28. Booth, "Docu-Trauma."

29. *New York Daily News*, August 20, 2004, http://www.nydailynews.com/entertainment/movies/moviereviews.

30. "*Uncovered: The War on Iraq*: A Movie Review by the Filmiliar Cineaste," February 10, 2005, http://variegate.com/.

31. Greg Bellavia, "Uncovered: The War on Iraq," November 17, 2004, *Film Threat*, http://www.filmthreat.com/.

32. Jonathan Trout, "Uncovered: The War on Iraq," October 25, 2004, http://www.bbc.uk.films/2004/10/22.

33. "*Uncovered: The War on Iraq*," February 10, 2005.

34. Bellavia, "Uncovered."

35. In his November 3, 2003, interview with *BuzzFlash*, Greenwald notes, "My favorite section of the film is when you see the Bushies try to switch the argument from weapons of mass destruction to programs that might develop WMDs. So now we went to war over a program?"

36. Bellavia, "Uncovered."

37. *"Uncovered: The War on Iraq,"* February 10, 2005.

38. Fiske, *Media Matters.*

39. Ibid.

40. Bellavia, "Uncovered."

41. Ibid.

"If you're keeping score at
the new political documer
Fahrenheit 9/11 (2004), v
"election" through the in
which examines Karl R
administration's policies:
the 2000 election, focus
Like these films and o
cinematic debate over
war. This year's cro
at the turn of the twer
"To understand wh
Lorenzo Nencioli arg
and negligent news o
war. This year's cro
void created by dere
least one reviewer s
nel, part of Rupert
tion not only for (
documentary film
televised politica
rest of the story'
Outfoxed take
Fox News Chan
decried in the o
contemporary
among thousa
policy in the
an unprecede
performance
commonly
Americans
them not t
Given i
Outfoxed s
lywood n
utterly ap
the stage
commur
tion like
perforn

Outfoxing th

Outfoxed: Rupert Mu.
apologetically partisan
enwald in 2004. Like &
Uncovered: The War on
Civil Liberties (2004), wh
cheaply, compiled collaboı
couple of years," the *New Yo*
of *Outfoxed*, "Greenwald ha:
filmmaking, creating timely p
gets and selling them on DVD
organizations like MoveOn.org.
oeuvre, *Outfoxed* can be seen as ro
that came to a head around the 2c
renaissance in documentary filmm
media reform.

The renaissance in documentary
increase in the number of feature-le.
wide distribution and critical acclaim, ı
the election. By all accounts, there were
and DVD sales, and "just more buzz" fo
ever before.² Many of these documentariı
or balance, and some of the most successful
As Ann Hornaday of the *Washington Post* qu

gests a solution to the problem: media consumers must declare they are "mad as hell" and take back the system, working as media watchdogs, reformers, and producers. The body of *Outfoxed*, couched in between, is a detailed and devastating critique of Fox News, the self-proclaimed "Fair and Balanced" channel produced in "America's Newsroom" and distributed to 88 million households worldwide.

Outfoxed combines interviews with former Fox News employees, commentary by communications analysts and media reform activists, internal memos written by Fox News management, and clips from Fox News broadcasts, all meticulously edited to advance the film's sobering thesis: that the Fox News Channel is in effect the news arm of the Republican National Committee and the Bush administration; that it consistently blurs the line between news and commentary in order to advance its right-wing agenda; that its viewers are systematically misinformed about issues of vital importance; and that the success of Fox News has led other news outlets to imitate it, to the detriment of journalism as an institution and to the peril of democracy.

In this chapter, we take a closer look at *Outfoxed* and the context of its production, distribution, and reception. In the first section, "Who Owns the Media?," we attempt to provide an institutional context some found lacking in the film by conducting a political economic analysis of ownership and concentration in the contemporary communications industry, focusing on News Corporation. In the second section, "Who's Afraid of Fox?," we survey popular press reviews of *Outfoxed* and examine the film as a documentary text, with particular attention to the levels of media analysis it explores and the cinematic devices it employs to advance its argument. In the final section, we examine the so-called Fox effect and attempt to situate both Fox News and *Outfoxed* in the ongoing debate over the myth of the liberal media.

Who Owns the Media?

News Corp. belongs to the handful of core media and communications firms that produce and disseminate most of the world's mass-mediated informational and cultural output. The oligopolistic structure of the media industry is a reflection of the dual economic structure of contemporary capitalism. For Samuel Bowles and Richard Edwards, the dual economy in the United States comprises a core of about 1,200 of the largest non-financial corporations, with about 20 million mid- and small-sized businesses constituting the periphery. The dual economy is the result of the logic of capitalist competition that produces a general tendency toward concentration as capitalists seek to command markets through horizontal and vertical integration in an effort to minimize risk and maximize profits. The core firms in the dual economy account for roughly half of all corporate sales. They employ the most workers, take the highest profits, and generate most of the nation's net output, giving them substantial market power.[9] The core firms are also dominant at the level of industry sector, forming oligopolies often more engaged in cooperation than in the apparent competition stressed in the business press and economics textbooks. Daniel Fusfeld argues that with the rise of big business and oligopolies, "Planning replaces the market as the coordinating mechanism."[10]

Douglas Kellner links the rise of corporate capitalism to the emergence of consumer society with its homogenization and standardization of consumption and life. Thus, a drive down "Anystreet USA" will look the same all over, a "generic America in the form of filling stations selling the same brands of gas, fast-food chains selling the same junk food, video stores renting the same (quite small) selection of films and chain stores selling the same goods everywhere."[11] The centralization, standardization, and homogenization of production and consumption is supported by advertising, the primary goal of which, Tibor Scitovsky argues, is to generate artificial differentiation between products that are basically the same while keeping consumers uninformed about genuine alternatives.[12] The main function of advertising is to create and maintain brand loyalty, a form of monopoly that results in economic concentration.

Kellner condemns the advertising industry from a critical theory perspective on the grounds that it is "parasitical, duplicitous and serves no real social needs or purposes."[13] At the same time, much of the mass media are advertiser-supported and therefore deeply integrated into the capitalist production and consumption process. And like consumer goods, the output of the mass media is homogenized, standardized, and artificially differentiated. Herbert I. Schiller noted long ago that "[t]hough no single program, performer, commentator, or informational bit is necessarily identical to its competitors, *there is no significant qualitative difference*."[14] Despite the obvious and constant increase in the number of communications sources, he continued, "the entertainment, the news, the information, and the messages are selected from the same informational universe by 'gatekeepers' motivated by essentially inescapable commercial imperatives. Style and metaphor may vary, but not the essence."[15]

Ben Bagdikian began analyzing media concentration and its effects in his 1983 book *The Media Monopoly*. At that time, he concluded that fifty national and multinational media conglomerates controlled most of the major media in the United States.[16] In *The New Media Monopoly*, published in 2004, Bagdikian found that the number was down to a mere five.[17] In 2005, the top five media companies in the United States were General Electric (owner of NBC Universal), Time Warner, the Walt Disney Company, Viacom, and News Corporation. They are strikingly similar in terms of ownership and management structures, media properties, and political activities. News Corp., the parent company of Fox News Channel, is exemplary.

News Corp.

In 2005, News Corp. had revenues of $24 billion, with assets totaling $55 billion based on operations in the United States, continental Europe, Britain, Australia, Asia, and the Pacific Basin.[18] In 2006, it was ranked eighty-sixth on the Fortune 500.[19] In 2004, Rupert Murdoch, News Corp.'s CEO and chair (number 27 on the 2004 Forbes 400 list, worth $6.9 billion), controlled 30 percent of the company's stock, and John C. Malone (number 142 at $1.7 billion), CEO of Liberty Media, controlled 19 percent. Liberty's other holdings included stakes in QVC, InterActive, Starz, Motorola, Sprint, and Time Warner.[20] Institutional shareholders included Fidelity Management and Research (6.6 percent) and Gabelli Asset Management (less than 5 percent).[21] The AE Harris Trust controlled another 29 percent of News Corp. voting stock. Since Murdoch could appoint directors to the trust's managing board, he had formal power to influence its votes (a fact Murdoch disclaimed in company filings).[22] Murdoch had been grooming his eldest son, Lachlan, to eventually take over the company when tensions between them over management issues led Lachlan to resign at the end of July 2005.[23] A daughter, Elisabeth, had left the company in 2000, leaving only youngest son James in the family business at the end of 2005. James served as the CEO of the London-based satellite company British Sky Broadcasting, of which News Corp. owned 34 percent. However, Lachlan remained on the board of the AE Harris Trust.

In 2004, News Corp. moved its corporate headquarters from Australia to the United States in order to increase trading liquidity and access to capital, but its 2005 board of directors retained an international presence, including the CEO of British Airways, a director of Rothschild Banking (UK), and board members of Ansell (rubber and plastic), Metcash Trading (food and consumer goods distribution), and RM Williams (bushwear), all of Australia. Additional corporate ties included Hewlett Packard, Six Flags, Ford, Intel, and Gateway. Academic ties included Colgate University and Georgetown professor of law Viet Dihn, who served as assistant attorney general for legal policy at the Department of Justice from 2001 to 2003.[24] Stanley S. Shuman, a News Corp. director since 1982, was also a managing director of Allen and Company, an investment banking firm that believes "there's no business like financing show business."[25] The investment bank has been involved in the financial dealings of some of the biggest media and technology companies, often facilitating mergers. It is run by Herbert A. Allen (number 321 on the 2004 Forbes 400 at $2 billion), who holds an annual retreat in Sun Valley,

Idaho, for media moguls and other economic and political elites. Attendees in 2004 included Michael Eisner, Richard Parsons, Bill Gates (number 1 on the 2004 Forbes 400 with $51 billion), Warren Buffett (number 2 with $40 billion), and Rupert Murdoch, who welcomed newcomer California governor Arnold Schwarzenegger. Sites such as this allow for formal business dealings as well as for the building of consensus regarding the primary mutual concerns of Big Media and big business.

News Corp. is a diversified media conglomerate divided for management purposes into eight segments: filmed entertainment (Twentieth Century Fox, Fox 2000, Fox Searchlight, Fox Animation, and 20 percent of New Regency Films); television (Fox Broadcasting Network, with 196 affiliates; thirty-five owned-and-operated television stations, including nine duopolies and twenty-five Fox affiliates; and television program production, distribution, and syndication in the United States and Asia); cable network programming (Fox News Channel, Fox Sports Net, FX, and international channels in Europe, Latin America, the Caribbean, and Asia); direct broadcast satellite (Sky Italia, BSkyB, and DIRECTV); inserts and magazines (free-standing inserts, in-store promotions, and the *Weekly Standard*); newspapers (the *Times*, the *Sunday Times*, the *Sun*, and *News of the World*, accounting for a third of all national newspapers sold in the United Kingdom; 110 daily, Sunday, weekly, and tri-weekly newspapers for the largest total circulation in Australia; and the *New York Post* in the United States); book publishing (HarperCollins, one of the world's largest English-language book publishers in fiction and nonfiction, including religious books); and other (pay-cable and broadcast television and radio stations, along with outdoor advertising, mostly in eastern Europe). News Corp. also owned 41 percent of Gemstar–TV Guide in 2005 and had stakes in Sky Brasil, Sky Mexico, and the National Geographic Channel.[26]

The range of policy issues facing News Corp. is as broad and varied as its lines of business, from station ownership renewals, ownership limits, cinema and television screen quotas, taxes, and foreign equity limits to the protection of copyrights, trademarks, and licenses. The company has been actively involved in protecting and promoting those interests. News Corp.'s lobbying expenditures peaked at almost $3.9 million in 2003, when Congress was considering cross-ownership limits and station ownership caps. Total lobbying expenditures from January 1998 to June 2004 were nearly $16 million. Despite the conservative reputation of Murdoch and such news outlets as the *London Times*, the *New York Post*, and the Fox News Channel, News Corp.'s campaign contributions between January 1998 and September 2004 overwhelmingly favored Democrats, with $2,675,000 (81 percent) going to Democrats and $622,000 (19 percent) to Republicans. The national Democratic Party committees were the top recipients, then the Republican committees, followed by John Kerry, Hillary Rodham Clinton, and Charles Schumer (D-N.Y.).[27] A breakdown of giving by News Corp. personnel explains part of this pattern, with most inclined to give to Democrats, especially president and chief operating officer Peter Chernin. However, News Corp. gifts attributed directly to Murdoch show overwhelming pro-Republican inclinations.[28] Murdoch's promotion of Roger Ailes, former media adviser to three Republican presidents, from chair and CEO of Fox News to chairman of Fox Television Stations in 2005, will give him more conservative company in the executive suite.[29] Nevertheless, Murdoch's participation in the political system is entirely pragmatic in terms of what is good for the bottom line. For example, he switched loyalties from Margaret Thatcher, who helped him with legislation allowing ownership of both the daily *Times* and the *Sunday Times*, to Tony Blair when Conservatives began proposing limits on media ownership in Britain. Similarly, he lunched with President Jimmy Carter in 1980 to gain an Export-Import Bank loan of $290 million U.S. tax-dollars for his foreign airline. But it was his deep affection for Ronald Reagan, who led the charge to deregulate the media, including eliminating the Fairness Doctrine, that led to the rampant blurring of the line between legitimate journalism and conservative politics and ideology in Murdoch's news outlets.

The Fox News Channel

News Corp. launched the Fox News Channel in October 1996. It was created as a "specific alternative to what its founders perceived as a liberal bias in American media" and "dedicated to presenting news in what it believes to be an unbiased fashion, eschewing ideological or political affiliation and allowing the viewer to reach his or her own conclusion about the news."[30] Murdoch tapped Ailes for the project, signaling that the effort to balance the "liberal media" would be a conservative, pro-Republican operation. Ailes had worked for Richard Nixon, Ronald Reagan, and George H. W. Bush and had helped come up with the devious Willie Horton commercials in Bush's campaign against Michael Dukakis in 1988. Ailes had also briefly produced Rush Limbaugh's television show. He brought the mentality of both attack politics and right-wing radio to Fox. Charlie Reina, a producer who worked at FNC for six years, wrote that, editorially, the newsroom was "under constant control and vigilance of management." The staff was made up of inexperienced and nonunion employees who had an "undue motivation to please the Big Boss [Ailes]."[31] Under Ailes, FNC evolved into what Seth Ackerman described as "a central hub of the conservative movement's well-oiled machine" that includes the GOP organization and its satellite think tanks and advocacy groups, the *Washington Times*, and the editorial page of the *Wall Street Journal*.[32] Along with direct mail—the original medium of choice for conservatives since the 1960s—the *American Spectator*, News Corp.'s own *Weekly Standard*, and now blogs and podcasts, there exists "a highly effective right-wing echo chamber where GOP-friendly news stories can be promoted, repeated and amplified."[33]

Ailes brought in an abundance of managers, producers, and journalists with strong conservative backgrounds to work at FNC. They, in turn, bring in the pundits or special report panelists that tend to lean heavily and obviously toward the Right. For example, a Fairness and Accuracy in Reporting (FAIR) study of the show *Special Report with Brit Hume* conducted between January and May 2001 found that of fifty-six partisan guests on the show, fifty were Republicans and six were Democrats—a greater than eight to one imbalance.[34] At the same time, Ackerman noted that "Fox's crew of 'liberal' pundits seems almost calculated to be either ineffective left-of-center advocates or conciliatory moderates."[35] Furthermore, its conservative pundits get extra time through various weekend specials. For example, Oliver North, after being interviewed by Neil Cavuto on war dead in Iraq (August 4, 2005), received a plug for "War Stories with Oliver North," a FNC Saturday night special. In the interview, both North and Cavuto insisted on referring to what most media call the Iraqi "insurgents" as "terrorists."[36]

At the time it was launched, FNC's main competitors were CNN, created by Ted Turner in 1980 and owned by Time Warner, and MSNBC, a joint venture of GE and Microsoft. Start-up costs were an estimated $475 million, most of it for distribution. News Corp. used its very deep pockets to reverse the normal dealings between program suppliers and cable operators by paying the operators ten dollars per subscriber per year for a specific, limited period. Additional costs were incurred in establishing the infrastructure for an international news operation and in buying video news images from Reuters, World Television News, and AP-TV.[37] It also enlisted the help of Sky-TV, News Corp.'s pan-European satellite service, and the company's newspapers from around the world. Between 1997 and 2003, Fox News spent $61 million and thousands of hours in promoting and advertising its brand through a global marketing campaign.[38] News Corp.'s investment in FNC quickly paid off, and it became profitable in the fourth quarter of 2000, one year ahead of schedule.

In December 2001, FNC's ratings beat CNN in prime time, even though CNN reached 22 million more households. By August 2004, FNC's coverage of the GOP convention (when the broadcast networks were not covering it live) attracted an estimated 3.9 million viewers, while CNN had 1.3 million and MSNBC had 845,000.[39] During the week ending September 4, 2005, FNC's ratings covering Hurricane Katrina beat not only the other cable news networks but also all advertiser-supported cable in both daytime and prime time, averaging 4.06 million viewers during prime time.[40] The last time this occurred had been April 2003, the first month of the Iraq war. By 2005, the channel was available in approximately 88 million households. It also ran a Web site (FoxNews.com) and Fox News Radio Network, a national network with hourly updates and long-form programs to distribute to local radio stations. In 2004, Fox radio signed a five-year exclusive deal with one hundred of Clear Channel's 1,200-plus radio stations. In September 2005, Fox News Radio was reaching 10 million listeners per week. The radio programs included current and former FNC news personalities, thus further amplifying the Fox effect.

The Small Media: Producing and Distributing Outfoxed

Robert Greenwald Productions (RGP), based in Culver City, California, operates in the shadows of the Big Media's filmed entertainment studios. Six major film production-distribution companies control the U.S. and world box offices and home video markets, the Big Five plus Sony. In 2004, their box office gross was $7.58 billion, while independents generated $1.05 billion (inflated by a hefty $300 million for *The Passion of the Christ*), giving the majors 88 percent of the market.[41] The average budget for a Hollywood film topped $60 million in 2005, with average marketing costs adding another $30 million. Because of such exorbitant production and distribution costs, as well as the tight control of the market by the majors, films that challenge the U.S. political economic structure have a harder time in the market, exemplified by Disney's refusal to distribute *Fahrenheit 9/11*. These barriers have prompted political filmmakers to get their films out through self-financing, word-of-mouth, the DVD market, churches and universities, and a national network of independent theaters. This guerilla method of independent movie-making and distribution is epitomized in the case of *Outfoxed*.

The $300,000 budget for the production of *Outfoxed* came from contributions of $80,000 from both MoveOn and the Center for American Progress.[42] Costs were kept down by the collaborative production process typical of independent filmmaking, and much of the content was pilfered FNC footage. In January 2004, twelve DVD recorders were set up to record FNC twenty-four hours a day, seven days a week for six months. After viewing the footage, Greenwald and a team of researchers came up with categories for dominant themes and techniques around which the film was eventually organized, along with the voice-overs and commentary. Volunteers from MoveOn matched content categories to the time of day and then coded. Greenwald hired five editors who normally get paid up to $1,000 a day but worked for $150 a day just for the chance to be a part of the project. The entire process, from when the DVD recorders started rolling until the film's premiere at the New School University in New York, took six months.[43]

The production of the film and its content was closely guarded out of fear that News Corp. would attempt to block it on the grounds of copyright infringement. It had already tried to suppress the distribution and sale of Al Franken's book *Lies and the Lying Liars Who Tell Them: A Fair and Balanced Look at the Right* a year earlier for infringing on its trademarked phrase "fair and balanced."[44] Although the case was dismissed as being without merit, Greenwald retained the services of a number of intellectual property lawyers ready to argue that the film fell within the Fair Use doctrine that allows for the use of excerpts of copyrighted works in the course of commentary and criticism. News Corp. probably could have killed the project by running up legal fees and keeping it in litigation indefinitely, but the publicity would have been bad, and there was the possibility of an unfavorable ruling. This would have been a major victory for advocates of greater access to intellectual property. With a broader and clearer definition of this type of fair use, the court could have taken away a powerful weapon in the arsenal of Big Media in protecting their property—the ambiguity that leads critics and commentators to self-censor out of fear of litigation or to give in to actual censorship out of the threat of litigation.[45] Rather than censoring through copyright, both Eric Clapton and Don Henley used their copyrights to support the project by giving permission to use music ("Layla" and "Dirty Laundry") at no charge. At the same time, a number of news organizations refused to license their clips, including CBS, which didn't want to be associated with criticism of Murdoch. WGBH, the Boston PBS station, refused to allow Greenwald to use excerpts from the show *Frontline* out of fear of looking "political."[46] In the case of PBS, we see the direct effects of the Right's attack media. Greenwald later released the interviews from *Outfoxed* and *Uncovered* under the Creative Commons Sampling Plus license, which will allow other filmmakers to use the material in new and creative ways.[47]

Like News Corp.'s launch of FNC, where the distribution model was turned on its head, RGP also turned the traditional model upside down by taking the film straight to DVD, as it had done with Greenwald's previous effort, *Uncovered*, before taking it to theaters. *Uncovered*, co-produced with Cinema Libre, was sold on DVD through the Web sites of various Left and liberal organizations including MoveOn, the Center for American Progress, *The Nation* magazine, Alternet.com, and BuzzFlash.com. The film was distributed further through an "upstairs-downstairs" distribution model with screenings in Washington, D.C., and an invitation to every member of Congress to attend. MoveOn mobilized its 2.2 million members, who held 2,600 house parties where the film was watched and discussed. The grassroots success allowed Cinema Libre to take *Uncovered* to the Cannes Film Festival, where DVD rights were sold for global distribution. The success of *Outfoxed* on DVD led Cinema Libre to pick it up for theatrical distribution in the United States. Here again, there are barriers to independents, as 80 percent of theaters are owned by major chains tied to the major distributors. Cinema Libre starts with independent theater chains, of which Landmark is the only national one; if successful there, Cinema Libre will try to interest the big corporate chains, where they may be rejected for political reasons, as Fridley Theaters, a Midwest movie chain, did with *Fahrenheit 9/11*. Philippe Diaz, founder of Cinema Libre, reported that *Outfoxed*'s theatrical run was a success, grossing $500,000, though after the costs of advertising and prints, the company broke even.[48] Cinema Libre generally loses money on theatrical distribution but makes up for it in DVD sales. It is a for-profit operation but is organized non-hierarchically with everyone getting paid the same.[49] The company's mission is to produce and distribute films that challenge social, political, and economic conditions in ways that the Big Media do not.

Who's Afraid of Fox?

When *Outfoxed* premiered in July 2004, political cartoonist Gary Trudeau devoted a week's worth of his widely syndicated comic strip, *Doonesbury*, to the film. Trudeau envisioned one of *Doonesbury*'s popular original characters, an amiable radio host named Mark, conducting a telephone interview about *Outfoxed* with Rupert Murdoch himself. "Mr. M., the film shows in detail how Fox News has effectively become the broadcast arm of the Bush White House," Mark begins. "Well, that's right Mark," Murdoch replies. "No administration has ever had its own network before. We saw a need." When Mark asks where he got this "amazing" idea, Murdoch explains, "Well, I own media in China . . ." Eventually, Murdoch grows leery of his liberal host and weary of the unproductive interview and hangs up. In the last strip, Mark invites listeners to phone in. The first caller is Fox News commentator Bill O'Reilly, who treats Mark much as *Outfoxed* suggests he does many of his own guests on Fox News: "*Shut up!* Okay? Just *shut up!*"

Critical Reception

The Fox News Channel was reported to have "reacted angrily" to *Outfoxed*, protesting the film's allegations of bias and nominally challenging its unauthorized use of clips from copyrighted broadcasts. For the most part, however, Fox treated the film as beneath its contempt. In a statement distributed at a press conference for *Outfoxed*, for example, Fox labeled the "low-level former employees" interviewed in the film as "hardly worth addressing."[50] The infamously combative O'Reilly—who, according to *Variety*, "seems to require little outside help in his demonization" in the film—refused Greenwald's invitations to engage in debates in a neutral setting.[51] Asked whether the director of *Outfoxed* would be invited to appear on *The O'Reilly Factor*, a representative reportedly replied, "Why would we book a has-been like Robert Greenwald on cable's highest-rated program? We wish him well on his road to extinction."[52]

Murdoch's *New York Post* adopted a recognizably Fox News approach in its review of the film, first declaring its own objectivity and then delivering a predictably partisan and vitriolic review: "*Outfoxed* may have the man who signs this critic's paychecks in its crosshairs," wrote Megan Lehmann, "but my job requires that I be fair." Lehmann goes on to refer to the film as a "furious finger-pointer's doc [that] is so one-sided, it undermines its own integrity." She dismisses the handful of former Fox employees whose identities are disguised in the film as "too yellow to identify themselves on camera." Finally, she argues, "Surely anyone watching the Fox News Channel can draw his own conclusions"[53]—a reference to the network's motto "We report, you decide" and a claim directly disputed by evidence cited in *Outfoxed* that Fox News viewers are disproportionately misinformed. (*Doonesbury*'s radio host couldn't resist this one: "Doesn't it bother you that you're actually making your viewers stupider?")

A hostile reaction from the Fox camp was, of course, to be expected. Most popular press reviews of *Outfoxed* were positive. *Variety* wrote succinctly that "Greenwald's film provides stimulating evidence of how thoroughly news can be skewed, political agendas served, and a climate of fear created by a news net selling itself as an objective information service but in reality offering little distinction between news and commentary."[54] The *Washington Post* found the film "often grave but sometimes hilarious" and generally "convincing."[55] A. O. Scott of the *New York Times* described his experience of viewing the film in one of its less conventional screening venues and concluded, "[Y]ou can catch a glimpse of the truth, even in a bar in Brooklyn on a muggy Sunday evening in July."[56]

It is nonetheless instructive to note the extent to which generally positive reviews of *Outfoxed* were consistent in their criticisms of the film. Most reviewers thought a variety of things were good about *Outfoxed* but agreed on what was bad about it. Common criticisms included obviously low production values, a tendency to preach to the choir, and an overall lack of fairness and balance. Taken together, these criticisms raise what O'Reilly might call "talking points" for a discussion of the film. We will address them briefly here and more fully in the textual analysis of *Outfoxed* that follows.

Quick and dirty. A number of reviewers pointed out that *Outfoxed* shows conspicuous signs of cost-cutting and haste-making, although few acknowledged the film's paltry production budget. The *New York Post* noted that *Outfoxed* "is a rush job—and it shows."[57] *Variety* remarked that "the film clearly came together in haste, reflected to an extent in its pedestrian structure."[58] The *San Francisco Chronicle* elaborated: "*Outfoxed* is a documentary obviously made on the cheap. . . . [I]t seems as if it were recorded on a camcorder and narrated by a guy sitting in his kitchen with a microphone. . . . Think of it as the cinematic equivalent of a pamphlet printed in somebody's basement." The *Chronicle* review does allow that the grunge look of *Outfoxed* "doesn't negate its effectiveness."[59] In fact, we will argue that *Outfoxed* wears its low production values like a badge of honor and equates Fox's flashy graphics and bombastic music with exploitative sensationalism and sanctimonious patriotism.

Preaching to the choir. Many critics complained that *Outfoxed* is (only) "enjoyable if you're a liberal and/or hate Fox News."[60] Writing about both *Outfoxed* and *Fahrenheit 9/11*, for example, a writer for the *Lancet* remarked, "I'm convinced there is truth in both these films, but their techniques are so heavy-handed as to ensure they preach only to the converted."[61] *Variety* predicted that *Outfoxed* "appears unlikely to reach beyond a liberal audience with an already vehement aversion to Fox News' partisan coverage."[62] A number of on-line reviewers agreed: "One obvious criticism to be made of agit-prop films such as this one is that—like Fox News itself—it serves as an echo chamber to an already entrenched point of view."[63] Some went so far as to suggest that the film's staunch stance made it not worth making: "*Outfoxed* simply tells everyone what they already know about Fox News."[64]

Unfair and unbalanced. Perhaps the loudest and most recurrent criticism of *Outfoxed* is that it has its own bias. A quick scan of headlines serves to illustrate this point: "Fair and Balanced, This Doc's Not," "Telling It Like It Isn't," "Crooked Angles in Sly Fox Exposé," and "Tilting at the Right, Leaning to the Left: Robert Greenwald's *Outfoxed* Has Its Own Slant on Bias."[65] Many reviewers commented on the film's "failure" to interview current Fox employees or to balance left-wing media reform activists with right-wing media analysts. The point that *Outfoxed* is partisan would seem to be rendered moot by the fact that (unlike Fox News) it announces itself as such. But the number of critics who faulted the film for not presenting "both sides of the story" merits further consideration. We will address this in a discussion of the "Fox effect" and the myth of the liberal media.

"The Problem We Face"

Outfoxed opens with an iconic image, the famous portrait of Al Pacino as Michael Corleone, slumped in the chair of the don, his eyes shrouded in shadows. The camera zooms in slightly on the still image, and over *Godfather*-like music we hear the voice of communications scholar and media activist Robert McChesney, who appears on-screen in a quick dissolve. A title identifies McChesney as "Founder of the Free Press/Author of *The Problem of the Media*," but he speaks with the familiarity and fondness of a regular movie buff:

> In the great 1972 film *Godfather 2*, there's a scene about halfway through where Hyman Roth and Michael Corleone and all the American gangsters are gathered in a patio in Havana. And it's Hyman Roth's sixty-seventh birthday and he's giving a slice of cake to each gangster: Louis from Chicago, you run the Copacabana; Frankie, you get the prostitutes. He's dividing the island among all the American gangsters, and appropriately enough, the birthday cake has an outline of Cuba on it. He's giving them a slice of Cuba. And while Hyman Roth is doing this, he says, "Isn't it great to be in a country that respects private enterprise?"

As McChesney speaks, we see another still image from *The Godfather*, this one from the Havana patio scene he so vividly describes. The camera pans down the figure of the gangster to reveal the knife in his hand and the cake he is poised to cut. The outline of Cuba isn't actually visible, but it doesn't matter. It is McChesney's animated recollection of the scene that brings the still images to life and that gives the metaphor he draws such resonance: "And that's how media policies have been done in the United States for the past fifty years, and it's increasing in the last twenty years. Extraordinarily powerful lobbyists duke it out behind closed doors for the biggest slice of the cake. The public knows nothing about it; it doesn't participate. And that's the problem we face."

The pre-title sequence in *Outfoxed* is less than one minute long. It merits detailed description here because it introduces a number of rhetorical strategies that will be used in the body of the film: (1) Likeable and knowledgeable if largely unfamiliar "talking heads" will comment on familiar sounds and images in a critical context, lending them new meaning. Viewers of *Outfoxed* are unlikely to watch Fox News again without recognizing at least some of the tactics the film claims the channel employs to advance its position. (2) Much will be done with little. The two still images from *The Godfather* occupy about ten seconds of screen time, and the accompanying music may or may not be lifted from the sound track, but a shared memory of the film will undoubtedly be evoked in many viewers. (3) Copyright concerns will be flouted. Most snippets of copyrighted sounds and images in *Outfoxed* are probably protected under Fair Use, but "If not, so what?" the film seems to say. (4) A problem is identified and posed as something "we," as citizens of a democracy, must face. Ominous (Fox-like) music accompanies the title credit, signaling the critical nature of the problem: *Outfoxed: Rupert Murdoch's War on Journalism.*

Levels of Analysis

The full title of the film invokes Rupert Murdoch as a private individual, the Fox News Channel as a media organization, and journalism as a social institution. From the beginning, then, *Outfoxed* signals its intent to operate at three distinct levels of media analysis, usefully distinguished by Denis McQuail in his influential text *Mass Communication Theory.*[66] Although *Outfoxed* conducts its investigation of Fox News at all three levels of analysis—and indeed, often moves fluidly between them—it strongly emphasizes the organizational over the individual and institutional.

Individual. According to McQuail, the individual level of analysis focuses on the human agent who carries out media work and is subject to certain requirements of the organization but also has some freedom to define his or her place within it. This level of analysis is sometimes regarded as the least sophisticated—the most likely to lead media analysts to rely on conspiracy theories, resort to ad hominem attacks, or fall into intentional fallacies. *Outfoxed* does not linger here. Despite his prominent placement in the title, for example, Rupert Murdoch as an individual is only occasionally invoked in the body of the film. There are animated graphics listing his vast holdings, snippets of news footage in which he appears as a company figurehead, and testimony from former Fox employees who recall that he "absolutely adored Ronald Reagan" or simply "couldn't stand the Kennedys." One media analyst in the film describes Murdoch as "foremost a politician," and another claims he "has contempt for journalism." But both speak of Murdoch primarily as a corporate capitalist who is more interested in power and profits than prestige, not as an evil individual intent on dismantling the fourth estate.

If anyone in *Outfoxed* is vilified as an individual, it is probably Bill O'Reilly, who holds the distinction of having his signature show described by Peter Hart of FAIR as "the perfect example of everything that's wrong with Fox News Channel." A lengthy scene in *Outfoxed* devoted to a single episode of *The O'Reilly Factor* is quite literally the centerpiece of the film; it is positioned precisely at the middle and occupies a full seven minutes of screen time. It is not surprising, then, that nearly every popular press review of *Outfoxed* comments on it. Scott's description in the *New York Times* is particularly salient: "Watching Bill O'Reilly's belligerent, boorish 'interview' with Jeremy Glick, whose father died in the attack on the World Trade Center and who came to oppose the administration's military response to 9/11, is enough to make you wish that the ghost of Joseph Welch would enter the studio and inquire, at long last, after Mr. O'Reilly's sense of decency."[67] Ty Burr of the *Boston Globe* added, "You don't have to work overtime to make the host of *The O'Reilly Factor* look like a jackbooted media thug."[68] Finally, though, Hart's description of O'Reilly as *exemplary* of Fox News rather than exceptional is more compelling. Even O'Reilly's propensity to cut guests off by telling them to "Shut up!" is contextualized in the film as pretty much in keeping with custom at Fox News. This leads us to the next level of analysis.

Organizational. The organizational level of analysis focuses on specific media organizations, emphasizing structural factors such as mode of production and chain of command. According to McQuail, researchers operating at this level of analysis ask questions such as "What degree of freedom does a media organization possess in relation to the wider society and how much freedom is possible within the organization? How do media-organizational routines and procedures for selecting and processing content influence what is produced?"[69] Or, in the case of *Outfoxed*, how is news defined, generated, produced, packaged, and even fabricated at the Fox News Channel?

The former Fox employees who tell their stories in *Outfoxed* contribute most to this level of analysis, which is the central focus of the film. Ten go on camera and on record; another three choose to remain anonymous. They are identified as writers, reporters, producers, anchors, regular contributors, and freelancers, representing a variety of areas of expertise and levels of influence. Although they speak as individual professionals, their function in the film is often to convey how little freedom they had to define themselves as such within the Fox News organization. Some of them may well be "disgruntled," as the *New York Post* alleged, but their anecdotes are buttressed by damning internal memos from Fox News management and illustrated with convincing clips from Fox News broadcasts. The testimony of former employees is crucial to a number of strategies the film uses to mount its argument about the Fox News Channel, one that is taken to an institutional level primarily by the participation of media analysts and activists.

Institutional. The institutional level of analysis concerns itself with the larger context in which media workers and organizations function, including the unwritten social and cultural guidelines they follow and the implicit ideological assumptions they make.[70] Researchers working at this level of analysis examine media organizations in relation to a wider society, assuming that both operate within a terrain that is formally or informally regulated or governed by normative expectations. "Such matters as the essential freedoms of publication and the ethical guidelines for many activities are laid down by the 'rules of the game' of the particular society."[71]

More than twenty media analysts and activists contribute to the institutional level of analysis in *Outfoxed*. They represent publications such as *The Nation*, the *Progressive*, *EXTRA!*, and *Mother Jones*, as well as a number of grassroots organizations active in the media reform movement including Free Press, Common Cause, Media Matters for America, Center for Digital Democracy, Center for Media Education, Center for Public Integrity, and FAIR. Journalist emeritus Walter Cronkite, Air America host Al Franken, and Vermont representative Bernie Sanders also put in appearances. These individuals raise institutional issues including journalistic ethics, social responsibility, and the vital role of media in a democracy. Their function in *Outfoxed* is to point to the far-reaching and often frightening ramifications of many all-too-familiar Fox News practices, especially in the context of the highly concentrated communications industry.

Documentary Devices

Back story. One way *Outfoxed* utilizes the testimony of former Fox employees is in the service of a device we call "back story." The film encourages viewers to deconstruct familiar Fox News stories by juxtaposing them with the narration of former employees who explain "what really happened" or "what was originally intended." In one scene, for example, a former West Coast anchor named John Du Pre tells of being assigned to "cover" the birthday of Ronald Reagan ("something akin to a holy day for Fox News Channel viewers") by reporting live from the Reagan Presidential Library in Simi Valley, where Fox management apparently assumed the Reagan faithful would gather. According to Du Pre, only a handful of individuals and a class of fourth graders showed up, "and I was frankly at a bit of a loss as to what to say or do to make it seem like there was a big celebration." We then see the broadcast as it aired: a series of medium and close shots show a child blowing up a balloon, a woman signing a banner, a cake with Reagan's image fashioned in the frosting, and a small group of children singing. Du Pre sounds convincing as he intones, "Since dawn they've been streaming in from all over the country and even parts of Canada and Mexico . . ." Casual viewers may not have noticed anything amiss, but Fox management did. Du Pre says that Senior Vice President John Moody called in, furious. "Apparently my live shots weren't celebratory enough," he explains. "I got in big trouble for that one. In fact, I was suspended."

Another back story is related by a former Fox employee who is represented on-screen by a microphone and identified as "Anonymous #3." The reporter tells of doing a feature story on immigration and naturalization. "I thought it was poignant to tell the stories of these people and all of the things that they had to go through to get citizenship," he says. As the reporter speaks, we see images that are indeed poignant: a diverse group of individuals smiling through tears, some wearing traditional clothing from other lands and carrying U.S. flags. "And the line I used in describing their efforts was 'folks seeking citizenship earned, not born.'" The reporter says that his managing editor reacted angrily to the story, exclaiming, "What have these people earned? They haven't earned a thing. They're just here for a free ride. They're just trying to take advantage of all our freebies." It is unclear whether the story actually aired as the reporter intended, landing him in trouble later (like Du Pre's live report), or if the piece was modified or censored by management before airing (more likely for a feature story). According to a transcript of *Outfoxed*, the images we see in this scene were actually taken from archival footage rather than a Fox News broadcast.[72]

In these cases, *Outfoxed* invites viewers to reexamine Fox News in light of privileged information provided by former employees. Both scenes encourage viewers to question the relationship between sound and image—to ask whether there is visible evidence to support the remarks of a reporter or, indeed, whether there is an ontological link between the image on-screen and the story at hand at all. In both cases, the former Fox employees invite skepticism on the part of critical viewers. Du Pre exposes his own on-air artifice and seems less offended by his assignment to treat Reagan's birthday as breaking news than by the fact that it proved difficult to do so under the circumstances. The testimony of "Anonymous #3" is compelling, but we don't see the reporter or the feature he produced. Finally, as the *Washington Post* commented on the claims of former Fox employees in *Outfoxed*: "Many of their allegations are hard to assess because they involve orders, or attitudes, by an unnamed 'they' at Rupert Murdoch's network."[73] A second device in the film attempts to make such allegations more tangible.

The memo. If there is a smoking gun in *Outfoxed*, it is undoubtedly the revelation of about a dozen leaked internal memos written by high-level Fox News managers and used to buttress the testimony of former "low-level" employees. A daily missive referred to simply as "The Memo" by insiders is introduced somewhat casually in the film by Av Westin, former vice president of ABC News: "I suspect your research has discovered the memoranda that were written by John Moody and by Roger [Ailes] in terms of setting the tone for the day," he ventures. "The message of the day is a very political device." We are then shown a series of reproductions of office memoranda. Each is read in decidedly sinister voice-over, and portions of some are highlighted or enlarged on-screen for emphasis. Each memo announces a topic for the day and makes clear just what the Fox News take on it should be.

"Let's spend a good deal of time on the battle over judicial nominations, which the President will address this morning," one reads. "Nominees who both sides admit are qualified are being held up because of their POSSIBLE, not demonstrated views on one issue—abortion. This should be a trademark issue for FNC today and in days to come." Another memo announces a meeting of the "so-called 9/11 commission" and instructs anchors, "Don't turn this into Watergate." One warns that a speech on the economy by John Kerry is "likely to move onto the topic of Iraq" and suggests that producers "see if other news at that time is more compelling." Another dictates official FNC language: "Let's refer to the US marines we see in the foreground as sharpshooters, not snipers, which carries a negative connotation."

The effect of these memos in terms of their influence on specific news broadcasts is not illustrated in this sequence. Rather, the memos are used to lend credibility to the claims of former employees such as Larry Johnson and John Du Pre about the chain of command at Fox News: "Every morning there was a detailed list of subjects to talk about and not talk about," according to Johnson. "There was nothing covert about the way the managing editors in New York or Washington operated," Du Pre adds. "They made it perfectly clear what they expected from us." The impact of The Memo sequence, placed early on, bleeds over into other scenes in the film. When a former Fox contributor remarks, "We were supposed to refer to suicide bombings as homicide bombings," we assume this was dictated in a memo. And when we see montages of different Fox News anchors using the exact same language, we suspect they were instructed to do so as well.

Rapid montage. The strategy of rapid montage involves identifying a seemingly innocuous word or phrase used routinely by Fox News commentators and editing short snippets of broadcasts together so that viewers of *Outfoxed* hear the phrase repeated with dizzying rapidity. It is seemingly self-incriminating because the montages are made up entirely of Fox News footage. The rapid editing emphasizes repetition and strongly suggests that the ideologically loaded use of key phrases is systematic—and thus organizational practice rather than individual choice. In some cases, the montage is commented upon by a media analyst, who makes the suggestion explicit.

One example of a rapid montage sequence is entitled "Some People Say." Peter Hart of FAIR explains that journalists occasionally use phrases like "some people say" or "officials say" to anonymously insert basic information into a story. "Fox does it a different way," Hart contends. "This is just sort of a clever way of inserting political opinion when you know it probably shouldn't be there." We are then presented with a series of news clips in which a variety of Fox anchors, reporters, and commentators use the phrase "Some people say," in some cases very clearly to introduce a conservative point of view: "Some people say [Alberto Gonzalez] would be a pretty good choice"; "Some people say [war protesters] might undermine what the U.S. troops are doing"; "Some people say John Kerry has some similarities to an earlier Massachusetts politician," and so on. In less than a minute and a half, more than twenty examples of Fox newscasters using the phrase flash before us. The last one is carefully chosen: "And some people say it's exploitative. What do you say to that?" Greenwald's point is made.

In another montage sequence, we are presented with a series of clips of Fox News interviewers cutting off their subjects—sometimes by literally demanding that their microphones be turned off, other times by simply shouting over them. A number of well-known Fox personalities, including Sean Hannity and Geraldo Rivera, are shown silencing a number of equally well-known guests, including Kerry campaign advisor Chad Clanton and comedian George Carlin. The scene culminates in a rapid montage of clips in which Bill O'Reilly says "Shut up!" nine times, immediately after he is shown denying such behavior. Like *The O'Reilly Factor* interview mentioned earlier, this scene was singled out by a number of reviewers for comment. For example, "Regardless of his political positions, anyone who bullies interview subjects by repeatedly bawling 'Shut up!' is an embarrassment to the trade."[74] But the sequence suggests, as Hart might have it, that O'Reilly the man is (merely) "the perfect example of everything that's wrong with Fox News."

Two montage sequences near the end of the film make the link between internal memos written by Fox management and the content of Fox News broadcasts more explicit—and both strongly suggest that managers take their cues from the White House. In the first, we see a snippet of a 2004 campaign speech in which Bush derisively paraphrases Kerry as saying "I actually did vote for the $87 billion before I voted against it." This is followed by a "Fox News Alert" featuring Dick Cheney saying almost the exact same thing. We are then given a memo from Moody alleging that "Kerry [is] starting to feel the heat for his flip-flop voting record." The memo is followed by a stunning series of Fox News clips in which reporters and commentators refer to Kerry as a "flip-flopper" nearly twenty times. One anchor even introduces a "new brand of summer footwear" over a graphic depicting Kerry's face and a pair of flip-flops with the caption "If the shoe fits."

A final montage sequence is devoted to the U.S. economy. Jeff Cohen, a former MSNBC/Fox News contributor and founder of FAIR, points out that the economy is always good or improving, according to Fox. "They select statistics that prove the economy's moving up and thank God for President Bush for doing it." We see clips of Bush proclaiming, "We're creating jobs," and Rupert

Murdoch declaring, "The economy is behaving like it's on steroids." A memo from Moody announces, "The President goes to Charlotte to talk about job training. Buoyed by the 300K job figure last week, he can boast his policies are working." Another rapid montage is composed of Fox News clips celebrating the supposed prosperity of the United States under Bush and warning that "the market is down on Kerry." One news anchor claims that "they're drinking the Maalox right out of the gallon bucket at the Kerry campaign."

Fox form. Mounting a critique of Fox News form appears simple enough at first in *Outfoxed*. Early in the film, there is a sequence entitled "Fox News Techniques" in which a number of media analysts call attention to the channel's use of "weird" banner wipes, "odd" animated graphics, and the ubiquitous waving U.S. flag. There are ample examples to illustrate these points through-out the film. "Graphics are always moving in the background," notes Hart. "They've sort of pioneered the use of the American flag as an icon of your news broadcast." Hart's use of the word "pioneered" here is telling, and the film's failure to note the zeal with which other news outlets adopted the flag as a logo in apparent imitation of FNC is a missed opportunity in the "Fox effect" segment.

In addition to the comments of media analysts, *Outfoxed* relies on the back stories of former Fox employees to deconstruct the channel's use of music and graphics. For example, a former Fox music supervisor recalls that he composed the ominous "Fox News Alert," a musical insignia often accompanied by a dramatic graphic, to convey a sense of urgency for important news stories, "specifically Columbine." The musician bemoans the fact that in the years since his departure from FNC, the Fox News Alert has regularly been "used for stories like Bennifer" (a reference to Fox's obsession with the romance between celebrities Ben Affleck and Jennifer Lopez and, by extension, an indictment of its conflation of information and entertainment). Here Greenwald gleefully supplies footage of Martha Stewart exiting a courthouse with her probation officer, urgently brought to our attention by the Fox News Alert. In this context, the music seems at best comical and at worst, in light of the tragedy that inspired it, obscene.

In an apparent reference to the John Kerry "flip-flop" graphic, an anony-mous former Fox employee submits, "So if you're the graphics department and you can put up a liberal flip-flopper as the chyron, hey, that's great, because the next time the graphics department has a discussion with management, manage-ment say, yeah, you guys have been doing a great job." The three anonymous former Fox employees in *Outfoxed* are represented on-screen by images of flamboyantly low-tech equipment: a badly smudged pushbutton telephone, a dusty audio recording console, and a large plug-in microphone. Here the film wears its own low production values like a badge of honor, contrasting them sharply with Fox's glitzy graphics and monumental music.

At the same time, however, *Outfoxed* works hard to be visually arresting and aurally compelling, sometimes resorting to the use of Fox-like techniques. At the beginning of the film, for example, there is a series of animated graphics in which Murdoch appears to boast of his vast holdings in the first person. A caricature of a dapper "Young Rupert Murdoch" hovers beside a list of acquisitions: "1954: I inherited my first newspaper. 1956: I bought my first magazine. 1958: I bought my first TV station," and so on. Each entry darts about the screen before finding its place. One announces, "1972: I bought my first politician." The charge is not elaborated on, and the innuendo is reminiscent of FNC's Kerry flip-flop. As on Fox News, graphics in *Outfoxed* are "always moving in the background," and titles are mostly red, white, and blue.

The "Fox Effect" and the Myth of the Liberal Media

Proving relationships between media ownership, texts, and audience effects is always problematic and contentious. Demonstrating the empirical effects of any single media outlet proves even more difficult. However, there is some evidence that Fox news is having a measurable effect both on news industry practices and on audience opinion. *Outfoxed* asks viewers to consider the "Foxification" of the news media as a whole—the proliferation of the Fox formula, including taking sides while denying it, blurring news and opinion, "tabloid sensationalism, zap-edits, in-your face graphics and sanctimonious displays of patriotism."[75] MSNBC, consistently ranking third among the cable news networks, soon began efforts to "out-Fox Fox" as its popularity grew.[76] In 1999, MSNBC hired a crew of conservative hosts for its daytime lineup, including Oliver North, John McLaughlin, and Laura Ingraham. In 2003, it hired controversial radio host Michael Savage, whose co-host was former Republican congressman Joseph Scarborough. MSNBC said it brought both in before the war in Iraq to bring better political balance to its programming.[77] At the same time, Phil Donahue's show was the top-rated program on MSNBC but was cancelled in 2003 for political reasons. According to an internal memo, executives feared that *Donahue* might make the NBC network look unpatriotic at the same time competitors were waving the flag at every opportunity.[78] Jeff Cohen, a founder of FAIR and on-air commentator at MSNBC, said that management ordered producers to include two prowar guests for every antiwar guest appearing on the channel.[79] Additionally, MSNBC added patriotic flourishes of its own: a regularly appearing American flag, a portrait of Bush, and a studio wall of snapshots of "America's Bravest" soldiers serving in Iraq. In 2005, MSNBC added a nightly talk show with

Tucker Carlson, host of PBS's weekly program *Tucker Carlson Unfiltered* and former conservative host of *Crossfire*.

In 2005, CNN's new president Joe Klein decided to address the Fox effect by projecting a return to hard news from shout-television, beginning with the cancellation of *Crossfire*, which had been sponsored by GE for many years. This came shortly after Jon Stewart of the *Daily Show* visited *Crossfire*, identifying himself as "someone who watches your show and cannot take it anymore." Dismissing allegations that he had been soft on Kerry in the weeks coming up to the election, Stewart reminded conservative host Tucker Carlson that there should be a difference between Comedy Central and CNN: "You have a responsibility to the public discourse, and you fail miserably."[80] But the look and tone Klein has sought since is quite Foxified; for example, it has more "emotionally gripping, character-driven narratives pegged to recent events" and is "more technically sound—with tighter introductions, better graphics and a more welcoming tone."[81] While the obvious counterstrategy to Fox would be to become more liberal, CNN claims to be "right down the middle" with moderates as its "sweet spot."[82] Finally, as a practical strategy, CNN reorganized its Headline News Channel so its two cable news channels were no longer offering competing newscasts during prime-time hours. Foxification at CBS News followed the departure of Dan Rather with a reduced focus on the anchor and more on the news team, including more "spontaneous give-and-take between [anchor Bob] Schieffer and the correspondents."[83] The long-term effect as cable and network news lowers the denominator by becoming more Foxified is a continual raising of the ante for the Fox News Channel to respond with more extremism.[84]

There is also empirical evidence of a Fox effect on the audience. FNC is an increasingly important source of national and international news, as a majority surveyed in 2004 said they turned to cable for breaking news more than to any other source.[85] Within the cable news audience, a Pew Research Center 2004 poll found that for the first time, FNC was the "regular" source of news over CNN (25 to 22 percent). The poll also found an "ideological splintering" of the audience as in no other news medium and more at FNC than anywhere else. More Republicans reported being regular cable news viewers, and specifically of Fox, than Democrats or Independents, suggesting that cable news "has come to resemble talk radio not only in content but in appeal."[86] One measure of Fox's impact on public attitudes is a decline in the number of viewers who find broadcast network news as well as CNN to be believable. Yet at the same time, of the respondents to a poll who said they were receiving most of their news from cable, half could not correctly answer two basic questions about the Democratic presidential candidates, with only local TV news viewers (14 percent) and morning news viewers (13 percent) doing worse.[87]

Another set of surveys conducted for the Program on International Policy Attitudes (PIPA) Research Center at the University of Maryland in October 2003 looked at the frequency of public misperceptions about the Iraq war according to media use. The questions focused on whether Iraq was involved with the September 11, 2001, attacks, al-Qaeda, and weapons of mass destruction. The study found that a significant portion of the respondents had misperceptions about these reasons for the war, both before and after the U.S. invasion, and that the higher the level of misperception, the stronger the support for war.[88] When examined by primary source of news, those who mentioned Fox had the highest average rate of misperceptions (45 percent) compared to National Public Radio (NPR)/PBS with the lowest (11 percent).[89] CBS viewers finished second (36 percent), followed by CNN (31 percent), ABC and NBC (30 percent), and then print news (25 percent). Furthermore, Fox viewers who paid greater attention to the news had increases in the likelihood of misperceptions.[90] The misperceptions could not be explained on the basis of political bias, since even those opposed to the president varied sharply in their misperceptions according to news source.[91] This study raises questions about whether network news audiences are more informed than those attending to cable, as suggested by the Pew center study. The evidence does suggest that the audiences of nonprofit, public media were most informed. Yet, following the summer hurricanes of 2005, congressional Republicans immediately began threatening to permanently eliminate funds for the Corporation for Public Broadcasting, which provides federal funds to PBS and NPR, to free up tax money for relief and rebuilding.[92]

The attacks on PBS and NPR have become linked to the myth of liberal media promoted by the Right for years. "Over the course of two decades," according to Hart, [conservatives] have forced media to internalize the 'liberal bias' critique, and in some cases to overcompensate to try and prove the critics wrong."[93] It is precisely the power of this myth that allows Fox to claim to be "fair and balanced" when, as documented in *Outfoxed*, it clearly is not. The myth of the liberal media is based on the assumption that the news media are supposed to be able to be "objective" in their reporting of issues and events. To some extent, both Fox News and *Outfoxed* work to subvert the journalistic canon of objectivity by flouting it. To a greater extent, they may be helping to further reify it, since both can be accused of being unfair and unbalanced. Since the origins of so-called objective journalism are rooted in economics—the need to appeal to advertisers by attracting the largest audiences with the right demographics—the persistence of the myth of objectivity, and therefore the liberal media, is functional for a profit-driven, largely advertiser-supported communications industry. The Big Media will always have more money, since they do not challenge hegemonic ideologies and practices. A truly democratic communications system cannot exist as long as culture, knowledge, and audiences are treated as commodities, produced primarily for their exchange value in the media marketplace.

Notes

1. Robert S. Boynton, "How to Make a Guerilla Documentary," *New York Times*, July 11, 2004.

2. Lorenzo Nencioli, "Indies Unleashed: Independent Documentaries Take On the Multinational Media Empires That Run Hollywood," *Dollars and Sense*, May/June 2005, 26–29.

3. Ann Hornaday, "*Outfoxed*: Another Documentary Salvo from the Left," *Washington Post*, August 6, 2004, C05.

4. Nencioli, "Indies Unleashed," 26.

5. Robert Roten, "Laramie Movie Scope: An Examination of a 'Fair and Balanced' Network," September 29, 2004, *Lariat*, http://www.lariat.org/AtTheMovies/new/outfoxed.html (accessed November 1, 2004).

6. Fox News is a division of News Corp. Fox News Channel is the subject of *Outfoxed*. We have used the terms interchangeably, since most of the material produced by Fox News is for Fox News Channel. We have borrowed the term "manufacturing consent" from Edward Herman and Noam Chomsky, *Manufacturing Consent: The Political Economy of the Mass Media*, 2nd ed. (New York: Pantheon, 2002).

7. Ronald V. Bettig and Jeanne Lynn Hall, *Big Media, Big Money: Cultural Texts and Political Economics* (Lanham, Md.: Rowman and Littlefield, 2003).

8. Aaron Sarver, "The Media Movement Matures," *In These Times* 29 (2005): 10.

9. Samuel Bowles and Richard Edwards, *Understanding Capitalism: Competition, Command and Change in the U.S. Economy*, 2nd ed. (New York: Harper Collins, 1993), 229–32.

10. Daniel Fusfeld, *Economics: Principles of Political Economy*, 3rd ed. (Glenview, Ill.: Scott, Foresman, 1988), 404.

11. Douglas Kellner, *Critical Theory, Marxism and Modernity* (Baltimore: Johns Hopkins University Press, 1989), 164–65.

12. Tibor Scitovsky, *Welfare and Competition* (Homewood, Ill.: R. D. Irwin, 1971), 398–410.

13. Kellner, *Critical Theory*, 165.

14. Herbert I. Schiller, *The Mind Managers: How the Master Puppeteers of Politics, Advertising, and Mass Communications Pull the Strings of Public Opinion* (Boston: Beacon, 1973), 20.

15. Ibid., 21.

16. Ben Bagdikian, *The Media Monopoly* (Boston: Beacon, 1983).

17. Ben Bagdikian, *The New Media Monopoly* (Boston: Beacon 2004), 27–50.

18. News Corporation, "Corporate Profile," 2005, *Newscorp.com*, http://www.newscorp.com/investor/index.html (accessed September 17, 2005).

19. "Fortune 500 2006," *CNNMoney.com*, http://money.cnn.com/magazines/fortune/fortune500/2006/full_list/ (accessed October 23, 2007).

20. Richard Siklos and Geraldine Fabrikant, "Liberty Media Completes Spinoff of Discovery State," *New York Times*, July 22, 2005, sec. C1, C2.

21. News Corp., Form 10-K, 89, 110, September 1, 2005, *Newscorp.com*, http://10kwizard.ccbn.com/fil_list.asp?TK=NWS&CK . . . (accessed September 17, 2005).

22. News Corp., Form 10-K, 2005, 27.

23. Richard Siklos, "Behind Murdoch Rift, a Media Dynasty Unhappy in Its Own Way," *New York Times*, August 1, 2005, sec. C1, C3.

24. News Corp., Form 14A, 5–9, September 1, 2005, *Newscorp.com*, http://ccbn.tenkwizard.com/filing.php?repo=tenk& . . . (accessed September 17, 2005).

25. "Overview: Allen and Company, Inc.," *Hoover's Fact Sheet*, 2005, http://hoovers.com/free/co/factsheet.xhtml? . . . (accessed September 19, 2005).

26. News Corp., Form 10-K, 2–18, 2005.

27. Center for Public Integrity, *Networks of Influence: The Political Power of Communications Industry* (Washington, D.C.: Center for Public Integrity, 2005), 144–45.

28. "News Corp. Ltd.—Political Campaign Contributions (1999–present)," *CampaignMoney.com*, July 6, 2005, http://www.campaignmoney.com/news_corporation.asp (accessed September 19, 2005).

29. Jacques Steinberg, "News Corp. Starts to Fill the Shoes of a Departed Murdoch," *New York Times*, August 16, 2005, sec. C1, C4.

30. *Fox News Network, LLC* v. *Penguin Group (USA) and Alan S. Franken*, Complaint, August 7, 2003 (Sup. Ct., N.Y.), *www.FindLaw.com*, p. 5 (accessed September 21, 2005.

31. Charlie Reina, "View Forum Post: Ex-Fox News Staffer on 'The Memo,'" Poynter Forums (posted by Jim Romenesko), *Poynteronline*, October 31, 2003, http://www.poynter.org/forum/view_post.asp?id=5976 (accessed September 21, 2005).

32. Seth Ackerman, "The Most Biased Name in News," *Extra!*, 14, no. 4 (August 2001): 10–12, 14–18, 10.

33. Ibid., 10.

34. Steve Rendall, "Fox's Slanted Sources: Conservatives, Republicans Far Outnumber Others," *Extra!*, 14, no. 4 (August 2001): 13.

35. Ackerman, "Most Biased Name," 11–12.

36. Author notes, Fox News Channel, August 4, 2005.

37. Neil Hickey, "Is Fox News Fair?" *Columbia Journalism Review* (March 1998): 30–35.

38. *Fox News* v. *Penguin*, 7.

39. Geoff Edgers, "Taking on Mainstream Media, Fox's Hume Faces Political Views Head-on," *Boston Globe*, September 1, 2004, A30.

40. Kate Aurthur, "Fox News Dominates Hurricane Coverage," *New York Times*, September 12, 2005.

41. Nencioli, "Indies Unleashed," 26–29, 26 (estimates from Kagan Research).

42. Robert S. Boynton, "How to Make a Guerilla Documentary," *New York Times Magazine*, July 11, 2004, http://www.nytimes.com/2004/07/11/magazine/11Fox.html . . . (accessed September 11, 2005).

43. Ibid.

44. *Fox News* v. *Penguin*, 2003.

45. Ronald V. Bettig, "Copyright and the Commodification of Culture," *Media Development*, no. 1 (2003): 3–9.

46. Boynton, "How to Make a Guerilla Documentary."

47. "Political Expression and Copyright," *www.creativecommons.org* (submitted by Glenn Otis Brown), September 15, 2004 (accessed September 21, 2005).

48. Nencioli, "Indies Unleashed," 28.

49. Ibid.

50. Dan Glaister, "Murdoch Accused over TV News 'Bias,'" *The Guardian* (London), July 14, 2004.

51. David Rooney, "*Outfoxed: Rupert Murdoch's War on Journalism*," *Variety*, July 13, 2004, http://www.variety.com/review/VE1117924372?categoryid=31& cs=1 (accessed November 1, 2005).

52. Robert Greenwald, "Big Bad Billy O," *RobertGreenwald.org* (accessed August 30, 2005).

53. Megan Lehmann, "Fair and Balanced, This Doc's Not," *New York Post*, August 6, 2004, http://www.nypost.com/movies/26331.htm (accessed November 1, 2004).

54. Rooney, "*Outfoxed*."

55. Hornaday, "*Outfoxed*," C05.

56. A. O. Scott, "Spin Zones, Flag Waving and Shouting to Catch a Fox," *New York Times*, July 20, 2004, http://www.nytimes.com/2004/07/20/

movies/200UTF.html?ex=1122177600&en=2f2 . . . (accessed November 1, 2004).

57. Lehmann, "Fair and Balanced."

58. Rooney, "*Outfoxed.*"

59. Mike Lasalle, "Crooked Angles in Sly Fox Exposé," *San Francisco Chronicle*, August 6, 2004.

60. See, for example, Matt Langdon, "*Outfoxed: Rupert Murdoch's War on Journalism*," 2004, *filmcritic.com*, http://www.filmcritic.com/misc/emporium.nsf/reviews/outfoxed-Rupert-Murdochs-War-on-Journalism (accessed October 23, 2007).

61. Faith McLellan, "Telling It Like It Isn't: Truth and Lies in a Post-9/11 World," *Lancet*, September 11, 2004, 927.

62. Rooney, "*Outfoxed.*"

63. Bruce Newman, "Murdoch '*Outfoxed*' by Cinematic Attack," *Mercury News*, August 13, 2004, http://ae.contracostatimes.com/entertainment/ui/mercurynews/movie (accessed October 23, 2007).

64. Langdon, "*Outfoxed.*"

65. Howard Kurtz, "Tilting at the Right, Leaning to the Left: Robert Greenwald's *Outfoxed* Has Its Own Slant on Bias," *Washington Post*, July 11, 2004, D01.

66. Denis McQuail, *Mass Communication Theory: An Introduction* (Thousand Oaks, Calif.: Sage, 1994).

67. Scott, "Spin Zones."

68. Ty Burr, "*Outfoxed: Rupert Murdoch's War on Journalism*: This Fox Hunt Is Direct and Effective," *Boston Globe*, September 18, 2004, http://www.boston.com/movies/display?display=movie&id=7252 (accessed November 1, 2004).

69. McQuail, *Mass Communication Theory*, 186.

70. Ibid., 188–90.

71. Ibid., 190.

72. "*Outfoxed: Rupert Murdoch's War on Journalism*: Full Transcript," *Outfoxed.org*, http://www.outfoxed.org/docs/outfoxed_transcript.pdf (accessed October 23, 2007).

73. Kurtz, "Tilting at the Right," D01.

74. Burr, "*Outfoxed.*"

75. Hornaday, "*Outfoxed.*"

76. Peter Hart, "Struggling MSNBC Attempts to Out-Fox Fox," *Extra! Update* newsletter, February 2005, 4.

77. Jim Rutenberg, "Cable's War Coverage Suggests a New 'Fox Effect' on Television Journalism," *New York Times*, April 16, 2003.

78. Hart, "Struggling MSNBC," 4.

79. Cited in ibid.

80. "Jon Stewart 'Crossfire' Transcript," *About.com*, http://politicalhumor. about.com/library/bljonstewartcrossfire.htm (accessed October 23, 2007).

81. Jacques Steinberg, "CNN Seeks New Ways to Battle Fox News," *New York Times*, March 23, 2005.

82. Ibid.

83. Alan Breznick, "The News Makes the News," *New York Times*, May 10, 2005 (advertisement).

84. Hornaday, "*Outfoxed*," C9.

85. Project for Excellence in Journalism, *State of the Media 2005*, 2005, www.stateofthemedia.org/2005/narrative_cabletv_intro . . . (accessed September 24, 2005).

86. Ibid.

87. Pew Research Center on the People and the Press, "Cable and Internet Loom Large in Fragmented Political News Universe," January 11, 2004 (cited in *State of the Media*).

88. Steven Kull, *Misperceptions, the Media and the Iraq War*, October 2, 2003, Program on International Policy Attitudes (University of Maryland) and Knowledge Networks (Menlo Park, Calif.), 2, 9.

89. Ibid., 12–13.

90. Ibid., 16.

91. Ibid., 17.

92. Stephen Labaton, "Departing Chairman of Public TV Defends Acts," *New York Times*, September 23, 2005.

93. Peter Hart, "Media Bias: How to Spot It and How to Fight It," in *The Future of Media: Resistance and Reform in the 21st Century*, ed. Robert McChesney, Russell Newman, and Ben Scott (New York: Seven Stories Press, 2005), 59.

Selected Bibliography

Contributors

Index

Selected Bibliography

Abel, Marco. "*Fargo*: The Violent Production of the Masochistic Contract as a Cinematic Concept." *Critical Studies in Mass Communication* 16 (1999): 308–28.

Alexander, William. *Film on the Left: American Documentary Film from 1931 to 1942*. Princeton, N.J.: Princeton University Press, 1981.

Anderson, Carolyn, and Thomas W. Benson. *Documentary Dilemmas: Frederick Wiseman's "Titicut Follies."* Carbondale: Southern Illinois University Press, 1991.

Aufderheide, Pat. "The Changing Documentary Marketplace." *Cineaste*, summer 2005, 24–28.

Aune, James Arnt. "Witchcraft as Symbolic Action in Early Modern Europe and America." *Rhetoric and Public Affairs* 6 (2003): 765–77.

Barnouw, Erik. *Documentary: A History of the Non-fiction Film*. 3rd ed. New York: Oxford University Press, 1993.

Barsam, Richard Meran. *Nonfiction Film: A Critical History*. Bloomington: Indiana University Press, 1992.

———, ed. *Nonfiction Film Theory and Criticism*. New York: E. P. Dutton, 1976.

Barthes, Roland. *Image-Music-Text*. Translated by S. Heath. New York: Hill and Wang, 1977.

Bazin, André. *What Is Cinema?* Translated by H. Gray. Vol. 1. Berkeley: University of California Press, 1967.

Beattie, Keith. *Documentary Screens: Non-fiction Film and Television*. New York: Palgrave Macmillan, 2004.

Benson, Thomas W. "Another Shooting in Cowtown." *Quarterly Journal of Speech* 67 (1981): 347–406.

———. "*Joe*: An Essay in the Rhetorical Criticism of Film." *Journal of Popular Culture* 8 (1974): 608–18.

———. "Looking for the Public in the Popular: Collective Memory and the Hollywood Blacklist." In *The Terministic Screen: Rhetorical Perspectives on Film*, edited by David Blakesley, 129–45. Carbondale: Southern Illinois University Press, 2003.

———. "Respecting the Reader." *Quarterly Journal of Speech* 72 (1986): 197–204.

———. "The Rhetorical Structure of Frederick Wiseman's *High School.*" *Communication Monographs* 47 (1980): 233–61.

———. "The Rhetorical Structure of Frederick Wiseman's *Primate.*" *Quarterly Journal of Speech* 71 (1985): 204–17.

———. "The Senses of Rhetoric: A Topical System for Critics." *Central States Speech Journal* 29 (1978): 237–50.

———. "Thinking through Film: Hollywood Remembers the Blacklist." In *Rhetoric and Community*, edited by J. Michael Hogan, 218–55. Columbia: University of South Carolina Press, 1998.

Benson, Thomas W., and Carolyn Anderson. *Reality Fictions: The Films of Frederick Wiseman.* 2nd ed. Carbondale: Southern Illinois University Press, 2002.

———. "The Rhetorical Structure of Frederick Wiseman's *Model.*" *Journal of Film and Video* 36, no. 4 (1984): 30–40.

———. "The Ultimate Technology: Frederick Wiseman's *Missile.*" In *Communication and the Culture of Technology*, edited by Martin J. Medhurst, Alberto Gonzalez, and Tarla Rai Peterson, 257–83. Pullman: Washington State University Press, 1990.

Bettig, Ronald V. *Copyrighting Culture: The Political Economy of Intellectual Property.* Boulder, Colo.: Westview Press, 1996.

Bettig, Ronald V., and Jeanne Lynn Hall. *Big Media, Big Money: Cultural Texts and Political Economics.* Lanham, Md.: Rowman and Littlefield, 2003.

Bhabha, Homi K. "Of Mimicry and Man: The Ambivalence of Colonial Discourse." Chap. 4 in *The Location of Culture.* New York: Routledge, 1994.

Blakesley, David, ed. *The Terministic Screen: Rhetorical Perspectives on Film.* Carbondale: Southern Illinois University Press, 2003.

Bluem, A. William. "The Documentary Idea: A Frame of Reference (1965)." In *Nonfiction Film Theory and Criticism*, edited by Richard Meran Barsam, 75–79. New York: E. P. Dutton, 1976.

———. *Documentary in American Television.* New York: Hastings House, 1965.

Booth, William. "Docu-Trauma: For Political Films, the Box Office Is More Bombo Than Boffo." *Washington Post*, November 2, 2004.

Borda, Jennifer L. "The Woman Suffrage Parades of 1910–1913: Possibilities and Limitations of an Early Feminist Rhetorical Strategy." *Western Journal of Communication* 66 (2002): 25–52.

Bordwell, David. *Making Meaning: Inference and Rhetoric in the Interpretation of Cinema.* Cambridge, Mass.: Harvard University Press, 1989.

———. *Narration in the Fiction Film.* Madison: University of Wisconsin Press, 1985.

Bruzzi, Stella. *New Documentary: A Critical Introduction.* New York: Routledge, 2000.

Buescher, Derek T., and Kent A. Ono. "Civilized Colonialism: *Pocahontas* as Neocolonial Rhetoric." *Women's Studies in Communication* 19, no. 2 (1996): 127–43.

Christensen, Christian. "The Politics of a Political Film." *Screen Education* 37 (2005): 20–24.

Combs, James E., and Sara T. Combs. *Film Propaganda and American Politics: An Analysis and Filmography.* New York: Garland, 1994.

Conway, Lorie. "Iraq War Documentaries Fill a Press Vacuum." *Nieman Reports* 59, no. 1 (2005): 106–8.

Cook, David A. *A History of Narrative Film.* 4th ed. New York: W. W. Norton, 2004.

Cooper, Brenda, and David Descutner. "'It Had No Voice to It': Sydney Pollack's Film Translation of Isak Dinesen's *Out of Africa.*" *Quarterly Journal of Speech* 82 (1996): 228–50.

Crowdus, Gary. *The Political Companion to American Film.* Chicago: Lakeview Press, 1994.

Culbert, David Holbrook, Richard E. Wood, and Lawrence H. Suid, eds. *Film and Propaganda in America: A Documentary History.* 4 vols. New York: Greenwood Press, 1990–91.

Cyphert, Dale. "Persuading the Body: A Rhetoric of Action in *The Fugitive.*" *Western Journal of Communication* 65 (2001): 161–83.

Davis, Lisa Selin. "Do-Something Documentaries: Effecting Change beyond Affecting Attitudes." *The Independent: A Magazine for Video and Filmmakers* 28, no. 3 (2005): 40–43.

DeLuca, Kevin Michael. *Image Politics: The New Rhetoric of Environmental Activism.* New York: Guilford Press, 1999.

Deming, Caren J. "*Hill Street Blues* as Narrative." *Critical Studies in Mass Communication* 2 (1985): 1–22.

Dixon, Wheeler W., ed. *Film and Television after 9/11.* Carbondale: Southern Illinois University Press, 2004.

Dow, Bonnie J. "Fixing Feminism: Women's Liberation and the Rhetoric of Television Documentary." *Quarterly Journal of Speech* 90 (2004): 53–80.

Economou, Rose. "Documentaries Raise Questions Journalists Should Ask Themselves." *Nieman Reports* 58, no. 3 (2004): 81–82.

Ellis, Jack C. *The Documentary Idea: A Critical History of English-Language Documentary Film and Video.* Englewood Cliffs, N.J.: Prentice Hall, 1989.

———. *John Grierson: Life, Contributions, Influence.* Carbondale: Southern Illinois University Press, 2000.

Elson, Robert T. "Time Marches on the Screen." In *Time Inc.: An Intimate History of a Publishing Enterprise, 1923–1941.* New York: Atheneum, 1973.

Farnsworth, Rodney. "John Wayne's Epic of Contradictions." *Film Quarterly* 52, no. 2 (1998–99): 24–34.

Fielding, Raymond. *The American Newsreel: 1911–1967.* Norman: University of Oklahoma Press, 1972.

———. *The March of Time: 1935–1951.* New York: Oxford University Press, 1978.

Finnegan, Cara A. "The Naturalistic Enthymeme and Visual Argument: Photographic Representation in the 'Skull Controversy.'" *Argumentation and Advocacy* 37 (2001): 133–49.

———. "Recognizing Lincoln: Image Vernaculars in Nineteenth-Century Visual Culture." *Rhetoric and Public Affairs* 8 (2005): 31–58.

———. "Social Engineering, Visual Politics, and the New Deal: FSA Photography in Survey Graphic." *Rhetoric and Public Affairs* 3 (2000): 333–62.

Fiske, John. *Media Matters: Race and Gender in U.S. Politics.* Minneapolis: University of Minnesota Press, 1996.

Foss, Karen A. "Celluloid Rhetoric: The Use of Documentary Film to Teach Rhetorical Theory." *Communication Education* 32 (1983): 51–61.

Frentz, Thomas S., and Thomas B. Farrell. "Conversion of America's Consciousness: The Rhetoric of *The Exorcist.*" *Quarterly Journal of Speech* 61 (1975): 40–47.

Gaines, Jane M. "Political Mimesis." In *Collecting Visible Evidence*, edited by Jane M. Gaines and Michael Renov, 84–102. Minneapolis: University of Minnesota Press, 1999.

Garver, Eugene. "Philosophy, Rhetoric, and Civic Education in Aristotle and Isocrates." In *Isocrates and Civic Education*, edited by Takis Poulakos and David Depew, 186–213. Austin: University of Texas Press, 2004.

Gianos, Phillip L. *Politics and Politicians in American Film.* Westport, Conn.: Praeger, 1998.

Giglio, Ernest D. *Here's Looking at You: Hollywood, Film, and Politics.* New York: Peter Lang, 2001.

Giovacchini, Saverio. *Hollywood Modernism: Film and Politics in the Age of the New Deal.* Philadelphia: Temple University Press, 2001.

Golden, Leon. *Aristotle on Tragic and Comic Mimesis.* Atlanta: Scholars Press, 1992.

Grant, Barry Keith, and Jeannette Sloniowski, eds. *Documenting the Documentary: Close Readings of Documentary Film and Video.* Detroit: Wayne State University Press, 1998.

Gregg, Richard B. "The Rhetoric of Political Broadcasting." *Central States Speech Journal* 28 (1977): 221–37.

Grierson, John. *Grierson on Documentary.* Edited by H. Forsyth Hardy. London: Faber and Faber, 1946.

———. "The Nature of Propaganda." In *Nonfiction Film Theory and Criti-*

cism, edited by Richard Meran Barsam, 31–41. New York: E. P. Dutton, 1976.

Gronbeck, Bruce. "Celluloid Rhetoric: On Genres of Documentary." In *Form and Genre: Shaping Rhetorical Action*, edited by Karlyn Kohrs Campbell and Kathleen Hall Jamieson, 139–61. Falls Church, Va.: Speech Communication Association, 1978.

Hall, Jeanne. "Realism as a Style in Cinema Verite: A Critical Analysis of *Primary*." *Cinema Journal* 30, no. 4 (1991): 24–50.

Hardy, Forsyth. *Grierson on Documentary*. Revised ed. Berkeley: University of California Press, 1966.

Hariman, Robert. "Civic Education, Classical Imitation, and Democratic Polity." In *Isocrates and Civic Education*, edited by Takis Poulakos and David Depew, 217–34. Austin: University of Texas Press, 2004.

Hariman, Robert, and John Louis Lucaites. "Public Identity and Collective Memory in U.S. Iconic Photography: The Image of 'Accidental Napalm.'" *Critical Studies in Mass Communication* 20 (2003): 35–66.

Harris, Thomas. "*Rear Window* and *Blow-Up*: Hitchcock's Straightforwardness vs. Antonioni's Ambiguity." *Literature Film Quarterly* 15 (1987): 60–63.

Haskins, Ekaterina V. *Logos and Power in Isocrates and Aristotle*. Columbia: University of South Carolina Press, 2004.

Hauser, Gerard A., and Amy Grim, eds. *Rhetorical Democracy: Discursive Practices of Civic Engagement*. Mahwah, N.J.: Lawrence Erlbaum, 2004.

Hendrix, Jerry A., and James A. Wood. "The Rhetoric of Film: Toward Critical Methodology." *Southern Speech Communication Journal* 39 (1973): 105–22.

Hill, Charles A., and Marguerite Helmers, eds. *Defining Visual Rhetorics*. Mahwah, N.J.: Lawrence Erlbaum, 2004.

Hogan, J. Michael. "Media Nihilism and the Presidential Debates." *Argumentation and Advocacy* 25 (1989): 220–25.

———. *The Nuclear Freeze Campaign: Rhetoric and Foreign Policy in the Telepolitical Age*. East Lansing: Michigan State University Press, 1994.

Holmlund, Chris, and Cynthia Fuchs, eds. *Between the Sheets, in the Streets*. Minneapolis: University of Minnesota Press, 1997.

Howard, John W., III, and Laura C. Prividera. "Rescuing Patriarchy or Saving 'Jessica Lynch': The Rhetorical Construction of the American Woman Soldier." *Women and Language* 27 (2004): 89–97.

Isaac, Jeffrey C. *The Poverty of Progressivism: The Future of American Democracy in a Time of Liberal Decline*. Lanham, Md.: Rowman and Littlefield, 2003.

Jacobs, Lewis, ed. *The Documentary Tradition*. 2nd ed. New York: W. W. Norton, 1979.

Jamieson, Kathleen Hall. *Dirty Politics: Deception, Distraction, and Democracy*. New York: Oxford University Press, 1992.

————. *Packaging the Presidency: A History and Criticism of Presidential Campaign Advertising.* 3rd ed. New York: Oxford University Press, 1996.

Jasinski, James. "Invention." In *Sourcebook on Rhetoric: Key Concepts in Contemporary Rhetorical Studies.* Thousand Oaks, Calif.: Sage, 2001. 327–30.

Juhasz, Alexandra, and Jesse Lerner, eds. *F Is for Phony: Fake Documentary and Truth's Undoing.* Minneapolis: University of Minnesota Press, 2006.

Karan, Tim. "Artists' Politics Are Portable." *Democrat and Chronicle,* October 29, 2004.

Kellner, Douglas. *Media Culture.* New York: Routledge, 1995.

Kennedy, George A. "Imitation." In *Encyclopedia of Rhetoric,* edited by T. O. Sloane, 381–84. Oxford: Oxford University Press, 2001.

Keyishian, Harry. *Screening Politics: The Politician in American Movies, 1931–2001.* Lanham, Md.: Scarecrow Press, 2003.

Koppes, Clayton R., and Gregory D. Black. *Hollywood Goes to War: How Politics, Profits, and Propaganda Shaped World War II Movies.* New York: Free Press, 1987.

Lefebvre, Martin. "Eisenstein, Rhetoric and Imaginicity: Towards a Revolutionary *Memoria.*" *Screen Education* 41 (2000): 349–68.

Leff, Michael. "The Idea of Rhetoric as Interpretive Practice: A Humanist's Response to Gaonkar." In *Rhetorical Hermeneutics: Invention and Interpretation in the Age of Science,* edited by Alan G. Gross and William M. Keith, 89–100. Albany: State University of New York Press, 1997.

Leyda, Jay. *Films Beget Films: A Study of the Compilation Film.* New York: Hill and Wang, 1964.

MacCann, Richard Dyer. *The People's Films: A Political History of U.S. Government Motion Pictures.* New York: Hastings House, 1973.

Mackey, Susan. "The 18-Minute Political Film Preceding Ronald Reagan's Acceptance Speech at the 1984 Republican National Convention." Ph.D. diss., Pennsylvania State University, 1988.

Mackey-Kallis, Susan. *Oliver Stone's America: "Dreaming the Myth Outward."* Boulder, Colo.: Westview Press, 1996.

————. "Spectator Desire and Narrative Closure: The Reagan 18-Minute Political Film." *Southern Communication Journal* 56 (1991): 308–14.

Mamber, Stephen. *Cinema Verite in America: Studies in Uncontrolled Documentary.* Cambridge, Mass.: MIT University Press, 1974.

McClure, Kevin R., and Lisa Laidlaw McClure. "Postmodern Parody: *Zelig* and the Rhetorical Subversion of Documentary Form." *Communication Quarterly* 49 (2001): 81–88.

McConnell, Bill, and John M. Higgins. "Sinclair under Siege." *Broadcasting and Cable,* October 25, 2004, 1–3.

McMullen, Wayne J. "Reconstruction of the Frontier Myth in *Witness.*" *Southern Communication Journal* 62 (1996): 31–41.

Medhurst, Martin J. "*Hiroshima, Mon Amour*: From Iconography to Rhetoric." *Quarterly Journal of Speech* 68 (1982): 345–70.

———. "Image and Ambiguity: A Rhetorical Approach to *The Exorcist*." *Southern Speech Communication Journal* 44 (1978): 73–92.

———. "The Rhetorical Structure of Oliver Stone's *JFK*." *Critical Studies in Mass Communication* 10 (1993): 128–43.

Medhurst, Martin J., and Thomas W. Benson. "*The City*: The Rhetoric of Rhythm." *Communication Monographs* 48 (1981): 54–72.

———, eds. *Rhetorical Dimensions in Media*. Dubuque, Iowa: Kendall/Hunt, 1984.

Mielke, Bo. "Rhetoric and Ideology in the Nuclear Test Documentary." *Film Quarterly* 58 (2005): 28–37.

"Moore Crafting 'Fahrenheit' Sequel." *CBSNews.com*, November 11, 2004, http://www.cbsnews.com/stories/2004/11/11/entertainment/main655200.shtml (accessed March 16, 2005).

Morreale, Joanne. *A New Beginning: A Textual Frame Analysis of the Political Campaign Film*. Albany: State University of New York Press, 1991.

———. *The Presidential Campaign Film: A Critical History*. Westport, Conn.: Praeger, 1993.

Muscio, Giuliana. *Hollywood's New Deal*. Philadelphia: Temple University Press, 1996.

Nadel, Alan. *Flatlining on the Field of Dreams: Cultural Narratives in the Films of President Reagan's America*. New Brunswick, N.J.: Rutgers University Press, 1997.

Neve, Brian. *Film and Politics in America: A Social Tradition*. London: Routledge, 1992.

Newman, Sara. "Aristotle's Notion of 'Bringing-before-the-Eyes': Its Contributions to Aristotelian and Contemporary Conceptualizations of Metaphor, Style, and Audience." *Rhetorica* 20 (2002): 1–23.

Nichols, Bill. *Blurred Boundaries: Questions of Meaning in Contemporary Culture*. Bloomington: Indiana University Press, 1994.

———. *Introduction to Documentary*. Bloomington: Indiana University Press, 2001.

———. *Representing Reality: Issues and Concepts in Documentary*. Bloomington: Indiana University Press, 1991.

O'Connell, P. J. *Robert Drew and the Development of Cinema Verite in America*. Carbondale: Southern Illinois University Press, 1992.

Palast, Greg. *The Best Democracy Money Can Buy*. London: Pluto Press, 2002.

Palmerton, Patricia R. "The Rhetoric of Terrorism and Media Response to the 'Crisis in Iran.'" *Western Journal of Communication* 52 (1988): 105–21.

Parry-Giles, Shawn J. "Mediating Hillary Rodham Clinton: Television News Practices and Image-Making in the Postmodern Age." *Critical Studies in Mass Communication* 17 (2000): 205–26.

Parry-Giles, Shawn J., and Trevor Parry-Giles. "Collective Memory, Political Nostalgia, and the Rhetorical Presidency: Bill Clinton's Commemoration of the March on Washington, August 28, 1998." *Quarterly Journal of Speech* 86 (2000): 417–37.

———. *Constructing Clinton: Hyperreality and Presidential Image-Making in Postmodern Politics.* New York: Peter Lang, 2002.

———. "Gendered Politics and Presidential Image Construction: A Reassessment of the 'Feminine Style.'" *Communication Monographs* 63 (1996): 337–53.

———. "Meta-Imaging, the War Room, and the Hyperreality of U.S. Politics." *Journal of Communication* 49 (1999): 28–45.

Parry-Giles, Trevor. "Ideology and Poetics in Public Issue Construction: Thatcherism, Civil Liberties, and 'Terrorism' in Northern Ireland." *Communication Quarterly* 43 (1995): 182–96.

Parry-Giles, Trevor, and Shawn J. Parry-Giles. "Political Scopophilia, Presidential Campaigning, and the Intimacy of American Politics." *Communication Studies* 47 (1996): 191–205.

———. *The Prime-Time Presidency: The West Wing and U.S. Nationalism.* Urbana: University of Illinois Press, 2006.

———. "*The West Wing*'s Prime-Time Presidentiality: Mimesis and Catharsis in a Postmodern Romance." *Quarterly Journal of Speech* 88 (2002): 209–27.

Pauley, Garth E. "Documentary Desegregation: A Rhetorical Analysis of *Crisis: Behind a Presidential Commitment.*" *Southern Communication Journal* 64 (1999): 123–42.

Plantinga, Carl R. *Rhetoric and Representation in Nonfiction Film.* New York: Cambridge University Press, 1997.

Pratt, Ray. *Projecting Paranoia: Conspiratorial Visions in American Film.* Lawrence: University Press of Kansas, 2001.

Prelli, Lawrence J., ed. *Rhetorics of Display.* Columbia: University of South Carolina Press, 2006.

Rabinowitz, Paula. *They Must Be Represented: The Politics of Documentary.* New York: Verso, 1994.

Reinhart, Mark S. *Abraham Lincoln on the Screen: A Filmography of Dramas and Documentaries Including Television, 1903–1998.* Jefferson, N.C.: McFarland, 1999.

Renov, Michael. *The Subject of Documentary.* Minneapolis: University of Minnesota Press, 2004.

Richardson, Glenn W., Jr. "Pulp Politics: Popular Culture and Political Advertising." *Rhetoric and Public Affairs* 3 (2000): 603–26.

Riggs, Karen E., Susan Tyler Eastman, and Timothy S. Golobic. "Manufactured Conflict in the 1992 Olympics: The Discourse of Television and Politics." *Critical Studies in Mass Communication* 10 (1993): 253–72.

Rosenthal, Alan. *The Documentary Conscience: A Casebook in Filmmaking.* Berkeley: University of California Press, 1980.

Rosteck, Thomas, ed. *At the Intersection: Cultural Studies and Rhetorical Studies.* New York: Guilford Press, 1999.

——. *See It Now Confronts McCarthyism: Television Documentary and the Politics of Representation.* Tuscaloosa: University of Alabama Press, 1994.

Rotha, Paul, and Richard Griffith. *Documentary Film.* 3rd ed. New York: Hastings House, 1963.

Rothman, William. *Documentary Film Classics.* Cambridge: Cambridge University Press, 1997.

Rushing, Janice Hocker. "*E.T.* as Rhetorical Transcendence." *Quarterly Journal of Speech* 71 (1985): 188–203.

Rushing, Janice Hocker, and Thomas S. Frentz. "The Rhetoric of *Rocky*: A Social Value Model of Criticism." *Western Journal of Communication* 42 (1978): 63–72.

Schlesinger, Arthur M., Jr. "The Fiction of Fact—and the Fact of Fiction." In *The Documentary Tradition*, edited by Lewis Jacobs, 383–91. 2nd ed. New York: W. W. Norton, 1979.

Schowalter, Daniel F. "Hallucination as Epistemology: Critiquing the Visual in Ken Burns' *The West*." *Communication and Critical/Cultural Studies* 1 (2004): 250–70.

Schwalbe, Carol B. "Jacqueline Kennedy and Cold War Propaganda." *Journal of Broadcasting and Electronic Media* 49 (2005): 111–27.

Scott, Ian. *American Politics in Hollywood Film.* Chicago: Fitzroy Dearborn, 2000.

Shapiro, Ann-Louise. "How Real Is the Reality in Documentary Film?" *History and Theory* 36 (1997): 80–101.

Shome, Raka. "Race and Popular Cinema: The Rhetorical Strategies of Whiteness in *City of Joy*." *Communication Quarterly* 44 (1996): 502–18.

Smith, Craig R. "Television News as Rhetoric." *Western Journal of Communication* 41 (1977): 147–59.

Snee, Brian J. "The Spirit and the Flesh: The Rhetorical Nature of *The Last Temptation of Christ*." *Journal of Media and Religion* 4, no. 1 (2005): 45–61.

Snyder, Robert L. *Pare Lorentz and the Documentary Film.* Norman: University of Oklahoma Press, 1973.

Solomon, Martha, and Wayne J. McMullen. "*Places in the Heart*: The Rhetorical Force of an Open Text." *Western Journal of Speech Communication* 55 (1991): 339–53.

Steven, Peter, ed. *Jump Cut: Hollywood, Politics, and Counter Cinema.* New York: Praeger, 1985.

Stott, William. *Documentary Expression and Thirties America.* New York: Oxford University Press, 1973.

Strachan, J. Cherie, and Kathleen E. Kendall. "Political Candidates' Convention Films: Finding the Perfect Image—An Overview of Political Image Making." In *Defining Visual Rhetorics*, edited by Charles Hill and Marguerite Helmers, 135–54. Mahwah, N.J.: Lawrence Erlbaum, 2004.

Terrill, Robert E. "Spectacular Repression: Sanitizing the Batman." *Critical Studies in Mass Communication* 17 (2000): 493–509.

Torry, Robert. "Politics and Parousia in *Close Encounters of the Third Kind*." *Literature Film Quarterly* 19 (1991): 188–96.

Tracey, Michael. *The Production of Political Television*. London: Routledge and Kegan Paul, 1977.

Trbic, Boris. "In the Realm of the Political Subtext: 'Control Room' and 'Outfoxed.'" *Screen Education*, 2005, 16–18.

Waldman, Diane, and Janet Walker, eds. *Feminism and Documentary*. Minneapolis: University of Minnesota Press, 1999.

Waugh, Thomas, ed. *"Show Us Life": Toward a History and Aesthetics of the Committed Documentary*. Metuchen, N.J.: Scarecrow Press, 1984.

Weinberg, David. "Approaches to the Study of Film in the Third Reich: A Critical Appraisal." *Journal of Contemporary History* 19 (1984): 105–26.

Willard, Barbara E. "Feminist Interventions in Biomedical Discourse: An Analysis of the Rhetoric of Integrative Medicine." *Women's Studies in Communication* 28 (2005): 115–48.

Williams, Dale E. "*2001: A Space Odyssey*: A Warning before Its Time." *Critical Studies in Mass Communication* 1 (1984): 311–22.

Williams, Linda. "Film Bodies: Gender, Genre, and Excess." *Film Quarterly* 44 (1991): 2–13.

Winston, Brian. *Claiming the Real: The Griersonian Documentary and Its Legitimations*. London: British Film Institute, 1995.

Ytreberg, Espen. "Moving Out of the Inverted Pyramid: Narratives and Descriptions in Television News." *Journalism Studies* 2 (2001): 357–71.

Zimmerman, Patricia Rodden. *States of Emergency: Documentaries, Wars, Democracies*. Minneapolis: University of Minnesota Press, 2000.

Contributors

Thomas W. Benson is the Edwin Erle Sparks Professor of Rhetoric at Penn State University. He is the former editor of the *Quarterly Journal of Speech* and *Communication Quarterly* and was founding editor of the *Review of Communication*. He is the author or editor of several books, including *Reality Fictions: The Films of Frederick Wiseman* (with Carolyn Anderson); *American Rhetoric in the New Deal Era, 1932–1945*; and *Writing JFK: Presidential Rhetoric and the Press in the Bay of Pigs Crisis*.

Ronald V. Bettig is an associate professor in the College of Communications at Penn State University. He is author of *Copyrighting Culture: The Political Economy of Intellectual Property* and coauthor, with Jeanne Lynn Hall, of *Big Media, Big Money: Cultural Texts and Political Economics*. He also has published a number of book chapters and journal articles on political economy, intellectual property, and media industries.

Jennifer L. Borda is an assistant professor of communication at the University of New Hampshire. She has authored articles on film and rhetoric and specializes in the critique of image politics, particularly those constructed by the feminist movement. Her research has been published in the *Western Journal of Communication*, *Women's Studies in Communication*, and the anthology *Rhetoric and Reform in the Progressive Era*.

Jeanne Lynn Hall is an associate professor in the College of Communications at Penn State University. Her research has been published in *Cinema Journal*, *Film Criticism*, *Film Quarterly*, *Creative Screenwriting*, and the *Journal of Communication Inquiry*. She is a coauthor, with Ronald V. Bettig, of *Big Media, Big Money: Cultural Texts and Political Economics*.

Susan Mackey-Kallis is an associate professor and the director of the graduate program in the communication department at Villanova University. She teaches courses in film, rhetoric, and media and culture and has a hobbyist interest in screenplay writing. The author of two books on film, *Oliver Stone's America: "Dreaming the Myth Outward"* and *The Hero and the Perennial Journey Home in American Film*, she has also published articles in national and regional communication journals on such topics as advertising, popular music, political campaign films, and the drug rhetoric of presidential administrations. Active in the National Communication Association and the Eastern Communication Association, she has served on the editorial boards of a number of national and regional journals, including *Communication Quarterly, Communication Education, Communication Research Reports,* and *Qualitative Research Reports in Communication.*

Martin J. Medhurst is Distinguished Professor of Rhetoric and Communication at Baylor University. He is the author or editor of twelve books, and his film criticism has appeared in *Rhetorical Dimensions in Media, Television Studies: Textual Analysis, The Films of Oliver Stone,* and *The Terministic Screen: Rhetorical Perspectives on Film.* He is also the founder and editor of the award-winning interdisciplinary quarterly *Rhetoric and Public Affairs.*

Shawn J. Parry-Giles is a professor of communication, an affiliate professor of women's studies, director of graduate studies, and the director of the Center for Political Communication and Civic Leadership at the University of Maryland. She is the author of *The Rhetorical Presidency, Propaganda, and the Cold War, 1945–1955,* and is the coauthor of *Constructing Clinton: Hyperreality and Presidential Image-Making in Postmodern Politics* and *The Prime-Time Presidency:* The West Wing *and U.S. Nationalism.*

Trevor Parry-Giles is an associate professor of communication and an affiliated scholar with the Center for American Politics and Citizenship at the University of Maryland. He is the coauthor of *Constructing Clinton: Hyperreality and Presidential Image-Making in Postmodern Politics* and *The Prime-Time Presidency:* The West Wing *and U.S. Nationalism* and the author of *The Character of Justice: Rhetoric, Law, and Politics in the Supreme Court Confirmation Process.*

Brian J. Snee is an assistant professor of communication at State University of New York–Potsdam. His research on film and media studies has appeared in *Communication Quarterly,* the *Journal of Media and Religion,* and the *Free Speech Yearbook.*

Roger Stahl is an assistant professor of communication at the University of Georgia. His research has been published in *Rhetoric and Public Affairs,* the *Quarterly Journal of Speech,* and *Critical Studies in Media Communication.*

Robert E. Terrill is an associate professor in the department of communication and culture at Indiana University. His research has appeared in *Critical Studies in Media Communication,* the *Quarterly Journal of Speech,* and *Rhetoric and Public Affairs.* He is the author of *Malcolm X: Inventing Radical Judgment* and a coauthor of *Reading Rhetorical Texts: An Introduction to Criticism.*